Social Rituals
AND THE
Verbal Art of
Zora Neale Hurston

LYNDA MARION HILL

Frontispiece: Zora Neale Hurston. Courtesy of Stetson Kennedy and Lucy Ann Hurston.

Social Rituals

AND THE

Verbal Art of

Zora Neale Hurston

LYNDA MARION HILL

HOWARD UNIVERSITY PRESS
Washington, D.C.
1996

Howard University Press, Washington, D.C., 20017

Manufactured in the United States of America

This book is printed on acid-free paper.

10 9 8 7 6 5 4 3 2 1

Library of Congress Cataloging-in-Publication Data

Hill, Lynda Marion, 1951–
    Social rituals and the verbal art of Zora Neale Hurston / Lynda Marion Hill.
        p.   cm.
    Includes bibliographical references and index.
    ISBN 0-88258-188-0 (cloth : alk.paper). —ISBN 0-88258-189-9 (pbk. : alk. paper)
        1. Hurston, Zora Neale—Criticism and interpretation.   2. Literature and
anthropology—United States—History—20th century.   3. Women and literature—
United States—History—20th century.   4. Rites and ceremonies in literature.
5. Manners and customs in literature.   6. Afro-Americans in literature.   7. Black
English in literature.   8. Speech in literature.   I. Title.
PS3515.U789Z715   1996
813'.52—dc20   96-14560
                                                                              CIP

Grateful acknowledgment is extended to the Hurston family for permission to reprint
program notes from *All De Live Long Day*, *The Great Day*, and *From Sun to Sun* and for permission to quote from selected correspondence of Zora Neale Hurston.

"Characteristics of Negro Expression" by Zora Neale Hurston is reprinted by permission
of the Hurston family.

The unpublished manuscripts "Barracoon," "Folklore," "Ritualistic Expression from the
Lips of Communicants of the Seventh Day Church of God," and "Uncle Monday" by
Zora Neale Hurston are quoted by permission of the Hurston family.

Dust Tracks on a Road by Zora Neale Hurston and "Uncle Monday," as published in *The
Complete Stories of Zora Neale Hurston*, are quoted by permission by HarperCollins
Publishers.

Cover photograph courtesy of Stetson Kennedy and Lucy Ann Hurston.

To my mother, Marion J. Hill,

and to the memory of my father, Paul Laurence Hill.

For the unspoken as well as the spoken.

EPIGRAPH

Every theoretical answer to the questions, What is an image? How are images different from words? seemed inevitably to fall back into prior questions of value and interest that could only be answered in historical terms.

W. T. J. Mitchell

In that story I gathered up the historical and psychological threads of the life my ancestors lived, and in the writing of it I felt joy and strength and my own continuity. I had that wonderful feeling writers get sometimes, not very often, of being with a great many people, ancient spirits, all very happy to see me consulting and acknowledging them, and eager to let me know, through the joy of their presence, that, indeed, I am not alone.

Alice Walker

So the struggle doesn't ever end. Her story, your story, the connections.

John Edgar Wideman

CONTENTS

✳

Contents

PREFACE

In 1988 I realized Zora Neale Hurston's ethnographic writing, particularly her essay "Characteristics of Negro Expression,"[1] was invaluable in a course I was teaching on black theater. At the time, I was interested in some very specific issues concerning authenticity, without knowing that eventually my interest would grow into this project. To myself, and to the students in my class in the Undergraduate Drama Department at New York University's Tisch School of the Arts, I asked whether the term 'authenticity' has any meaning when talking about African-American forms of expression, and if so, what. Would it be useful to create, perform, or interpret various texts with a notion of authenticity in mind, and if so, how would authenticity be judged or defined?

Introducing questions of authenticity into discussions about how and why black theater has developed as a tradition that is both part of and separate from American theater, inevitably led to further questions. Trying to define authenticity seemed to require a consensus about how to define originality, reality, and imitation. I know that these are large issues; indeed, they have been the subject of numerous years of contemplation. In an effort to specify the significance of these terms for black theater, I attempted to trace the issue of authenticity as it has developed, historically, in black arts movements, as well as in literature concerned with American identity. In the black theater class, we approached the issues through the plays. Not only can written dramas be interpreted from various perspectives, but presenting plays in performance raises questions as to how black experience offers a cultural and historical basis for defining originality.

Students in the black theater class read Hurston's essay "Characteristics of Negro Expression" and were asked to study her ideas about authentic African-American expression. I asked them to read various authors' plays depicting diverse aspects of black experience. Using their own judgment as actors, directors, and playwrights in training, the students were to decide whether Hurston's ideas would be helpful in creating performances from written texts. Hurston's ideas, and the specific examples she gives of African-American language and everyday-life behavior sensitized students to subtleties in black expression and equipped them to interpret techniques playwrights used to render black experience. Perhaps most important, the drama students were drawn in by the storyteller's voice. Because Hurston reports all the significant details in a voice that never loses its casual manner, simple humor, and warmth, the students were readily convinced that "authenticity" has a meaning associated on some level with a genuine admiration for black expressive forms, along with a way of knowing how to show others that appreciation. This was, for them, knowledge that could be translated into practice.

Lynda M. Hill

ACKNOWLEDGMENTS

I owe a great deal to important authors whose work has made it possible for me to gain insights into Hurston's life and work. Even when I dare to look critically at some of their ideas I am ever conscious of my own need to have a strong sense of conviction before straying from proven grounds. Some of these authors include Houston Baker, Henry Louis Gates, Jr., Trudier Harris, Robert Hemenway, Barbara Johnson, Alice Walker, Cheryl Wall, and Susan Willis. For sustained intellectual support and encouragement, I am indebted to Michael Taussig, whose work on a history of the senses helped me with the sympathetic magic portions of Hurston's work. The colloquium he initiated on Mimesis and Alterity: Race and Gender, in 1988 at New York University, provided a forum for me to present my work at an early stage; the experience had an enormous value to me. I am grateful to Barbara Kirshenblatt-Gimblett for her rigorous reading and for being especially attentive to the history of folklore studies and its place in Hurston scholarship. John Roberts contributed to my understanding of issues pertaining to essentialism as it is currently applied to the sorts of identity questions Hurston's work raises. Richard Schechner and Peggy Phelan offered helpful critical comments for which I am grateful. For perceptive readings of all or portions of this work from its earliest to more recent versions, I also thank Arnold Rampersad, Lynda Hart, John Lowe, and Sandra Richards. A version of Chapter Six was first published in *Acting Out: Feminist Performances* edited by Lynda Hart and Peggy Phelan (Ann Arbor: University of Michigan Press).

Individuals whose lives have touched this project in a personal way will never be forgotten. Among them I include the late George Houston Bass, a profoundly inspiring thinker whose death in 1990 was a loss to the theatrical vision shared by everyone committed to creating the sort of drama Hurston longed to see produced in her day. Without the undying enthusiasm of students in my fall 1988 black theater class, in the Department of Undergraduate Drama at New York University, I might never have conceived of Hurston's work as a basis for a Performance Studies methodology. Ron Argelander, who was Chair of Undergraduate Drama at the time, offered much encouragement and support for the course. I thank Lucy Ann Hurston for being so understanding and gracious. Similar appreciation is extended to all of Zora Hurston's heirs for enabling her legacy to continue.

I appreciate the patience of people who, through conversations, shared their knowledge on key topics. They include Anne Cattaneo, Lincoln Center Theater Dramaturg, and Ed Burbridge, the set designer for Lincoln Center's production of *Mule Bone*. I am also grateful to Ruby Dee, Elizabeth Van Dyke, Laurence Holder, Mari Evans, Wanda Shell, Barbara Speisman, Cynthia Hodges, Kathy Perkins, Beverly Robinson, Charles Blockson, Michael Schultz, N.Y. Nathiri, and Stetson Kennedy. Peninah Petruck-Jacobson kindly let me borrow some invaluable art history books. Karen Jefferson was generous with her time at an early stage of my research.

Various institutions and individuals therein have helped my research go smoothly at different stages. Esme Bhan's knowledge of Hurston was invaluabe to me while researching the Alain Locke Papers in the Manuscript Division of the Moorland-Spingarn Research Center at the Howard University Library. At the University of Florida Library, the Director of Special Collections, John Ingram offered assistance, as did Laurel Garber. Archivist David Reddy at the Florida Bureau of Folklife Programs provided help with the Florida Folklore Project collection. Ngadi Npocou at the Beinecke Rare Books and Manuscript Library at Yale University kindly assisted, and Patricia Willis, Curator, helped to guide the permissions process. Kathleen Reich at Rollins College graciously provided me with access to the Archives and Special Collections; George Grant, Director of the Rollins College Library, extended himself on my behalf, as well. I am grateful for the proficiency of the staffs in the Manuscript Division, the Prints and Photographs Division, and the Folklore and Folklife Center of the Library of Congress; the Southern Historical Collection of the Manuscripts Department at the University of North Carolina at Chapel Hill; the American Philosophical Society; the Billy Rose Theater Collection, New York Public Library for the Performing Arts at Lincoln Center; the Schomburg Center for Research on Black Culture; the American Museum of Natural History

Acknowledgments

Library; the Department of Special Collections at Fisk University
Library.

I thank the Ford Foundation for generous support of this project and
the National Research Council. A Temple University Grant-in-Aid of
Research made it possible for me to travel to collections to obtain the
art work, including photographs, reproduced in the book. My colleague
Carolyn Karcher deserves special thanks for her supportiveness during
this phase of my work.

Robin Rones, formerly of Howard University Press, Managing Editor
Renee Mayfield and Marilyn Nelson have guided me through the publication process in all phases with great skill. Howard University Press
Director Edwin J. Gordon has my respect and gratitude for bringing the
project to fruition.

I have held onto the prayers and words of wisdom from Jeffrey N.
Leath, and I appreciate Susan Leath's kindness. Without my family's
love and generosity I would have written very few words. God knows.

XIII

LIST OF ILLUSTRATIONS

INTRODUCTION

Born January 7, 1891, in Notasulga, Alabama, Zora Neale Hurston spent the greater part of her childhood in Eatonville, Florida, a small town often referred to as the first all-black town to be incorporated in the United States. Her father, a Baptist preacher, was Mayor of Eatonville for three terms beginning in 1899. From 1894 until 1904, when her mother died, Hurston enjoyed a sheltered childhood in the closely knit community, situated on a lake, "in a raw bustling frontier" (*Dust Tracks on a Road: An Autobiography*) five miles north of Orlando.[2] She received her early education at the Hungerford School, modeled after Tuskegee Institute, with its guiding principles of discipline and hard work; Hungerford's founders had studied with Tuskegee's founder Booker T. Washington.

Hurston developed into an avid reader and an attentive listener, a fan of myth, legend, and local lore. While reading aloud one day in school, she was moved to dramatize the Greco-Roman tale of Persephone; she delivered her words with such feeling, two visiting white northern women recognized her talent and, consequently, sent Hurston a box of books.[3] Included in the package were the types of fanciful stories she cherished, notably Grimm's fairy tales, Greek and Roman myths, and her favorite, the Norse tales. During this early period of her life, Hurston fed her imagination. Much has been made of how profoundly the men gathering to tell stories on the porch of Joe Clarke's store impressed young Hurston. Joe Clarke, the legendary Mayor and store-owner of Eatonville, appears as a fictional character in much of Hurston's work. Defying her parents' orders to stay away, she took every opportunity to situate herself on Clarke's store porch, where she could hear "the menfolk holding a 'lying session.' That is, straining against each other in telling folk tales. God, Devil, Brer Rabbit, Brer Fox, Sis Cat, Brer Bear, Lion, Tiger, Buzzard and all the wood folk walked and talked like natural men" (*Dust Tracks* 47). Little did she know at the time, this early stage of her life would help to shape her into a professional folklore collector and author.

When her father remarried, Hurston's relationship with him, already strained because she was a feisty child favored by her mother, declined. Moreover, she could not live under the same roof with her stepmother, because of their incompatible personalities and an argument which ended in a violent confrontation. Dejected and displaced, deeply affected by the loss of her mother, Hurston entered a period of instability, of wandering—"Not so much in geography, but in time. Then not so much in time as in spirit" (*Dust Tracks* 65). Gradually emerging from this "transcendental homelessness" with a renewed commitment to follow her mother's challenge to "jump at de sun," Hurston, in 1915, found employment with a Gilbert and Sullivan traveling musical theater group.[4] There she worked as a personal attendant for a singer and actress who, observing Hurston's intelligence and wit, encouraged her to resume her education.

From the Morgan Academy to Howard University Preparatory School and College, Hurston was propelled into the lap of the black literati. She majored in English and joined a literary club which brought her into contact with Alain Locke, a philosophy professor. She then published her first short story, "John Redding Goes to Sea" (*Stylus* 1921). Hurston met other young black writers in Washington, DC, and published a second story "Drenched in Light" (1924) in *Opportunity*, edited by Charles Johnson, whose intellectual support further buttressed Hurston's literary aspirations. After placing second in an *Opportunity* contest for her story "Spunk" and her play *Color Struck*, Hurston moved to New York and became part of the literary scene popularly called the "Harlem Renaissance." She met the poet Langston Hughes, among other notable artists, at the *Opportunity* award banquet.

Meeting prominent individuals became crucial to Hurston not only because of the friendships she developed but also because she received financial and moral support for furthering her education and career. With aid from the Jewish writer Annie Nathan Meyer, Hurston enrolled at Barnard College of Columbia University in 1925. She studied anthropology with Franz Boas, the father of American anthropology, affectionately called Papa Boas by his protégés, who included Margaret Mead, Ruth Benedict, Melville Herskovits, and Zora Hurston. In 1927, Hurston embarked on a field research trip to the South, sponsored jointly by Boas and Carter G. Woodson, director of the Association for the Study of Negro Life and History. During this time, she continued publishing stories, as well as another play, *The First One* (*Ebony and Topaz* 1927). One development had an immense impact on Hurston's career aspirations: she obtained financial support from Charlotte Osgood Mason, a rich, white patron of the arts, who had an interest in preserving Native and African-American cultures. Mason also supported Hughes, Locke, and a host of white artists, among them Miguel Covarrubias, whose illustrations adorn Hurston's folklore collection *Mules and Men* (1935).

Hurston simultaneously pursued at least three lines of work. In addition to her fiction writing, her apprenticeship as a social scientist led to professional obligations, and her fascination with becoming a playwright intensified. Receiving her B.A. from Columbia in 1928, she continued her field research in Florida, Alabama, Louisiana, and the Bahamas. Funded in part by Mason, the research culminated in journal articles, notably one on Bahamian songs, dances, and lore (*Journal of American Folklore* 1930) and 100 pages on "Hoodoo in America" (*Journal of American Folklore* 1931). A premonitory development in her career as a dramatist, her collaboration with Langston Hughes on the play *Mule Bone, a Comedy of Negro Life*, began in 1930 and ended, along with their friendship, in 1931; as Hughes noted on the title page of his copy, the play was never finished because he "fell out" with Hurston.[5]

Between 1931 and 1934, Hurston busily pursued a theater career but grew increasingly frustrated with what I argue was her driving ambition during the most formative part of her professional life. Whether collaborating with other artists or creating shows of her own, she never realized her theatrical pursuits to her complete satisfaction.[6] One researcher has estimated Hurston composed "close to twenty plays," twelve of them between 1930 and 1935, and for three years "became obsessed" with producing her revue *The Great Day* (1932).[7] Two early commercial theater ventures in New York—J. Rosamond Johnson's *Fast and Furious* (1931), in which Hurston's skit "The Court Room" appeared, and her own *Jungle Scandals* (1931), both revues—closed almost immediately after opening. She did, however, gain recognition for her production of *The Great Day*. Originally titled *In the Beginning, The Great Day* opened at the John Golden Theatre, on Broadway, and was performed at other locations in New York, including the New School. Composed of vignettes depicting the songs, dances, and lore of life in a railroad camp, the revue was a showcase of Hurston's folklore collecting. In several versions, under different titles (*From Sun to Sun, All de Live Long Day, Singing Steel*), the production had a favorable reception not only in New York but also in Chicago and in Orlando, Winter Park, and elsewhere in Florida. Hurston, nevertheless, was unable to earn a living as a playwright or director. Although she occasionally taught drama, her goal was the commercial stage, not the classroom. These and other episodes in Hurston's quest to be a dramatist I explore as a point of departure, alongside her active work as a field researcher and an author of seven books.

The energy Hurston directed toward the theater was not exhausted, in my view, but diverted into her writing. The printed page becomes the stage upon which dramatized folk tales, games, sermons, jokes, hexes, songs, and even dances are enacted. According to Hurston, daily life in black communities she had visited and inhabited consisted of "little plays by strolling players," dramatic and beautifully rendered scenes illustrating everything one would need to know to get "what your strengths would bring you." (*Dust Tracks* 46) Her early life had taught her how to understand and appreciate the rich meanings of adult behavior and had made her rather precocious. "There were no discreet nuances of life on Joe Clarke's porch. There was open kindness, anger, hate, love, envy and its kinfolks, but all emotions were naked, and nakedly arrived at." (*Dust Tracks* 46) In other words, a great depth of wisdom could be garnered from folk appearing to be quite simple and communicating in candid terms. Her training as a field researcher, on the other hand, taught her to unlearn her adult assumptions and her Ivy League language to become humble enough to submit herself to apprenticeships as a Voodoo initiate, a folk singer, a Bahamian dancer, or whatever a given situation seemed to require. She was both observer and participant, as scholars have shown. The many commentaries on Hurston's skill translating both the participant and observer perspectives into her writing have opened myriad possibilities for looking at her text as examples of modernist narrative.[8] To add to the knowledge that has been gained by seeing Hurston's texts as exchanges between the ethnographer and the fiction writer, it is helpful to look at the ways ethnography and fiction, anthropology and art, converge.

Using performance as a bridge between the two forms of writing, Hurston created performative language to emphasize that ritualized behavior is preeminent in the black cultures she studied, which led her to conclude that drama is the ultimate quality of life among blacks "the world over." Characterizing black culture using an Aristotelian idea of drama as imitative, Hurston aggravates some perpetual problems associated with representation in black arts. The theater historian M. Francesca Thompson has noted:

> Frequently, Blacks have been rated as 'natural-born actors,' without any real conception of what that designation, if true, actually means. Disparagingly, it could mean a recognition of the Black man's restriction to the interpretative, as distinct from the creative, aspect of drama; it could indicate a confinement, in terms of a second order of talent. It could mean a reducing of his talent to that of a mere mimic.[9]

Drama, after all, is the ritualizing of "reality," set off from ordinary "reality," framed or more specifically, staged; however, the question of whose reality shall be represented cannot be separated from issues pertaining to social, economic, and political factors influencing what spectators see—indeed, who the spectators are. Black musical theater such as the kind Hurston and her colleagues produced during the early 1930s, was vulnerable to critics' disparaging remarks about black shows appearing to imitate white productions.[10]

A great deal of sensitivity still surrounds references to black culture as imitative, which harkens to the period during the first quarter of the twentieth century. With a legacy from nineteenth century minstrel performers, artists, black and white, during the early twentieth century struggled to rectify their perceptions of "reality" with mainstream perceptions of what constituted acceptable varieties of imitation. As Jessie Fauset wrote in 1925, "There is an unwritten law in America that though white may imitate black, black even when superlatively capable, must never imitate white. In other words, grease-paint may be used to darken but never to lighten."[11] Hurston's idea that drama is the cornerstone of black cultures "the world over" and imitation and mimicry the sources of "high art," needless to say, produces a stir of discomfort wherever a concern for cultural authenticity and its representation in the arts exists. Her thwarted career in the theater, in my view, can be seen as symptomatic of unresolvable aesthetic questions arising when authenticity is a dominant objective for producing drama and other performances. Hurston was able to resolve the aesthetic dilemma in writing—an accomplishment in no small measure attributable to her remarkable verbal skills and insights into the relationship language has to para- and extra-linguistic communication, as well as to nonverbal systems of signification.

In her writing, Hurston translates spoken language, already rich in metaphors, into graphically drawn word-pictures of daily life, just as the people who provided her inspiration "sat around on the porch and passed around the pictures of their thoughts for the others to look at and see" (*Their Eyes Were Watching God* 81). Using pictures to describe is not an end in itself, but a means to understanding on a deeper level, in conjunction with the other senses, especially hearing, through sound—speech and song. " 'You heard her, you ain't blind,' " is Walter's challenge to Joe to hear not only with his ears and to see with more than his eyes alone. "The fact that the thought pictures were always crayon enlargements of life made it even nicer to listen to" (*Their Eyes* 81). Borrowing from the theater, Hurston composes her texts using histrionics, as if words are realized through dramatic performances. Indeed, "Janie wanted to hear the rest of the play-acting and how it ended" (*Their Eyes* 109), as each occasion when people gather becomes a drama of everyday life, more compelling than the day's events when "big picture talkers were using a side of the world for a canvas" (*Their Eyes* 85).

Performativity, the capacity of language to recreate action, is an idea used in various critical perspectives. In literary criticism, performance has been viewed as a technique authors adopt to show how personal traits are masked, how individual character is elusive, how subjectivity is not singular but differs according to situations.[12] Although performativity in language has had an impact in philosophical approaches to rhetoric and theories of action,[13] the idea of performance I am applying to Hurston's writing combines the philosophical definition with concepts of performance used in studies of social behavior, literature, culture, and drama. Thus, while recognizing the economy of terms which when uttered commit a speaker to a particular course of action—such as, saying "I do" to get married or to be sworn in as a witness—I am concerned with the way words imply actions through metaphors. Here, John MacAloon's definition of "cultural performances" supplies the juncture I see connecting Hurston's different forms of writing with her conception of drama in black cultures. "Cultural performances are culture 'in action,' " according to MacAloon; they come in many genres.[14] To use "cultural performances" as a category of analysis is to stress that various expressive forms combine to make a single form; thus, writing is not sharply detached from singing, for instance. Similarly, words may reproduce dances and other "ritualistic expressions." Music combined with language in *The Souls of Black Folk*[15] leads the literary critic Houston Baker to replace Du Bois's term "culture" with "cultural performance"; Baker remarks that the latter term "always signifies a distinctively Afro-American sounding of events."[16] Baker connects the idea of cultural performance with a notion of masking in his explanation of expressive forms bridging the late nineteenth and early twentieth centuries. Masking is seen as a vehicle through which African-Americans transmute the minstrel mask into cultural performances which are at once linguistic, artistic, and politically informed. Building on these concepts of cultural performance, with their implications for adaptability through individual, creative responses to social circumstances, I argue that Hurston's work exemplifies the way in which language is a vehicle not only for cultural knowledge, but also for cultural transformation and individual survival.

Much of what appears in this book explains how Hurston's career as a dramatist and performing artist relates to her work as a folklorist. Central to her public image was her wish to see African-American folk songs, dances, and lore revealed to the world at large, in mainstream theaters, which is to say, major commercial venues. Although the public knows her primarily as a fiction writer and to an extent as a folklorist, she considered writing plays and directing primary parts of her professional identity, and she performed as a dancer and singer. This dimension of Hurston's career for the most part coincided with the height of her productive period as a field researcher and author. Her theatrical ambitions, in my view, help to explain why her public image has been characterized as a stagelike persona sometimes considered controversial. Not only did her contemporaries observe her tendency to exaggerate, as she confesses in *Dust Tracks*, but her critics have suggested that Hurston exploited the mask and used it as a means for achieving personal goals, particularly through gaining support from wealthy patrons. This view demonstrates a limited notion of "masking." In a theatrical and a psychological sense, a mask can be donned not simply to conceal one's motives but also to expose one's awareness that, however unfortunate, deception is all too often at the core of social interaction.

Technical terms for actors, dancers, singers can be conflated in the single term "performer." When used in reference to Hurston, the term "performer" takes different meanings, some pertaining to the stage, as mentioned, others not—for example, she was a storyteller and eventually mastered the skills required for communicating with and organizing activities among people of diverse backgrounds. Above all, Hurston wrote fiction, folklore, and an autobiography as if her words were meant for the stage. Her language suggests that performances, including activities such as migrant farming and railroad labor, give substance to the beliefs, ideas, and desires of individual black people and their communities. In a sense, all of Hurston's work can be read as dramatic literature. The varieties of performance appearing in her work, along with theoretical approaches used to interpret them, promise to renew our understanding of Hurston's place in American cultural history. The primary notion of performance I am using suggests the types of theatrical work Hurston produced—revues including songs, skits, dances, rituals, and games based on information she collected while conducting field research in the rural South and the Caribbean.

According to Richard Schechner, a performance can be distinguished from daily behavior because it repeats or "restores" previous behavior.[17] This is the meaning of enactment—a ritualization of behavior. In the theater, behavior is ritualized through rehearsals, where actions are frequently repeated. Some definitions of performance emphasizing ritualistic—repetitive—behavior offer insights into Hurston as a person who understood how cultural traditions change. They change in part because people bearing the traditions are influenced by circumstances beyond their immediate environment and, therefore, develop unique versions of apparently customary behavior. Powerful examples in Hurston's work are to be found in religious, healing, and magical practices. In *Their Eyes*, for example, during her husband Joe Starks's illness, Janie Starks trusts only the advice of a modern physician, whereas Joe, against Janie's wishes, confers with a root-doctor, who intimates that Janie might have had him "fixed," cursed

> He made new alliances too. People he never bothered with one way or another now seemed to have his ear. He had always been scornful of root-doctors and all their kind, but now she saw a faker from over around Altamonte Springs, hanging around the place almost daily. Always talking in low tones when she came near, or hushed altogether. She didn't know that he was driven by a desperate hope to appear the old-time body in her sight. She was sorry about the root-doctor because she feared that Joe was depending on the scoundrel to make him well when what he needed was a doctor, and a good one. She was worried about his not eating his meals, till she found out he was having old lady Davis to cook for him. She knew

that she was a much better cook than the old woman, and cleaner about the kitchen. So she bought a beef-bone and made him some soup.

"Naw, thank you," he told her shortly. "Ah'm havin' uh hard enough time tuh try and git well as it is."

The conflict illustrates the "two-headedness" of conjurers considered healers, on the one hand, and practitioners of magic, on the other. The dual power to heal and to curse attributed to some conjure doctors becomes a metaphor for the dual edge sharply dividing past from present and future. Joe's and Janie's different perceptions of traditional medicine escalate into a conflict which cannot be reconciled. Their marriage becomes one of numerous instances when characters refuse either to accept or to release themselves from time-worn beliefs with obscure origins. Janie repeatedly resists conventional attitudes, as when she leaves her marriage with Killicks and when she criticizes the town's treatment of Matt Bonner's mule. When "everybody was having fun at the mule-baiting" (*Their Eyes* 89), Janie could not join in the fun. "A little war of defense for helpless things was going on inside her" (*Their Eyes* 90). The politically conscious thought that "people ought to have some regard for helpless things" seeps into Janie's awareness through the narrator (*Their Eyes* 90). Hurston illustrates that not all customary behavior is innocuous; individuals invent conventional wisdom.[18]

Focusing on Hurston's texts as dramatic literature makes it possible to examine her multiple careers. The composition techniques she used in writing her fiction and folklore draw heavily from techniques she acquired through scientific research and through her efforts to write for the stage. For example, *Their Eyes Were Watching God* (1937) includes episodes from *Mule Bone* (1931), co-authored by Hurston and Langston Hughes; the play, in turn, is based on an early story of Hurston's, "The Bone of Contention." Consequently, her texts dramatize the conflicts implicit in crossing cultural, disciplinary, and generic boundaries—particularly in combining science and art, but especially in attempting to bring often arcane worlds to public notice. Using a performance-centered approach when conducting research often means becoming actively involved as a participant in the events being studied. Hurston was avidly engaged in participatory research, and it is interesting to consider how she is aligned with anthropologists of her period, as well as with contemporary anthropologists who have since the 1970s focused attention on the poetics of writing ethnography. Their work reflects a disenchantment with scientific empiricism, as they acknowledge that their own roles as field researchers makes them interpreters, hence, mediators and inventors of cultures.[19] Hurston is situated in an active period in the development of field research methodology for the study of non-Western cultures during the 1910s, 1920s, and 1930s.

Hurston's work is rich with the type of conflict the anthropologist Victor Turner calls "social drama." Social drama is Turner's term for a situation in which a break occurs in the way people habitually behave; as a result, a crisis sometimes arises which must be resolved through "redressive" procedures, involving ritualized behavior.[20] According to Turner, much of what gets communicated during the process of redressing a crisis is encoded in the body—through gestures, facial expressions, and other physical and mental responses understood affectively by first-hand participation in the events.

The process in which Hurston was engaged—studying African-American cultures through "the spyglass of Anthropology" (*Mules and Men* 1)—meant that she was often walking into situations wrought with conflict. Consequently, she discerned limitations in scholarly writing, which she saw as inflexible to the spontaneous and unpredictable episodes encountered while in the field. Dissatisfaction with an academic style of presenting culture caused Hurston to pursue alternatives. Much has been made of Hurston's affinity with the folk she studied, and indeed Hurston offered herself as an informant to fellow folklorists on the Folklore Project of the Federal Writers' Project. In this way, her work is instructive. Inasmuch as "one learns through performing, then performs the understanding so gained,"[21] Hurston's work opens a learning process. Through enacting the songs, stories, and dramatic episodes she witnessed, she learned firsthand from the people she studied, then translated her knowledge into forms a broad audience could grasp.

To read Hurston's texts as plays means to examine them as a dramaturg reads a script—with sensitivity to the various contexts a text suggests. One must be able to see words as worlds and to envision these worlds animated through enacted scenes. A dramaturg borrows knowledge from various sources to analyze a script. History is a primary source. The study of dramatic literature also borrows knowledge from anthropology, as mentioned, as well as from linguistics, sociology, psychology, and art history. Linguist and folklorist Dell Hymes has defined performance as a process of assuming responsibility for presentation.[22] Whereas conduct requires norms and rules and ordinary behavior is "anything and everything that happens," performance, according to Hymes, calls for initiative and special abilities on the part of the performer.[23] These are the skills dramaturgs, directors, and actors rely on to create convincing examples of ordinary and extraordinary events.

The sociologist Erving Goffman explains performance as a process whereby people control their public images in much the same way Hurston has been accused of doing, as an actor upon a stage. Goffman characterizes social life and the workplace as stages upon which people present themselves according to the impression they wish to make on others.[24] Using what has been called a world-as-stage metaphor, Goffman extends his research to show how behavior is organized into categories or levels of communication and "framed."[25] His concept of performance, rooted in psychological approaches to human behavior, assumes that face-to-face interactions, which include countless nonverbal signs,[26] are far-from-random episodes. Although it almost goes without saying that people on a day-to-day basis are enacting patterns learned early in life and oft repeated in activities such as morning rituals, the idea that human interactions such as negotiating the power relations in a marriage are enactments of "scripts" can be viewed with skepticism. Nevertheless, methods from sociology are helpful in interpreting dramatic literature.

The method of interpreting texts orally has been used to emphasize that performance is an integral part of reading and comprehending, and this emphasis is only another way to give credence to the idea that written texts do not have a privileged position. A written script is only one aspect of a performance. Moreover, a play is not only a script but the sum of meanings a script has acquired through time.[27] Though written in 1931, like *Mule Bone*, for example, a text will be inseparable from its production history—an accumulation of all the performances between then and now which have presented the play in different guises. In addition to its theatrical history, a given drama includes various subtexts directly related to interactions between performers and audiences during particular performances. This dynamic of performance is not only specific to the theater but has parallels with ceremonies such as church services, ritualistic festivals, sporting events, carnivals, and political rallies, along with numerous other activities requiring an audience. Hurston's work is composed of events falling under almost all these categories.

Seeing patterns in human behavior has long been established as a reliable starting point for drawing inferences about cultures, as Hurston
well knew.[28] During her early fieldwork she tried to assess the presence
and meaning of behavior patterns. Boas's influence is evident in his correspondence with Hurston, in which he urged her to seek "essentially
new" material—namely "methods of dancing, habitual movements in
telling tales, or in ordinary conversation."[29] Hurston responded to Boas
with her own theory of singing and drumming in "primitive music."[30]
"Singing was an attenuation of the drum-beat," she noted, which singers
continue until they "can maintain the attenuation independently of,
and unconscious of, the drum."[31] Her notion of attenuation involved
imitation, the cornerstone of her histrionic conception of black culture.

> I mean by attenuation, the listener to the drum will feel the space be-
> tween beats and will think up devices to fill those spaces. The between-
> beat becomes more and more complicated until the music is all
> between-beat and the consciousness of the dependence is lost.[32]

Although Boas refuted Hurston's theory because it "does not explain in
any way the origin of the intervals which is one of the essential features"
of the music,[33] it is possible to see how a pattern of "between-beats" is
similar to the beats in a performance—when gestures and expression
fill a pregnant silence written into the script as a pause. Spectators are
silent, for example in *Their Eyes*, when "Daisy is walking a drum tune,"
since "you can almost hear it by looking at the way she walks" (*Their Eyes*
105). Furthermore, gestures and expressions take on a language to
such an extent that it is possible to draw conclusions when variations in
these nonverbal patterns occur. The dynamic between pattern and variation appears not only in nonverbal behavior but—significantly to
Hurston's work—in verbal forms. Thus, the difficult procedure of classifying stories she collected into "tale types," as a folklorist is expected
to do, for her becomes a challenge to figure out how tales she remembered from a time past have taken new forms. "The type of tale has
veered from the animal tale to the exaggeration tale, wherein stupen-
dous feats of strength or quickness are performed,"[34] she writes.
Performance is part of a tale's telling. "The tales are dramatized to a
great extent," she writes, "Many sentences are elided and gestures substituted." Thus, patterns and variations can be observed in the teller's
performance, but departure also carries an implicit commentary; if
fleeing from routine is part of a story's content, the status quo is being

mocked. "The tellers like to tell of running away," she writes: "They boast of running away from danger as some other tales are full of courageous stands. 'Cold strolling' means extremely swift flight." Taking flight is a prominent theme in Hurston's early plays, including "The Fiery Chariot," performed as a scene in *From Sun to Sun* and *The Great Day.*

Verbal forms such as the dozens, jokes, and sermons appear in all of Hurston's work, along with work songs and their progeny, the blues, and have been crucial to literary studies of her work. Bridging oral traditional and written forms, Baker as well as the literary and cultural critic Henry Louis Gates, Jr., have multiplied the options available for interpreting literature, by using vernacular expression as an analytic category. Baker's analysis of the blues as a vehicle for lyric commentary on the skills required to survive, shows how cultural performances have an epistemological foundation. His book *Blues, Ideology and Afro-American Literature: A Vernacular Theory* provides an elegant argument for a critical approach to African-American literature formulated in an understanding of the sensibility that goes along with vernacular lyric style.[35] Similar epistemic values are attached to Gates's tracing of the Yoruba Eshu Elegbara's transmutations across the Atlantic Ocean and his appearances in African-American vernacular traditions, particularly the use of signifying, in oral poetry. Insight into the vernacular practice of signification and its many manifestations enables Gates to show how Hurston's use of free indirect discourse in *Their Eyes* represents the tension between oral and written narrative forms where the oral wins out by inscribing its style upon the written text.

Hurston devoted substantial time looking for ways to represent the diversity of Afro-American cultures; she had collected folklore from, among other places, the Bahamas, Louisiana, and Florida and had a strong motivation to exhibit her findings. The stage, in Hurston's view, was an ideal medium for presenting to the public the dramatic ways of life she encountered in the field. Her life was a quest for equilibrium among three major pursuits—literature, social science, and theater. At times, working in three disciplines produced conflicts of interest for Hurston.

She was not alone, however, working in these realms. At each stage of her multidisciplined career, she figured prominently in major intellectual developments. Her literary career positions her behind male and female progenitors such as Charles Chesnutt, Paul Laurence Dunbar,

Mark Twain, Frances Harper, and Harriet Beecher Stowe. She can be contrasted with her contemporaries Jessie Fauset, Nella Larsen, Fannie Hurst, Richard Wright, Langston Hughes, and Carl Van Vechten. In social science, Hurston's contributions bear the markings of her apprenticeships with pioneering anthropologists Franz Boas and Melville Herskovits and with public sector folklorist such as Benjamin A. Botkin and John Lomax. In theater, Hurston's collaborations with J. Rosamond Johnson, Hall Johnson, and Langston Hughes brought her notoriety. Her theater aspirations also gained strength from her associations with Alain Locke, Charles Johnson, Paul Green, and others committed to developing an indigenous American theater. Like her counterparts, she wanted to see a particular brand of theater, where African-Americans would be represented in ways departing from the minstrel tradition dominating American popular entertainment since the nineteenth century.

Because many black and white artists were motivated to refigure depictions of blacks in popular entertainment, the number of blacks participating in the arts increased during the 1910s, 1920s, and 1930s. James Weldon Johnson attributed this increased participation to the unique contribution African-Americans had made to American music—ragtime, in particular. Thus, ragtime is identified with the burgeoning of black musical entertainment during the 1910s and 1920s. This development did not arise spontaneously but was an outgrowth of increasing fascination with local color as a pathway to American art. White and black playwrights, novelists, poets as well as visual artists and musicians, sought to produce work reflecting American lifestyles. Mirroring life as lived by common people became a fascination with early twentieth century artists. It is here where the aesthetic issues I explore in subsequent chapters converge into what I argue are unresolved, politicized contests over what constitutes authenticity. On one side of the issue are people holding to an idea of cultural, racial, or ethnic identity as a fixed point of reference, even a geographical point of origin, against which to measure the authenticity of various forms of expression. On the other side, are people convinced that diversity among people identified as a monolithic group is more pervasive than the similarities among them and that too many factors are involved in shaping expressive forms for one to be more definitive than another. Between these two positions are gradations—perspectives leaning toward essentialism, on the one hand, or relativism, on the other. But to date, no comfortable position emerges, in my view;

rather a continuing debate needs to be tracked to gain a clearer under-standing of the way artists such as Hurston have grappled with these is-sues in the past and how their work points toward a vision of aesthetics as not in the least separate from the power politics of everyday life.

My argument begins, in Chapter One, with the critical year 1934, when Hurston's ethnography was introduced to the world-at-large, through her essay "Characteristics of Negro Expression," and other se-lections appearing in Nancy Cunard's *Negro* anthology. Also the year of Hurston's debut as a novelist, 1934, marks a turning point in political and economic developments affecting the masses of Americans. What do Hurston's publications during that year tell us about why Hurston's work has come to have increasing importance at the end of the twenti-eth century? I argue that her work prefigures a growing awareness of the manufactured quality of ordinary reality. Not only does she make clear that distinctions between art and life are fabricated, but also as-sumptions about folklore and folklife being separate from sociopolitical turmoil are not easily supported through a close reading of Hurston's work, even when she seems to be laughing in the face of disaster. My analysis of "Characteristics of Negro Expression" shows the challenges Hurston confronted in 1934 amounted to a dense wall of racial am-bivalence. Her response was to rattle the wall; rather than trying to dis-mantle it, she left every inch of contradiction and ambiguity in place. The result is that her work constantly reminds us of unresolved tensions surrounding any mention of racial, cultural, social, and sexual differ-ences and of the power struggles they engender in American society.

Hurston's ideas on imitation and mimicry are not only an elabora-tion of a world-as-stage metaphor but also a nod toward carnivalesque humor. Here, a vigilance of analytic authority is cloaked with crafty puns. Her theory of imitation, as I title Chapter Two, can be called, in contemporary parlance, a performance theory—an application of the-atrical principles to various expressive forms. In Chapter Two, I show how Hurston uses mimicry and parody to express opposition. Through my analysis of her ironic metaphors, her shifts in point of view, and other literary techniques, her resistance to dominant "scientific" views on assimilation becomes apparent. I also make clear that tensions be-tween "imitation" and "originality" correspond with historical debates over how to define American culture, as either one homogenized "melt-ing pot" or a multiplicity of distinctive cultures. I explore why her con-flicts over how to define culture are related to her quest for the ideal medium, drama, as a vehicle for representing traditional African-American expressive forms.

In Chapter Three, "Negotiating the Field," I discuss key field research projects in an effort to illustrate the source of Hurston's conflict over how to represent African-American cultures. I show how pursuing fieldwork, as well as producing ethnographic texts and other documents, led Hurston to seek a career in theater. She considered the stage to be the only medium truly conducive to presenting the forms of expression she saw ritualized in everyday life. Part of my aim in the chapter is to allow Hurston's texts to speak for themselves, to illustrate the dynamic her variety of field research and ethnography represent.

Looking further at some issues related to aesthetics and cultural production (explored in Chapters One, Two, and Three), I give an overview in Chapter Four of an ongoing debate over authenticity, as it pertains to the arts, particularly black arts, in twentieth century America. I position Hurston in the debate, and discuss its impact on developing supportive critical and artistic traditions, as well as the significance of Hurston's legacy in the social and cultural survival of African-American expressive forms. I pursue a more detailed discussion of ritualistic expression in Hurston's traditional tales, in Chapter Five, where I assess the significance of her research on sympathetic magic and techniques she borrows from traditional religion in crafting her conjure stories. A semiotic interpretation of intertextuality across genres, particularly the folktale and fictional story, exposes her transpositions of linguistic structures from one genre to another. I, further, attempt to show how Hurston's concept of African-American language as "hieroglyphics" is a metaphorical way of describing verbal expression as performance. I also explore distinctions between structural aspects of folktales and myths, and speculate about the extent to which Hurston's texts, as symbols of her life, are testaments to the way that traditional knowledge is embodied, recreated, and transmitted from one generation to another. In Chapter Six, to demonstrate some implications of the argument presented in the preceding chapters, I show the impact of Hurston's iconography in a current revival of interest in her work, exemplified by some major theater productions based on her life and work. Special attention is given to the Broadway debut of *Mule Bone*, in 1991. Here, her influence on contemporary theater practitioners is illustrated within the history of African-American theater, in general, and the roles of African-American women, in particular.

CHAPTER ONE

The Drama of Everyday Life

※

When Hurston published her essay "Characteristics of Negro Expression" in the 1934 anthology *Negro*, edited by Nancy Cunard, it was one of numerous contributions reflecting some of the perplexing issues related to race pervasive during a pivotal moment in U.S. history. A photograph of two black men dangling by ropes from a tree, surrounded by a mob, appears on the page facing Hurston's essay at the end of the preceding article "Aftermath of a Lynching," by William Pickens, with a caption that begins: "A lynching in America, of which roughly some 60 or more, in one form or another, take place every year, not necessarily with the same ceremonial as here shown."³⁶ Among various topics included in the book, pertaining to black life in the United States, the Caribbean, South America, Europe, and Africa, discussions of race relations and lynching figure as prominently as articles on education, ethnology, folklore, and the performing and plastic arts. The lynching photo juxtaposed to Hurston's essay symbolizes the extent to which dramatically contrasting depictions of black life were represented in the *Negro* anthology and in the world at large.

ESSENTIALISM IN A TIME OF TURMOIL

Intellectual developments in society, some of which influenced Hurston's thinking while she was writing "Characteristics of Negro Expression," suggest answers to glaring questions raised by controversial generalizations she makes in the essay and shed light on her motivations for writing it. Hurston deliberately argues from an essentialist point of view, while mocking the rhetoric of acculturation current at the time. Her brand of essentialism can be viewed as a way of establishing herself at once as a spokesperson and an authority on a group with which she is ostensibly affiliated.[37] Essentialism, according to Webster's, is "a theory that gives priority to essence over existence." As applied to human beings, essentialist theories attribute various traits to groups of people. Terms such as "Oriental" and "Occidental," for example, divide the globe geographically while carrying implicit assumptions about differences among cultural and racial groups inhabiting the East and the West. Indeed, according to Edward Said, the West has produced a whole system of Orientalist thinking which reduces diverse cultural groups to an imaginary prototype.[38] Said's notion of Orientalism, the process by which the West has created an idea of the East, can be taken as a model for the type of critical issues essentialism raises. To what extent do people characterized by stereotypical views of their culture have power to alter the terms used to classify them? Appropriating the terminology of essentialism, as Said does to explain the impact Orientalist theories have had on cross-cultural relations between East and West, is a first step toward critiquing the problems essentialist thinking presents for cultural analysis.[39] In discussing "characteristic" Negro behavior, Hurston displays essentialist ideas of her time while illustrating the contradictions implicit in racialist conceptions of culture. In her efforts to come to terms with what at the time was referred to as "primitive man," what Hurston intended and what she actually accomplished in adopting an essentialist stance provide a focus for examining key disputes over black cultural development then and now. For it is at the juncture between ethnological fascination with "primitives" and sociopolitical pressures related to "the Negro problem" that her work becomes entangled with major intellectual developments of the century. Such developments and the debates surrounding them have been critical to studies of Black Aesthetics throughout the twentieth century. Indeed, it is impossible to view artistic movements such as the Harlem Renaissance of the 1920s and the Black Arts Movement of the 1960s and 1970s apart from concurrent perspectives on culture being formulated in academia—as by-products of enlightenment thinking.

Although 1934 is a focal point, many of the texts included in Cunard's *Negro* anthology reflect issues spanning the late 1920s and early 1930s, just as Hurston's essay is based on field research from the juncture between the two decades. An investigation of circumstances influencing Hurston's development as a folklorist and theater artist suggests she hoped to achieve, in writing the essay, a resolution to the problem of authenticity. Moreover, her ideas have ramifications beyond her historical period, since the issue of authenticity remains an enigma just as the essentialism Hurston espoused has been challenged by relativistic views of culture.[40] Deciphering the then-versus-now meaning of "Characteristics" becomes an issue with each new reading of the essay, as with Hurston's work on whole. Perspectives on how to characterize American culture generally have been in flux, particularly during the twentieth century since ethnic studies have had increasing influence on cultural debates pertaining to "race."[41] A close reading of "Characteristics," focusing on Hurston's central argument concerning imitation and mimicry among African-Americans, exposes the controversies implicit in efforts to classify people ethnographically.

"For Hurston, the distinction between originality and imitation is a false distinction," according to Gates, "and for the black writer to suffer under the burden of avoiding repetition, revision, or reinterpretation is to succumb to a political argument that reflects a racist subtext."[42] Gates's statement underscores a key problem Hurston's essay presents to contemporary readers, for it would seem the "racist subtext" causing Hurston to insist that there is a fixed definition of black culture based on mimetic performance produces as much anxiety as her implying that imitation is a key to resolving questionable claims about originality or its absence. Gates explores the relationship between imitation and originality to illustrate differences between black writers such as Langston Hughes and Sterling Brown, who considered their work original because they drew from African-American folk idioms and expressive styles, versus writers such as Richard Wright and Charles Chesnutt who claimed their literary predecessors were European. Gates writes: "If Hurston sought to relieve her fellow black authors' worries about their complex relationships to the Western tradition on the one hand, and to the Afro-American vernacular and formal traditions on the other, then she clearly failed."[43]

Departing from the idea that she was trying to assuage her colleagues, one could say Hurston was trying to come to terms with scientific and popular definitions of race and culture prevalent at the time, particularly as such terminology pertained to "the Negro." Gates positions Hurston's essay in a discourse on signification in black literature and culture. Her article also can be seen in the context of political alliances on the one hand and, on the other, social scientific debates over the extent to which classifying people into racial groups could be accomplished by observing their physical characteristics or whether such categories could in any way be considered static. Views of key figures such as Franz Boas and Alain Locke, former teachers of Hurston's, show how research on race and culture intersected with political debates of the period and, consequently, had repercussions in the sphere of cultural production.

Scientific and popular ideas of race were curiously intertwined during the early twentieth century. Although this is a topic historians have examined at length, a few salient points concerning the relationship between science and popular imagination serve as further grounding for delineating the narrowness of the tightrope upon which Hurston was obliged to maintain her precarious balance. Racial classifications based on inherited traits developed into the eugenics movement, which lent a scientific veneer to discriminatory practices and became a backdrop against which dramatic episodes in American popular culture were enacted. Popular fiction, such as Thomas Dixon's *The Klansman* (1905) had sought since the postreconstruction era to reinforce perceptions of blacks as barbaric, subhuman. When *The Klansman* was adapted as the film *Birth of a Nation* (1915) by the innovative American director D. W. Griffith, images of unruly blacks fed the fears and political attitudes of mass audiences. These developments in combination aroused conservative racial attitudes that were at odds with scientific research challenging the status quo, as did the work of Franz Boas and his protégés. At the same time, as the historian Audrey Smedley has noted, Boas's scientific rationalism did not preclude his having personal biases—a fact apparent in the ambiguities documented not only in Boasian references but throughout the work of other anthropologists pursuing similar ideas considered progressive at the time.[45]

People researching black culture, from Boas to Melville Herskovits to Locke and Hurston, were consciously—or perhaps unconsciously in Hurston's case—polarized against racial conservatives such as Lothrop Stoddard, whose influential book *The Rising Tide of Color Against White World Supremacy* (1921) was repudiated in print both by Boas and Locke, although Stoddard's outspoken views against immigration of all but "Nordic" Europeans, his "proofs" of racial superiority and inferiority based on Army intelligence tests, and his eugenics theories continued to hold sway well into the twentieth century.[46] The period "was marked by the rise of racism as a political factor," against which "Boas spoke out with the authentic voice of the scientist, yet with the passion that the misuse of science always aroused in him."[47] Similarly Locke, in accordance with his method of cultural critique, astutely observed that the color line Stoddard insisted should be maintained to prevent racial fusion had never been "blood tight" and "is notoriously not a blood barrier but a culture barrier," adding "that the real cause for frenzy and alarm among the advocates of White Supremacy is based upon [the] real threat of economic and cultural competition."[48] The question arises: where exactly can Hurston's views be positioned among the divergent racialist agendas of the period?

RACE AND CULTURE

Comparing Hurston's essay "Characteristics" with an essay Boas published in 1934, "Aryans and Non-Aryans," places contested issues concerning race in a cross-cultural context. An analysis of why "it is a fiction to speak of a German race," Boas's essay was part of his response to the rise of fascism—"authoritarianism, based on a false philosophy of race," which "challenged all he stood for as a scientist and citizen" and "came the closer home because, as one of Jewish origin, his many relatives in Germany were among the proscribed."[49] Moreover, both Boas's and Hurston's essays are important because they show how membership in a cultural group, along with historical circumstances affecting the group, combine to form an ideological basis for social scientific research and analysis.

In a manner similar to the instructive tone he would take in letters directing Hurston's field research during the late 1920s and early 1930s, Boas argues in his article:

> Naturally, bodily forms are not alike in separate regions or in different classes of society, but in every population may be found such utterly different types that it would be difficult to assign any one individual with certainty, solely by means of bodily form to the local or social group to which he belongs. Yet every region and every group has a fairly definite mental character. It has never been proved that this is determined by the physical type of the people, but there are many observations indicating that it is due to the unifying cultural bond which unites the people.[50]

Here Boas presents ideas for which he had been well-known since 1911 when he delivered his paper "The Instability of Human Types" at the First Universal Race Congress in London, where he argued that physical characteristics of American-born and European-born members of the same family vary due to environmental differences. As part of a process of Americanization, such changes led him to conclude that one's mental make-up "may be considerably influenced by his social and geographical environment."[51]

His research gradually developed, during the late nineteenth and early twentieth centuries, into a careful application of physical science methodology to the study of language and customs which according to Boas were more reliable categories for interpreting human behavior than were physical traits such as head sizes and skin colors. Measuring head sizes, which Hurston had done in Harlem, was a method used to collect anthropometric statistics, particularly to correlate physical growth patterns with the development of intelligence. "In the few cases in which the influence of culture upon mental reaction of populations has been investigated," he wrote in 1932, "it can be shown that culture is a much more important determinant than bodily build."[52] Although an individual's physical form and mental capacity relate in some way, the parallel cannot be generalized to whole populations. Boas's awareness of the limits of biological methods in studying human behavior produced the striking observation that while "animal forms develop in divergent directions, and an intermingling of species that have once become distinct is negligible in the whole developmental history," human culture is different.[53] "Human thoughts, institutions, activities may spread from one social unit to another. As soon as two groups come into close contact their cultural traits will be disseminated from the one to the other."[54] This idea of diffusion as a primary attribute of cultural groups in part accounts for Boas's reputation as a cultural relativist.

When Hurston studied with Boas while she attended Barnard, and later pursued field research under his supervision, she had already been Locke's student at Howard University and a protégée of his while developing her creative talent during the "New Negro" period identified with the Harlem Renaissance of the 1920s.[55] Locke, who had been strongly influenced by Boas's work, particularly since the First Universal Race Congress, had begun to develop slightly different ideas about race and culture by 1916.

> Boas believed that the solution to the racial problem required that we deemphasize race in modern life and assimilate ethnic groups totally into the dominant American stock. But Locke wished to retain the concept of race. He did not accept the proposition that race was either a permanent biological entity or nothing at all: people often possessed a race or group

6

sense that contributed to group esteem and power. Second, Locke moved beyond the cultural relativism of Boas to analyze race within the context of modern imperialism. For Locke, race was not simply a theoretical question, but a practical issue affecting social relations in the United States.[56]

Whereas Boas's views reflect a relativistic idea about the variability of traits among people within cultural groups, Locke argued for retaining a notion of racial and cultural distinction for the practical reason that certain social and political needs could be met only through group identification. To the extent that Locke and Boas were influential in Hurston's development, the strength of their views on race and culture bear significantly on her theoretical ideas in "Characteristics of Negro Expression."

If folklore was, as Boas defined it, "the science of all the manifestations of popular life,"[57] Hurston makes clear from the opening of her essay, under the subheading "Drama," she intends to distance herself from conventions of "scientific" exposition, although she retains pseudoscientific generalities. She begins: "The Negro's universal mimicry is not so much a thing in itself as evidence of something that permeates his entire self. And that thing is drama" (see Appendix, p. 243). As with other terms used when a large number of people are categorized according to racial, cultural, or national "characteristics," the term "Negro" draws attention to the problem of defining group identity. The term "Negro," having gained prominence at the time, can be seen as a sign of some political ramifications associated with classifying people into racial and cultural groups and defining the characteristics which supposedly make it possible to determine whether or not a particular person belongs to the group. An anthropological classification forms part of Hurston's perspective, combined with a popular or conventional sense of the term.

The distinction between two senses of the term "Negro" is illustrated in a footnote to "The Trend of the Races," a 1922 essay by George Edmund Haynes, founder of the National Urban League. He writes:

> The use of *Negro* as a race designation is to take both terms ["Negro" and "race"] in their conventional, popular meaning. The terms are not used in an ethnological sense based upon complexions, hair forms, or head forms or upon cultural types, because all types are found in the group and because in language, literature, art, religion, industry, and other items, Negroes have very largely appropriated and assimilated the culture around them. They have, however, developed a solidarity and race consciousness which make a group life and a Negro world of feeling, thought, and attitude.[58]

7

Whereas Haynes disparages what he calls the "ethnological sense" of the term "Negro," Hurston, following her Boasian training, begins with the social scientific, even biological, classification to show how cultural patterns emerge among people sharing social, geographical, and linguistic factors in common. Haynes's assessment illustrates how conflicts concerning terminology are integral to debates over what role scientific theories should play in social issues. The widely held belief that blacks emulate white American culture for Haynes is countered by political alliances but for Hurston is countered by distinctive cultural patterns, which are evidence of environmental influences continuously rather than conclusively modifying inherited traits. Thus, Hurston interprets blacks' assimilating behavior manifested among members of the dominant culture as "universal mimicry." Her argument is not just an explanation of how a minority culture absorbs a dominant culture by mimicry but a reification of the idea that inherited traits are modified through patterned responses to dominant environmental influences.

"UNIVERSAL MIMICRY" AND "ORIGINALITY"

Hurston's reference to "universal mimicry" and her commentaries on "originality" and "imitation" (appearing further along in the essay) seem to be directed against views favoring acculturation and assimilation as dominant patterns in African-American culture. "It has been said so often that the Negro is lacking originality that it has almost become a gospel," she writes (*see* Appendix, p. 250). Although she continues, "outward signs seem to bear this out" (*see* Appendix, p. 250), to a certain extent her objective was to challenge popular interpretations of what Boas scientifically called "diffusion." Thus, she cleverly adds that "if one looks closely [the] falsity [of such views] is immediately evident" (*see* Appendix, p. 250).

She ineffectively uses the idea of mimicry, however, if she seriously wanted to oppose the assimilationist view. Only her use of irony, revealed through careful analysis of her word choices and seen within the context of ideological conflicts implicit in terms used to address race and culture can account for her equating "mimicry" and "imitation" with "originality." Using ironic language, recognizing "the problematic nature of language, the potential foolishness of all linguistic characterizations of reality,"[59] becomes for Hurston a way to engage indirectly in politicized disputes. Working under conflicting pressures, she apparently felt the need to distance herself from the mainstream of black political thought. Because she uses ironic language as "a self-conscious mode that senses the failure of all sophisticated conceptualizations,"[60] examining her passages on mimicry and originality exposes the larger significance of distancing as a means of self-empowerment.

Drama, as Hurston describes it in "Characteristics," is based on the everyday-life behavior she observed while pursuing ethnographic field research. She uses drama as a model—a world-as-stage metaphor—to explain patterns of expressive behavior. She uses images to produce scenes that correspond to the enacted scripts, "little plays by strolling players" she reads as the subtexts of everyday life, "acted out daily in a dozen streets in a thousand cities" (*see* Appendix, p. 244). Based on this model, she interprets everyday-life behavior by translating her perceptions into terms that visually reproduce gestures, movements, and styles—dramatic action. "To read everyday life, what Hegel called 'the prose of the world,' is . . . to become engaged in an act of *poesis*."[61] Hurston transforms "the prose of the world" into theatrical verbal expressions, by using a form of composition that corresponds with Aristotle's definition in the *Poetics*.[62] Whereas verbal expression in the *Poetics* conveys thought through language, in Hurston's work verbal expression gives form to the "little plays by strolling players." Combining popular and conventional views with anthropological explanations, she attempts to criticize prevailing notions about "culture," by appropriating and attempting to invert the meanings of key terms.

If "everyday life harbors the texture of social change" and if "to perceive it at all is to recognize the necessity of its conscious transformation," then African-American language is a cultural process, as well as the means through which a primary text—behavior called everyday-life drama—is enacted.[63] Hurston writes: "His very words are action words. His interpretation of the English language is in terms of pictures. One act described in terms of another" (see Appendix, p. 243). Language becomes a vehicle for transforming meaning, for translating behavior into words and converting everyday-life drama into written texts which are also performances. Rather than translating everyday life into expository prose, Hurston's language converts everyday-life drama into signs that extend the spatial and temporal boundaries of prose, multiplying the dimensions through which a reader enters the text and understands its meaning.

"Hieroglyphics" become a vehicle through which social order changes. The English language is appropriated and undergoes transformation through verbal expressions produced and given meaning within African-American communities, particularly, according to Hurston, among all but middle-class members of the group defined by the (contested) term "Negro."[64] The dramatic text of everyday life finds its equivalent in "action words" which are visual representations— whereby "the speaker has in his mind the picture of the object in use" (*see* Appendix, p. 244). Also, a transformation from the mundane to the preternatural occurs through language, because "the Negro thinks in hieroglyphics" (*see* Appendix, p. 244). Thus, the simile "one at a time, like lawyers going to heaven" (*see* Appendix, p. 245) implies a processional, suggesting a ceremonial rite and an authority rooted in secular power, aspiring to sanctity in a sacred realm. Through "the conveying of a truth by asserting its opposite,"[65] irony is produced; a commentary on lawyers' motivations is juxtaposed to a metaphysical reference. The allusion to ritual and ceremonial recurs in Hurston's lexicon, drawing attention to various actions in everyday life, actions that challenge assumptions about consistency, balance, and order in the world. In this sense, Hurston's notion of social change corresponds with the "cultural ideology" Locke promoted during the 1920s as the means to achieve progress or to transcend social circumstances; Hurston's work reflects some key differences, however.

Locke's "cultural ideology" of "racial pride" is a conscious "tool for building group esteem and solidarity."[66] His promoting art as a vehicle for change has a basis in the cultural pluralism and pragmatism espoused by the philosopher William James. According to Jeffrey Stewart, "By arguing for the creation and recognition of a distinctive African American culture, even when Locke's own analysis reflected the overwhelming assimilationist stance of most black people, Locke was acting like a good pragmatist and inventing a racial tradition whether or not one existed."[67] In his pragmatism, Locke stood apart from Hurston and enjoyed a wide sphere of influence over the young African-American artists published in *The New Negro* (1925) anthology he edited. But because of his broad education and exposure, he also formed alliances with influential whites to advance his ideological agenda.[68] One example of Locke's efforts to collaborate to advance a cultural agenda involved the formation of an interracial Committee for the Establishment of a Permanent Negro Repertory Theater in 1931, which had among its stated goals the education of whites and "the fostering of a more en-lightened understanding between the races."[69] Moreover, Stewart points out that

> Locke's movement away from criticism of white paternalism and toward an essentialist view of racial character may have been influenced by his in-creasing dependence in the late 1920s on the financial support of Charlotte Mason, a white millionaire, who, in addition to being a fierce anti-Marxist, also believed that blacks and Indians were noble primitives who could reform Western civilization.[70]

Furthermore, and perhaps more important, Locke did not use eco-nomic class to establish whether a person represents an "authentic" member of the group.

Unlike Locke, Hurston cannot be considered a pragmatist, although she, too, was supported by Charlotte Osgood Mason and deliberately embraced an essentialist view. Hurston's essentialism, rather than being born from a commitment to furthering a collective political agenda, was an expression of racial and individual pride as an end in itself. She was devoted to her own individualized goals over and above the objectives of people with whom she collaborated, such as Mason and Boas.[71]

Hurston's essentialist position, based on a theory of imitation, reflects the kind of "human ambivalence toward imitation" that shifts between two attitudes toward mimesis which seem not only to be irreconcilable but indelibly linked.[72] Although a "preoccupation with origins, pedigrees and process leads . . . to exalt[ing] derivation as tradition," there is a "dis-dain and mistrust [for] 'imitations,' 'copies,' and 'facsimiles,' the 'artifi-cial,' the 'ersatz' and the 'typical.' "[73] Unlike Locke, Hurston seeks to differentiate blacks who imitate "for the love of it" from "slavish" imita-tors. To an extent, then, although she hardly attempts to copy nature in her writing style, Hurston can be seen as a mimetic critic because she evaluates the texts of everyday-life expressive forms according to whether they recreate what she considers authentic behavior.[74]

If "originality" is intangible because "most of us do no more than per-ceive originality as a quality of our attention, which is enlivened or shocked by an experience that pushes all others either into second place or out of sight," how are we to interpret Hurston's notions of im-itation and originality in relation to each other?[75] Her essay "Characteristics," as well as her other texts, can be construed as what Edward Said calls "writing that brings together, as in the novel, conti-nuity and originality"; continuity is suggested in the systematic cultural patterns she translates, originality in her combinations of verbal and visual forms. Said also explains *how* originality means (to play on Albert Scheflen's semiotics of behavior) "an endless, perhaps occasionally violent, substitution of one experience for another."[76] According to Said, in certain texts, an author's theory of originality is demonstrated through his or her textual practices. Thus, in Hurston's essay, we can come to terms with her theoretical discussion only by examining the intersections among various systems of knowledge present and absent in the text. For, again, as Said argues, "the value of writing as an object of analysis is that it makes more precise the almost anonymous alternation of presence and absence we impressionistically and perceptually associate with originality."[77] Perhaps it is important to note Said's point that "presence and absence cease to be mere functions of our perception and become instead willed performances by the writer."[78]

Hurston's own practice of imitation and the degree of her originality, then, must be investigated as well as her theory. When she frankly states "it is obvious that to get back to original sources is much too difficult for any group to claim very much as a certainty" (*see* Appendix, p. 250), she pays homage to the teachers who seem to have been most influential in her career. More problematic, however, is her statement immediately following—"What we really mean by originality is the modification of ideas"—which seems to insist on a notion of authenticity which, unfortunately, can hardly be distinguished from racial conservatism, as attributed to white southerners, including John Lomax, a collector of African-American folklore slightly predating Hurston's period; she collaborated with Lomax as well as with his son, Alan, during the Works Progress Administration (WPA).[79] The other possibility is that Hurston had no allegiance to a Platonic conception of originality as an ideal but was closer to understanding it as "a variation within a larger, dominating pattern."[80] According to Said, key thinkers such as Nietzsche, Marx, and Freud have attempted in their work to assess originality in relation to a dominating tendency "to regularize, pattern, and schematize the conditions of human experience."[81] But if originality cannot be attributed to forms of expression or, more pertinently, to ideas which are "highly valued and relatively rare, which appear for the first time, which have no similar antecedents, which may serve as models for others, and which to this extent deserve to be regarded as creations," as Foucault defines them, then what terms could Hurston or any of her contemporaries use to define American culture, black or white?[82]

To show how American culture relies for its authenticating standards on "authoritative" European models, Hurston writes: "The most ardent admirer of the great Shakespeare cannot claim first sources even for him. It is his treatment of the borrowed material" (43). Here, she emphasizes what is often taken for granted, "the metaphorical handing-along of something which we prize"—a presumption that an authoritative standard for originality exists, based on European origins of American culture, a normalized sense of which "original" forms of expression should be passed along through tradition.[83] Shakespeare becomes a sign for the dichotomy between high and low culture.

Like Hurston, Anthony J. Buttitta in his essay "Negro Folklore in North Carolina," immediately following Hurston's in the anthology, also refers to Shakespeare in one example he uses to illustrate how certain cultural patterns occurring among blacks and whites are interpreted according to different standards. "The Negro's fear of ghosts has been sufficiently ridiculed by the American films," he writes and continues, "All people believed in ghosts at some time, even Hamlet, or shall we call that a technical trick on the part of Shakespeare?"[84]

In light of the historical context and other developments related to folklore research at the time, Hurston's reference to Shakespeare shows that, like her contemporaries in the field, she was not immune to dominant critical and cultural trends. Citing numerous references from Lomax's research on African-American music, for example, Jerrold Hirsch points out that making analogies "between Western high culture and Black folk art" was in the 1930s "a radical attack on the prestige attached to high culture produced in the Old World—a prestige that blinded Americans to the value of their own culture."[85] But such comparisons could not escape reinforcing the standards they sought to challenge, as Hirsch observes: "One implication was that indigenous African-American folksong could only be regarded as art if it could be compared to true art—Western high culture."[86] Thus, classical references, no less than the concepts and terms available to a person pursuing research on African-American culture at the time, reflect a desire to revise existing views amid overwhelming opposition to change.

A PARADOX

Some of Hurston's statements seem too self-consciously humorous to be interpretations of black culture based on documented research. In contrast with her former teachers, who consciously labored to relieve themselves and the world from the burdens of racial antagonism through eloquent academic prose, Hurston deliberately unlearned the language she acquired through her academic training. Her first field research expedition to Florida taught her to do so, because her "carefully accented Barnardese," alienated "the men and women who had whole treasuries of material just seeping through their pores" and brought minimal results, as she recalls in her autobiography *Dust Tracks on a Road* (128). The playful tone so noticeable in "Characteristics" is absent from "The Florida Expedition," an early field research report she sent to Boas, which in contrast with the opening of "Characteristics," begins: "While a large number of tales were found, not nearly so many are current as before the literate era of the Negro. The bulk of the population now spends its leisure in motion picture theatres or with the phonograph and its 'blues.' "[87] More so than the playful voice in "Characteristics," the sober tone in the unpublished "Florida Expedition" essay resembles Buttitta's style of prose in the *Negro* anthology. He writes:

> It comes as a surprise to many people that the Negro of North Carolina, though possessing a sufficiently colorful folklore, is not as much the all-believing creature as he has been carelessly pictured in literature. Investigations of the elements that go into the making of his folklore shows that the Negro is not as superstitious as the corn-fed mountaineer of the Blue Ridge section or the 'po' white trash' of the bottom lands and swamps. In many cases he shows more intelligent reaction to various signs and omens; especially does he show a more scientific approach in his medical lore.[87]

Although the comparative analysis suggests a similar defensiveness as arises in the Shakespeare analogies and although elsewhere in his essay Buttitta's racial essentialism matches Hurston's, his narrative style is expository. In contrast, Hurston strives to reproduce what Boas called in his preface to her folklore collection *Mules and Men* (1935), "the intimate setting in the social life of the Negro" (x). Also, what in Boas's view could be called a "revealing style" helps to give the reader "knowledge of the true inner life of the Negro" (x).

Examining Hurston's texts reveals a style rooted in conventions of African-American oral and written narrative—particularly the practice of imitation or borrowing and revision, which has been extensively discussed by Houston Baker, Henry Louis, Gates, Jr., and others.[89] The hallmark of this practice in Hurston's work, "the speakerly text"—"whose

rhetorical strategy is designed to represent an oral literary tradition"—
accounts for her being considered an innovator in African-American
literature.[90] In her folklore texts, the "revealing style" Boas notes in
Mules and Men, varies from one text to another, but the texts share in
common a blending of social scientific analysis and Hurston's renditions of folktales, sayings, and beliefs she collected and remembered
from her childhood as well as behavior she observed and assigns verbal
equivalents, representing in written form the lexicon of oral "hieroglyphics." Just as in her novels and other fiction she uses her imagination in combination with folklore, in her folklore texts she appropriates
fictional techniques. Therefore, the prose style used in "Characteristics"
resists the sort of lucidity ordinarily associated with scientific writing and
revels in ambiguity. Based on her idea of "universal mimicry," for example, the following statement seems to be an oxymoron. "So if we look
at it squarely, the Negro is a very original being" (*see* Appendix, p. 250).
Does originality reflect an origin, a past, a long-standing tradition, or a
first? Is "a very original being" an essentialist reference, positing an
ideal type, or is a higher value placed on tradition than on newness or
invention? To echo Hurston, "*if one looks closely* [the statement's] *falsity
is immediately evident.*" As with Gregory Bateson's discussion of the message communicated in the statement "This is play," the terms used to define "originality" in Hurston's lexicon result in a paradox which seems
to be a function of syntax: If the statement is true, then it must be false.
"If it be false, then it must be true."[91] To understand Hurston's theory
of originality and to evaluate the originality of her texts "is to look not
for first instances of a phenomenon, but rather to see duplication, par-
allelism, symmetry, parody, repetition, echoes of it."[92] For she makes the
point that "while he [the Negro] lives and moves in the midst of a white
civilization, everything that he touches is re-interpreted for his own use"
(*see* Appendix, p. 250). Thus, [*"if one looks closely"*] she empowers herself
as an author by appropriating Boas's notion of diffusion to illustrate
[*"its falsity is immediately evident"*]. Her reasoning leads to the conclusion
that African-Americans participate in cultural processes through conscious appropriation and inversion of cultural forms.

In addition to "Characteristics," Hurston's first novel *Jonah's Gourd
Vine* also appeared in 1934, when the severity of the economic depression, escalating since 1929, had reached a critical point throughout the
United States. The years between World Wars I and II have been acknowledged as a period fraught with racial tension and violence, which

many of the more provocative submissions to the *Negro* anthology address; however, public debates over just how to resolve ambivalent and unstable social relations continued to intensify. For this reason, according to David Levering Lewis, Hurston's translation of folklife into language, as represented in *Jonah's Gourd Vine* was "irrelevant in 1934." [93] If the same could be said of her essays in the *Negro* anthology, it was an "irrelevance" of enough importance to foreshadow the launching of a national folklore research project four years later, under the WPA. This is not to say her work influenced the WPA folklore project's coming into existence; rather, a combination of causes led to its creation. But it is to say that folklore research during the late 1920s and early 1930s did not diminish in importance with increasing economic and social pressures.[94] Hurston's work in 1934, along with that of the folklorists Sterling Brown and Anthony Buttitta, is significant in part because it illuminates a particular historical moment anticipating developments in documentary expression during the 1930s.[95]

For all of its purported failings, *Jonah's Gourd Vine* captures the spirit of indigenous culture in the making. In writing the novel, Hurston had seized an opportunity to celebrate the triumph culture was having over destabilizing economic and social forces. Although the novel serves Hurston personally, by being a medium for her family history and by allowing her the freedom, through fiction, to reimagine that history, it also satisfies a broader need for conceiving and representing American cultural diversity. Criticism of the novel reflects a political climate that cannot accommodate unruly rumblings from southern backwoods.

SUNDAY EVENING, JANUARY 10, 1932

ZORA HURSTON

Presents

"THE GREAT DAY"

A PROGRAM OF ORIGINAL NEGRO FOLKLORE

With a

CHORAL AND DRAMATIC CAST

Ensembles and Vocal Effects under the direction of "Wen" Talbert
Musical Arrangements by Porter Gainger

FIRST PART

1. LEIGH WHIPPER
2. IN THE QUARTERS.   WAKING THE CAMP.
   Shack Rouser .... Percy Punter
   Joe Brown .... Male Chorus
3. LEIGH WHIPPER
4. WORKING ON THE RAILROAD
   a. Captain Keep a-Hollerin'
   b. Oh, Lulu!
   c. Can't You Line It?
   d. Mule on de Mount.
   e. East Coast Blues.
   f. Black Gal.
   g. John Henry .... lead by Percy Punter
5. LEIGH WHIPPER
6. BACK IN THE QUARTERS.   DUSK DARK.
   a. Children's Games.
   b. Chick - mah - chick.
   c. Mistah Frog .... sung by Sadie McGill
7. ITINERANT PREACHER AT THE QUARTERS
   a. Death Comes a-Creepin'.
   b. Sermon .... Leigh Whipper
   c. All You People Got To Go.
   d. You Can't Hide.

INTERMISSION

SECOND PART

8. LEIGH WHIPPER
9. IN THE "JOOK."   BLACK DARK
   a. Cold Rainy Day.
   b. Frankie and Albert.
   c. Halimuh Fack.
   d. Palm Beach.
   e. Let de Deal Go Down.
   f. Alabama Bound.

2. The Great Day, *Program notes.*

10. LEIGH WHIPPER

11. CONJURE CEREMONY
    Pea-vine Candle Dance.
    9 Hairs in the Graveyard.

12. LEIGH WHIPPER

13. IN THE PALM WOODS
    Fire Dance.
    a. Bellamina.
    b. Wasp Bite Noby.
    c. Evalina.
    d. 1. Jumping Dance.
       2. Ring Play.
    e. Crow Dance . . . . by Joseph Neeley

14. LEIGH WHIPPER
15. GROUP FINALE
    Deep River.

Piano Accompaniment . . . . . . "WEN" TALBERT

NOTE—From Stephen Foster to contemporary Broadway the folkways and folk-arts of the American Negro have been presented in tinctured and adulterated approximations. That they have seemed characteristic and have been so movingly effective is, in view of this fact, all the greater testimony to their power and originality in the pure undiluted folk-forms that for generations have been in the shrewd and disarming custody of the common people. These folk have always had two arts,—one for themselves and one for the amusement and beguilement of their masters. And seldom, if ever, can the white man or even the sophisticated Negro break through to that inner circle so well-guarded by the instinctive make-believe and "possum-play" of the Negro peasant.

"Great Day" is a stage arrangement of part of a cycle of Negro folk-song, dance and pantomime collected and recorded by Miss Zora Hurston over three years of intimate living among the common folk in the primitive privacy of their own Negro way of life. It is thus a rare sample of the pure and unvarnished materials from which the stage and concert tradition has been derived; and ought to show how much more unique and powerful and spirit-compelling the genuine Negro folk-things really are. That this legacy has not been irrevocably lost or completely overlaid is good news of the highest spiritual and practical importance for all who wish to know and understand the true elements of the Negro heart and soul.   —Alain Locke.

ACKNOWLEDGMENT—The complete cycle of which this concert material is a part was collected by Miss Zora Hurston during four years' travel (1927-31) in the far South.

Throughout these years, this work of salvaging some of the supriving portions of the original primitive life of the Negro has had spiritual and material support from Mrs. R. Osgood Mason of New York.

THE CAST

ALFRED STROCHAN	ROSINA LEFROY	JAMES DAVIS
LEONARD STURRUP	MURIEL AMBRISTER	JAMES ARNOLD
JOHN DAMSON	ZORA HURSTON	VAN JACKSON
JOSEPH NEELEY	OLLIE HOPKINS	HAROLD SMITH
EDWARD WILSON	HATTIE KING REAVES	JOHN ROBINSON
JAMES WHITE	MABEL HOWARD	WILLIAM SANDRIDGE
JAMES BETHEL	DORA THOMPSON	PERCY PUNTER
NEHEMIAH CASH	HELEN DOWDY	DORA BACOTE
CAROLYNE RICH	RED DAVIES	VIOLA ANDERSON
LUCILLE SMITH	GEORGE SIMMONS	ROSETTA CRAWFORD
MARY SANDS	JAMES LORING	SADIE McGILL
BELLE FERGUSON	WILLIAM WINTER	SARA EVANS
CLEMENTINE WILLS	JAMES PARKER	JOHN MOBLEY
ANNA WASHINGTON	LEIGH WHIPPER	WILLIAM POHLAMUS

2. The Great Day, *Program notes.*

3. *Performers from* The Great Day.

To my Godmother, The Mother of the Primitive, in Faith and Devotion — Zora Hurston

THE NEW SCHOOL PRESENTS

"FROM SUN TO SUN"

A Program of Original Negro Folklore

PRODUCED BY ZORA HURSTON
WITH A CHORAL AND DRAMATIC CAST

ENSEMBLE AND VOCAL EFFECTS UNDER
THE DIRECTION OF GEORGETTE HARVEY
MUSICAL ARRANGEMENTS BY PORTER GRAINGER

TUESDAY EVENING
MARCH 29 AT 8:30
RESERVED SEATS NOW
ON SALE $1.50—$1.00

NEW SCHOOL AUDITORIUM
66 WEST 12TH STREET • NEW YORK

4. From Sun to Sun, *Program notes. (Credit: Zora Neale Hurston Papers, Moorland-Spingarn Research Center, Howard University.)*

PROGRAM

1. IN THE QUARTERS—WAKING THE CAMP
   a. Shack Rouser . . . . Percy Punter
   b. Joe Brown . . . . Male Chorus

2. WORKING ON THE RAILROAD
   a. Captain Keep a-Hollerin' . . led by James Davis
   b. Oh, Lulu! . . . . . . led by William Winters
   c. Can't You Line It? . . . . led by James Davis
   d. Mule on de Mount . . . led by William Winters
   e. East Coast Blues . . . . sung by Georgia Burke
   f. Black Gal . . . . . . led by William Winters
   g. John Henry . . . . . sung by William Davis

3. BACK IN THE QUARTERS—DUSK DARK
   a. Children's Games
   b. Chick - mah - chick
   c. Mistah Frog . . . . sung by Rosetta Crawford

4. ITINERANT PREACHER AT THE QUARTERS
   a. Death Comes a-Creepin'
   b. Sermon . . . . Richard Huey
   c. All You People Got To Go
   d. You Can't Hide

INTERMISSION—TEN MINUTES

5. IN THE "JOOK"—BLACK DARK
   a. Cold Rainy Day . . . led by Rosetta Crawford
   b. Frankie and Albert . sung by Rosetta Crawford,
                          Oline Hopkins and Viola Anderson
   c. Halimuh Fack . . . . . sung by Georgia Burke

---

4. From Sun to Sun, *Program notes. (Credit: Zora Neale Hurston Papers, Moorland-Spingarn Research Center, Howard University.)*

d. Palm Beach . . . . sung by Rosetta Crawford, Oline Hopkins and Viola Anderson

e. Let de Deal Go Down . . . led by Joseph Neely

f. Alabama Bound . . . . led by William Davis

g. Guitar Solo . . . . by John Dawson

6. THE FIERY CHARIOT

Original Negro Folk Tale . Georgette Harvey, Joseph Neely and William Davis

7. IN THE PALM WOODS—FIRE DANCE

a. Bellamina . . . . led by Joseph Neely

b. Mama Don't Want No Peas, sung by Leonard Sturrup

c. Evalina . . . . led by Joseph Neely

d. 1. Jumping Dance . . . . led by Joseph Neely

2. Ring Play . . . . . . led by Joseph Neely

e. Crow Dance . . . . . . led by Joseph Neely
(Cutamahcah — Thomas Lee)

PIANO ACCOMPANIMENT — ELINOR BOXWILL

GUITAR ACCOMPANIMENT—JOHN DAWSON AND ALFRED STROCHAN

THE CAST

Reginald Alday	John Dawson	Joseph Neely
Viola Anderson	Sarah Evans	Inez Persand
Dora Bascote	Georgette Harvey	Percy Punter
James Bethel	Oline Hopkins	Carol Rich
Berleana Blanks	Bruce Howard	Alfred Strochan
Georgia Burke	Richard Huey	Leonard Sturrup
Nehemiah Cash	Zora Hurston	James White
Rosetta Crawford	Van Jackson	Clementine Wills
James Davis	Thomas Fletcher Lee	William Winters
William Davis	Estelle Miller	

4. From Sun to Sun, *Program notes. (Credit: Zora Neale Hurston Papers, Moorland-Spingarn Research Center, Howard University.)*

NOTES ON THE PROGRAM

MISS ZORA HURSTON spent four years (1927-1931) in the far South collecting the material used in this production, in an effort to assemble an authentic Negro folk-cycle of representative songs, dances, tales and rituals. Throughout these years, this work of salvaging some of the surviving portions of the original primitive life of the Negro has been actively supported by Mrs. R. Osgood Mason of New York.

THE WORK SONGS in the second number on the program are representative of the songs sung to the rhythm of the work as the men labor on the railroads, in the saw mills, in the phosphate mines. The words often merely add body to the tunes, but all the songs fit some definite rhythm—the swinging of a pick . . . the driving of a nail . . . the sawing of a log.

THE SERMON BY AN ITINERANT PREACHER is a study of Negro religious expression, shown by a scene in a village church, with the congregation working itself to fever pitch, exhorting, and finally breaking into several original and moving spirituals.

THE JOOK SONGS are commonly known as "blues," but many of them tell stories and belong in the ballad class. They originate in the places of entertainment, or jooks, of the South and travel by word of mouth from one jook to another. Few of them are ever heard by a person literate enough to preserve them in writing.

THE CROW DANCE is a primitive and exciting folk dance performed by a group from the Bahama Islands.

--- --- --- --- --- --- --- --- --- --- --- --- --- --- --- ---

THE NEW SCHOOL
for Social Research
66 WEST 12TH STREET
NEW YORK, N. Y.
Tel.: ALgonquin 4-2567

I am enclosing a check for $............................for............................tickets to Zora Hurston's production "From Sun to Sun" on March 29.

Name ....

Address ....

---

4. From Sun to Sun, *Program notes. (Credit: Zora Neale Hurston Papers, Moorland-Spingarn Research Center, Howard University.)*

ROLLINS COLLEGE

Dramatic Art Department

PRESENTS

ZORA HURSTON

IN HER ALL-NEGRO PRODUCTION
OF AFRO-AMERICAN FOLKLORE

"ALL DE LIVE LONG DAY"

An unique and authentic representation of
real negro folk life by talented
native artists

❖

A RETURN ENGAGEMENT WITH
A NEW PROGRAM AND A NEW CAST

❖

All Students (College and Public School) ____$ .35
Reserved Seats _____$ .75 & $ .50

(Reservations may be made by mail, or through
The Bookery, Winter Park.)

❖

RECREATION HALL,   ::   ROLLINS COLLEGE
FRIDAY EVENING AT 8:15
JANUARY 5, 1934

5. All De Live Long Day, *Program notes.*

PROGRAM

❖

1. MAKING THIS TIME—DAYBREAK

   a. "Baby Chile"
      Pauline Foster and Female Ensemble

   b. "I'm Goin' to Make a Graveyard of My Own"
      Gabriel Brown, guitarist, and Male Chorus

2. WORKING ON THE ROAD

   a. "Cuttin' Timber"

   b. "You Won't Do"
      Buddy Brown and Ensemble

   c. "John Henry"
      A. B. Hicks, tenor-baritone

   d. "Please Don't Drive Me"
      Buddy Brown and Ensemble

   e. "Halimuhfack"
      Bernice Knight, soprano

   f. "Fat Gal"
      Mellard Strickland, A. B. Hicks, and Oscar Anderson

   g. "Water Boy"
      A. B. Hicks, tenor-baritone

3. "DE POSSUM'S TAIL HAIRS"—A ONE-ACT FOLK PLAY

   De Possum _____ Maggie Mae Fredericks
   Brer Noah _____ Lewey Wright
   Ham _____ Gabriel Brown

4. SPIRITUALS

   a. "O Lord"

   b. "I'm Going Home"
      Ensemble

   c. "Sit Down"
      Buddy Brown and Ensemble

   d. "Swing Low"
      A. B. Hicks, tenor-baritone

   e. "All My Sins"
      Ensemble

   f. "Go Down Moses"
      A. B. Hicks, tenor-baritone

   g. "I'm Your Child"
      Ensemble

INTERMISSION

5. All De Live Long Day, *Program notes.*

5. "FUNNIN' AROUND"

    a. "Ever Been Down?"
        Female Quartet—Bernice Knight, Willaouise Dorsey,
        Maggie Mae Fredericks, Billy Hurston

    b. Harmonica Solo

    c. "Let the Deal Go Down"

    d. Guitar Solo
        Gabriel Brown

    e. Buck and Wing Specialties
        Curtis Bacott, Willie Matthews, Alphonso Johnson

    f. "St. Louis Blues"
        Bernice Knight, soprano

    g. Piano Solo
        Curtis Bacott

    h. "Break Away"—Folk Dancing
        Ensemble. John Love, fiddler

6. STRING BAND IN THE NEGRO MANNER

    Banjo _____S. E. Boyd
    Fiddle _____ John Love
    Guitar _____Bubble Mimms

7. ON THE NIGER

    a. Ahaco

    b. Bellamina

    c. Mamma Don't Want No Peas

    d. Courtship—"Jumping Dance"
        George Nichols, Maggie Mae Fredericks,
        Lewey Wright

    e. Crow Dance
        ZORA HURSTON

    f. Fire Dance
        Ensemble. George Nichols, African drummer, and
        Oscar Anderson, "Kuta-Mah-Kah" (beating the off
        rhythm on the rear end of the drum).

5. All De Live Long Day, *Program notes.*

Rollins College is delighted again to extend its hospitality to Miss Zora Hurston and her company for a return engagement at Recreation Hall. Last year's performance was so creditable to the negro race, which composed, produced, and acted the various features of the evening's entertainment, that I hope Miss Hurston will be able to extend her performances to other audiences throughout the State.

HAMILTON HOLT.

❖

"From Sun to Sun" was a remarkable revelation of the negro heart and mind. In its primitive spontaneity, its exaggerated rhythms, its intermingled melodies and its vivid coloring it produced a riotous spectacle that thrilled the audience. Zora Hurston and her group of Negro Chanters reveal, as has never been done before, the native instinct of the negro for art expression.

EDWIN OSGOOD GROVER.

❖

The folk lore concert given by Zora Hurston and her company of negroes at Rollins College last year was one of the outstanding events of the season for me both from the artistic and entertainment standpoint. Anyone wishing to get a real glimpse into negro life in Florida should not miss the performance to be given in Recreation Hall on the evening of Jan. 5th. It is a real event.

R. W. FRANCE,
Professor of Economics.

5. All De Live Long Day, *Program notes.*

CHAPTER TWO

Hurston's Theory of Imitation

Hurston heralds imitation as the basis for a theater practice; her concept of imitation, however, runs counter to ordinary meanings of the term. Her clever twist on imitation can be interpreted as meaning that to mimic is to achieve originality. To Hurston, purity of origins is incompatible with truly innovative style, and she presents her argument as if it is a universal idea. The theatrical metaphor (of imitation for the love of it) gets played out in Hurston's simultaneous careers. Her theater career requires full consideration because it is such a little-known, though formative, dimension of her work. In her personal drama of juggling demanding professional pursuits, 1934 becomes a threshold. Not only did Hurston's production *All De Live Long Day* appear on stage in Florida at Rollins College in Winter Park, another of her productions, *Singing Steel*, was staged at the Chicago Women's Club Theater and at the University of Chicago. These productions, like their predecessors *The Great Day* and *From Sun to Sun*, delighted audiences with elegant renditions of songs, dances, games, and storytelling, performed under Hurston's diligent direction in a naturalistic style imitating, if anything, the beauty of simplicity.[96] During that year, she taught dramatic arts at Bethune-Cookman College in Daytona Beach, Florida; sought a faculty position as director of an experimental theater at Fisk University in Nashville; and staged a performance at the First National Folk Festival in St. Louis. The publication of *Jonah's Gourd Vine* and the appearance of "Characteristics" that year merely represented Hurston's compromises with high art and science. Although she had written *Jonah's Gourd Vine* in about three months and had turned over selected essays to Cunard for inclusion in the *Negro* anthology as an entree into the international avant-garde, these writings have never been taken to exemplify Hurston's pinnacle as a fiction writer or ethnographer.

"Characteristics," a theoretical, highly inventive, playful essay, not only departs from but also casts a jaundiced eye toward scientific writing.[97] Overall, Hurston's contributions to the *Negro* anthology can be seen as an experiment with form, a residual outcome of her efforts during the early 1930s to publish the results of her field research for an academic audience—"to re-write and arrange the material for scientific publications," as she said, before realizing "the pity of all the flaming glory of being buried in scientific journals."[98] Hurston's argument in "Characteristics" implies that staged productions, not written texts, are the ideal medium for presenting African-American cultural performances. Imitation becomes her focal point for demonstrating her antipathy toward acculturation, but particularly assimilation, as a solution to social and political problems stemming from "racial" or cultural differences. She sees the problems of defining race and culture and deciding how to present the information one collects as inseparable from the problem of deciding whether the medium one uses to present expressive behavior is compatible with the cultural milieu being displayed. Her statements in "Characteristics" often seem to mock scientific generalizations while making direct statements about black life. In contrast, *All De Live Long Day* and *Singing Steel* are performances showing the poetical side of daily life among hardworking rural people, without the ambiguity of meaning articulated in "Characteristics." A favorable review of *All De Live Long Day* in the Rollins *Sandspur*, credited the play with presenting its characters "in a direct unvarnished manner." Similar to Hurston's previous productions, *All De Live Long Day* takes place in a railroad camp, where the rhythms of life are enacted with equal emphasis given work, play, and ceremonial rites. The reviews Hurston's productions received, when contrasted with reviews of other black musicals of the 1930s (including *Fast and Furious*), suggest her shows offered distinctive portrayals of intimate scenes rare to the public eye.

All De Live Long Day recreates a railroad-camp day through a series of ballads, work songs, a one-act play called "De Possum's Tail Hairs" dramatizing a story she includes in *Mules and Men* as "How the Possum Lost the Hair off His Tail," spirituals, blues songs, instrumental folk tunes, and dances. The day is roughly sketched out from dawn to the middle of the night. Rather than following a plot structure, the narrative mimics everyday-life rhythms in a effort to show how love, labor, religious ex-

pression, fun, games, and devotion to tradition are components of ordinary existence. Secular and sacred rites of passage are rendered. Thus,
the first section of the show—"Making this Time (Daybreak)"—invokes
birth and death through the songs "Baby Chile" and "I'm Goin to Make
a Graveyard of My Own," whereas the final section and climax ("On the
Niger") invokes the Middle Passage and African cultural transformations
in the West. Music dominates the program, which is more an adaptation
of existing "scripts" than a play, more a concert than a musical, but above
all is unique in relation to early twentieth-century folk plays by authors
such as Randolph Edmonds, Willis Richardson, and Ridgeley Torrence
or landmark musicals such as Marc Connelly's *Green Pastures* (1930) and
Du Bose and Dorothy Heyward's *Porgy* (1924)—perhaps closest to James
Weldon Johnson's *God's Trombones: Seven Negro Sermons in Verse* (1927),
with Hurston's work adding a secular dimension.

The representation of songs, dances, and ceremonies Hurston studied on her field research trip to Nassau, Bahamas, distinguishes her
staged work from American drama and entertainment of the period,
where "primitive" culture was caricatured, as in Eugene O'Neill's *The
Emperor Jones* (1925), about a black ruler of a Caribbean island in the
middle of an uprising. It is worth noting, though, that mainstream critics did not perceive distortions in the characterization of Brutus Jones,
the play's central character. Charles Gilpin's performance in the lead,
playing what is said to be the first serious role for a black actor, brought
dignity to the "noble savage" figure. This is the background against
which audiences witnessed Hurston's productions. Presenting
Caribbean dances aligns her with Katherine Dunham, the African-
American dancer and choreographer who, like Hurston, spent considerable time in the Caribbean and staged her findings during the 1940s.
Hurston asserts in her article "Dance Songs and Tales from the
Bahamas": "These songs accompany the exceedingly African folk dance
called the fire dance." As if describing the final scenes in *All De Live
Long Day*, or similar scenes in her other productions, she adds:

> In either form of this dancing [the jumping dance or the ring play], the
> players form a ring, with the bonfire to one side. The drummer usually
> takes his place near the fire. The drum is held over the blaze until the skin
> tightens to the right tone. There is a flourish signifying that the drummer
> is all set. The players begin to clap their hands. The drummer cries,
> 'Gimbay!' (a corruption of the African work *gumbay*, a large drum) and
> begins the song. He does not always select the song. The players more

often call out what they want played. One player is inside the ring. He or she does his preliminary flourish, which comes on the first line of the song, does his dance on the second line, and chooses his successor on the third line and takes his place in the circle. The chosen dancer takes his place and the dance goes on until the drum gets cold. What they really mean by that is, that the skin of the head has relaxed until it is no longer in tune. The drummer goes to the fire and tunes it again. This always changes the song.[99]

Rather than working from a script, Hurston coached performers in singing and dancing their roles; they were trained not to act in a professional sense but to dramatize the gestures and movements one might observe among people in their own environment—in short, she taught them to perform "with unselfconscious simplicity," as the *Sandspur* described it. Hurston's collecting expeditions had supplied her not only with the material for the show but also with a visual concept of how people engaged in the activities she presents manage to perform—that is, sing, dance, play cards, and so forth—without putting on masks in the "disguise" sense. Thus, the show tries to imitate the absence of character masks and feigned personas in everyday life. At the same time, the idea is to capture the depth of experience implicit in ordinary expressions. Simplicity is the face profundity wears, but simplicity is in no way to be taken as simple minded, much less carefree. This goes against the grain of criticism stressing Hurston's romanticism, where critics assume that her use of folklore in literature proves her failure to acknowledge that racism and segregation are severe facts of life for black folk.[100] It has been said enough without my needing to elaborate here that Hurston's reactionary political stance on segregation was one mark setting her apart from the mainstream of black thought. It is worth reiterating, however, that she shows through her work that segregation and discrimination need not be definitive in characterizing black reality.[101] Neglecting to write in the social realist tradition, she nevertheless opts for a realism that depicts the damaging consequences of slave mentality in the character Ned Crittenden, of *Jonah's Gourd Vine*, with as much keen insight as the most self-hating characters in Richard Wright's early work. The complaint against Hurston for her refusal to blame whites for social problems plaguing blacks, stresses her essentialism, her insisting that pure and authentic black folkways flourish merrily on the margins of mainstream society. Her rendition of the fire dance in *Jonah's Gourd Vine* might be taken as a case in point:

So they danced. They called for the instrument that they had brought to America in their skins—the drum—and they played upon it. With their hands they played upon the little dance drums of Africa. The drums of kid-skin. With their feet they stomped it, and the voice of Kata-Kumba, the great drum, lifted itself within them and they heard it. The great drum that is made by priests and sits in majesty in the juju house. The drum with the man skin that is dressed with human blood, that is beaten with a human shin-bone and speaks to gods as a man and to men as a God. Then they beat upon the drum and danced (29).

The scene suggests that the Alabama rural folks gathered around the fire, playing their guitars and banjos and clapping their hands, are transported to a primeval time and place. Africa is invoked and the Middle Passage is seen as a backdrop against which the spirit of survival through performance is enacted, whereby, " 'I, who am borne away to become an orphan, carry my parents with me. For Rhythm is she not my mother and Drama is her man?' "(30). The dance is rendered not simply as an evening's entertainment but as an occasion for the author to display her understanding of African-American music's parallels with African performance traditions. She writes: "Furious music of the little drum whose body was still in Africa, but whose soul sung around a fire in Alabama"(30). Describing improvised rhythms as "hollow-hand clapping for the bass notes," she hints at transplanted African cultures swirled together in the nocturnal drama: "Ibo tune corrupted with Nango. Congo gods talking in Alabama"(30). The participants in the dance achieve something like "spontaneous communitas," until, Hurston reminds us, "the shores of Africa receded," and the night ends.

Sharing a fascination with Africa, Hurston and the intellectuals showcased in the *Negro* anthology had little in common with Broadway producers.[102] While the black and white writers in *Negro* were offering various perspectives on aspects of numerous black cultures, commercial theater producers and directors valued black expression for its capacity to be commodified. The stage was a place where sensational style had priority, and although Harlem's black renaissance seemed to profit in the 1920s because of the long-running musical *Shuffle Along*'s novelty and popular appeal, by the 1930s, black musicals—including those exposed in Broadway's glitter—were disparaged for their hackneyed repetitions of 1920s formulas. Although reviews of performances cannot be taken as definitive, they can be quite influential in determining the life spans of shows, despite the uneven relationship between positive critical reception and commercial success. In her exhaustive work on *The Great Day* and *From Sun to Sun,* Hurston channeled energy she previously had expended without much reward on *Fast and Furious* and *Jungle Scandals*—lesser work she deemed necessary to get public recognition for her talents as a dramatic artist.[103] She had sacrificed time as well as her financial resources for her New York debut as a dramatist and continued the same pattern of overextension during her Rollins College production of *From Sun to Sun,* though with greater institutional support than the New York ventures. Rollins College sponsored Hurston's productions and supplied her with space and technical staff; she had only to train and rehearse the performers. By the time *All De Live Long Day* was mounted, Hurston had developed her techniques for presenting the material and was poised for her highest achievements in the theater.

Singing Steel, harkening once again to a railroad camp, appeared in Chicago in November 1934, to enthusiastic notices and was, like its progenitors, touted for its genuine beauty. A Chicago reviewer who deemed the show superior to its contemporary counterparts on commercial stages called Hurston "an anthropologist for and of her race," because she was discerning enough to include a tough-toned blues song ("Mama Don't Want No Peas") which "accomplished quickly and easily what a generation of Tin Pan Alleyites have only tried to do."[104] The same reviewer designates the performance of "Let the Deal Go Down" as "a somber haunting progenitor of Bert Williams' famous solo poker game and as full of drama too as the bereft bully dealt his cards and called off a series of threats as to what the card augured toward his 'two-timing' girl and her paramour."[105] Hurston had, while staying at the YWCA, directed the show with local talent (dramatic arts and sewing students at the YWCA), novices to professional theater whom Hurston no less than the critics found more "authentic" than seasoned artists (which to Hurston meant corrupted).[106] "The large chorus is not the typical trained group—they are authentic unsophisticated singers and performers and the effect is truly artistic and entertaining," said one reviewer of the cast (clippings file, Rollins College archive). In an ultimate tribute to the spell of fine performance and the type of breakthrough theater, Hurston is alleged to have fantasized creating with Hughes, another critic praises *Singing Steel* for its lucid portrayal of the proletariat: "The vehicle, packed with folklore, drama and dancing, brings to the public not only the song and drama of a working day, but all the pathos, joy and innate feeling of freedom so characteristic of and inherent to the worker. From the chant of the shack-rouser just before the break of day until the end of the fire dance at midnight, it is a remarkable revelation of the laborer's heart and mind."[107]

As Hemenway explains, Hurston's theatrical career ostensibly ended at the apex of her achievement due to the inordinate time and energy required to get the results she desired. Since her writing talents were in demand, she was able to take advantage of the notoriety her theater presence ensured. She was able to continue her quest for a performance-centered understanding of black culture, through language. Her goal did not change, but the attention she devoted to creating performances shifted from stage to page. Her performance-centered approach accounts for difficulties critics perceive in her work because she omits political commentary, combines the fictional and the factual, and narrates from a first-person omniscient point of view. All her texts, like her staged productions, in part become auto-texts or auto-performances—displays of scripts filtered through their creator who also inserts herself at intervals. A controlling first-person point of view permeates the narrative, stemming from Hurston's self-conscious role as a mediator, as a social scientist required to report information authoritatively while appearing disinterested. The glossary at the end of *Jonah's Gourd Vine* suggests a taxonomic analysis has been applied to the Alabama and Florida communities portrayed in what otherwise is presented as a fiction, subsequently known to be autobiographical. Including a taxonomy of linguistic terms is Hurston's way of signalling readers to the translation process necessary for cross-cultural understanding to occur. As Werner Sollors notes, when writers either deliberately or inadvertently become interpreters of culture for uninformed readers, "footnotes, lengthy asides, explanations which at times seem superfluous or even offensive to some readers, bibliographies and glossaries become the signposts of this situation.[108] Any attempts to reduce the objectives of social scientific research to cause-and-effect formulas, or to deploy causal analysis as a way of making sense of human lives, are held up for scrutiny.

SCIENCE, HUMANISM, AND PARODY

The question of whether so-called "scientific" approaches to folklore research can be helpful in solving social problems is crucial to an understanding of the broad humanistic agenda underlying the folklore research Hurston and many of her contemporaries pursued. Whether humanistic objectives for research can be reconciled with social and economic problems of cultural groups being studied and how the question is related to, or influences, the products of research is a central concern in my analysis of "Characteristics." The essay's ethnological terms, along with the definitions proffered, are replete with parodic references, recalling what James Clifford calls "Ethnographic Surrealism," in his discussion of French anthropology during the 1920s and 1930s. His definition of ethnography helps to clarify the transition occurring in anthropology, when empirical research involving fieldwork was beginning to be more widely practiced. Ethnography, according to Clifford, is not to be equated with ethnology—the latter being another term for anthropology or "human science" and its empirical methods, noted for taxonomic systems of organizing cultural facts and artifacts. ("Cultural" and "social" anthropology are the corresponding terms in the United States and England, respectively.) The ethnographer, in Clifford's sense, rather than describing and attempting to explain "the unfamiliar," reexamines assumptions about "the familiar." By showing the oddities abounding in ordinary existence, ethnographic surrealists were demonstrating that reality is not a given but, rather, is "contested" and that "ethnographic evidence and an ethnographic attitude could function in the service of a subversive cultural criticism."[109]

I would like to suggest that Hurston is somehow aligned with the ethnographic approach Clifford describes as surrealist; although she does not use collage or concentrate on grotesque imagery, she employs shock techniques, an approach that Clifford argues is the ethnographer's provenance in efforts to make "primitive" culture not merely comprehensible but recognizable to the mind of "civilized man." An analogy also arises in connection with Negritude poet Aime Cesaire's use of neologisms; as Clifford notes, coined words and phrases in Cesaire's poetry—and I would add, in Hurston's writing—become metonyms for cultural transformation, creolized language, hybrid identity, and meta-discourses on the "nature" of writing.[110] Hurston no doubt was unaware of her affinity with the ethnographic style Clifford attributes to French anthropologists Michel Leiris, Marcel Mauss, Marcel Griaule, and Alfred Metraux collaborating with the poet George Bataille, but her resistance to the dominant school of empiricism, particularly its representational style—the scientific article—is evident in the creative license she takes. What is most interesting in the parallel between Hurston and the French anthropologists is the significance artistic license came to play as a primary basis for diminishing the scientific credibility of her work. Increasing the orientation toward empiricism meant the "consolidation of a paradigm," in Clifford's terms, which in turn "depends on the exclusion or relegation to the status of 'art' of those elements of the changing discipline that call the credentials of the discipline itself into question."[111] Thus, being identified primarily as an artist is presumed to be counter-scientific, though this negative judgment need not be the case. The interplay between artistic and scientific judgments can, as Clifford argues, be a fruitful alternative to reproducing conventional dichotomies between "civilized" and "primitive" societies.

Hurston attempts to debunk the stereotype that African-Americans adapt to social circumstances by mimicking white-American "norms" of behavior. Her theory of imitation mocks social scientific explanations of cultural diffusion and assimilation. How her theoretical ideas are translated into practice through staged performances that similarly revise common stereotypes is not immediately apparent because of assumptions about what was or was not the "norm" at the time. Challenges related to medium, social context, framing, audience, and economics, which were highly constraining when Hurston pursued her theatrical work, indicate the extent to which Americans historically have resisted changing stereotypes and, by extension, changing social circumstances; resistance to change causes prevailing views to be reproduced in various media.[112] Whether performances in any way contribute to changing social relations or solving social problems is difficult to establish. If Hurston's intention was to revise stereotypes through staged performances rather than texts, to what extent was she able to achieve her goal? And, subsequently, have other artists been able to do so? The potential success of her theory was to a large extent inseparable from the ideology underlying efforts in the scientific community to advance cultural development among African-Americans—an early example being Boas's 1906 proposal for an African Institute.

Boas maintained that African-Americans' social problems could in part be attributed to "the economic, mental, and moral inferiority of the [black] race in America," relative to blacks in Africa.[113] This position, along with the belief that white Americans' attitudes "in regard to the Negro might be materially modified if we had a better knowledge of what the Negro has really done and accomplished in his own native country," prompted Boas to propose to Andrew Carnegie, in 1906, creating an "African Institute" to "contribute materially to the solution of these problems."[114] The proposed institute was to present exhibitions and publications and would have separate divisions devoted to the study of African anatomy and collecting statistics on African-Americans.

Boas's effort to establish an African Institute is significant in this context because as the person who "more than any man defined the 'national character' of anthropology in the United States,"[115] he influenced a generation of anthropologists. Hurston worked with at least three of them, including Ruth Benedict, Otto Klineberg, and Melville Herskovits, all of whom addressed racial issues in their work and helped to bring about a humanistic direction in a field racked by contestable assumptions implicit in "scientific" notions of "race" and culture.[116] In her radio address "Race Prejudice in the United States" (1946), Ruth Benedict's argument shows that progressive scientific research on race, inspired by Boas, had discredited ideas concerning superiority and inferiority of people based on biological traits, but that "the old jealous tribalism of the untutored savage has not died out even in our literate industrial world."[117] Thus, even the scientifically trained, like the unnamed anthropologist Benedict describes, must explain cultural and racial differences in ways "more complicated than we need to be," because of an underlying, ever present human bias.[118] The interest in humanistic issues also bears directly on Hurston's work and that of folklorists and artists who, according to Jerrold Hirsch, began in the 1930s to develop a pluralistic notion of American culture, promoting diversity rather than absorption into a homogenized "melting pot."[119] Hurston's work occurs at a pivotal moment when an emphasis on pluralism was gaining prominence in the sphere of public-sector folklore; her work manifests aspects of both the older and newer ways of thinking. Boas's work also can be interpreted as bridging the two perspectives; according to Roger Abrahams, Boas departed from nineteenth century "reductionist thinking," based on social evolutionist ideas influencing biological research.[120] Hirsch argues that by the time folklorists were working for the Federal Writers' Project (FWP) in the mid-1930s,

> They were influenced by cultural relativism, the emphasis on a plurality of historically conditioned cultures *rather than a hierarchical evolutionary scheme of a universal culture in which different groups occupied higher and lower rungs*—the idea of culture as an integrative force *and the concept of acculturation, which characterized the work of Franz Boas, Ruth Benedict, and their students.*[121] [Emphasis mine.]

As Hurston had been influenced by Boas and Benedict and as Hurston's work illustrates, she was to a large extent developing her own position on anthropological doctrines taught at Columbia University and Barnard College.

Nowhere are Hurston's efforts to come to terms with the cultural anthropologists' arguments on acculturation more evident, in my view, than in "Characteristics." Herskovits wrote in his 1927 article "Acculturation and the American Negro" that acculturation is "a body of people accepting *in toto* the culture of an alien group" and that "the American negro shows himself to be essentially American, and scarcely at all negro."[122] Unlike Herskovits, who addressed himself to "insistent claims from some quarters" that studies on acculturation were important "for what has come to be termed 'applied anthropology,' "[123] Hurston includes no explicit social agenda in her work—in contrast also with the Columbia anthropologists already mentioned and progressive FWP folklorists, whether their emphasis was on acculturation or pluralism.[124] To make the case that Hurston's work presents a model for understanding how social scientific research, humanistic objectives, and solutions to social problems are related means demonstrating that she shared a similar agenda with some of her colleagues, although she communicated her objectives differently. As I stated in Chapter One, her words recreate "hieroglyphics," action words, behavior made explicit through visual analogies. It is through her interpretation and use of action words, which is to say dramatic analogies, that she demonstrates a critical method. Thus, the results of her thinking and evidence of a social or political consciousness are structurally embedded in her work and are implicit in her terms and the meanings they produce.

The question of how research on social behavior can be used to analyze and resolve social problems has no conclusive answer. As Hirsch has noted, the optimistic outlook that New Deal folklorists had for a future when cultural democracy would prevail was not worked out in practical plans: "The FWP offered no programs for achieving the ideal relationship described in their mythic view of the role arts had played in the American past and could play in the future" and "was unable to face the issue of whether the revitalized American culture they hoped for could be created without changes in social and economic arrangements."[125]

Between Boas's plan for an African Institute in 1906 and the FWP folklorists' 1935 vision of a future where culturally diverse groups would coexist in a world of social equality, is Hurston's position, which parallels views attributed to John Lomax. According to Hirsch, Lomax considered technological society "a destroyer of folk tradition" which "broke down isolation and exposed members of folk cultures to other traditions and to popular culture."[126] To Lomax, "cultural interaction was a form of contamination resulting in impurity."[127] In this thinking, cultural differences are valued without regard for how they are related to social and economic problems. Folklore "purists" such as Lomax and Hurston, according to Hirsch, held a romanticized view of folk culture, which in a strangely inverted way, "privileges" the lower class rural folk as bearers of traditions worth preserving in their untouched forms. "Untouched," in this analysis means unalleviated from the burdens of poverty. Changing economic relations through social scientific research is not part of the agenda in this romanticized view, although attempting to improve social relations through educating people about their own and other cultures was a broad objective for Hurston.

Seeing folklore as a process that exposes dynamics of social interaction among people makes it possible to speculate about how such knowledge can be translated into concrete plans for social change.[128] Cultural forms can be taken as models for adaptability, as Hurston's assessment of "Negro Folklore" suggests; folklore is "not a thing of the past," she writes. "It is still in the making. Its great variety shows the adaptability of the black man: nothing is too old or too new, domestic or foreign, high or low, for his use" (*see* Appendix, pp. 248–9). By creating a frame for behavior within specific social contexts, Hurston tries to show how forms of expression slip across boundaries.

> God and the Devil are paired, and are treated no more reverently than Rockefeller and Ford. Both of these men are prominent in folklore, Ford being particularly strong, and they talk and act like good-natured stevedores or mill-hands. Ole Massa is sometimes a smart man and often a fool. The automobile is ranged alongside of the oxcart. (*See* Appendix, p. 249.)

By showing how boundaries defining social context are flexible, she equalizes the categories ("old," "new," "domestic," "foreign," "high, "low") and diverts the reader's attention away from the economic and political power relations influencing cultural production. The analogy that rich men such as Ford and Rockefeller are like stevedores and mill-hands is characteristic of Hurston's analogical method. Culture, art, and community are contained within boundaries that preclude examining complicated political forces affecting communities and cultural groups and their relations with the world at large. Whether forms of folk expression are useful in reconstituting the world is a contested issue, as mentioned at the end of Chapter One. According to Jay Mechling,

> Folklore may not be an effective source of resistance against the hegemony enjoyed by the dominant culture. If the double bind is a structural mode of maintaining hegemony, then language games will have no effect on the dominant culture or even in the intercultural encounter with other marginalized groups. 'Masking' may be a form of resistance, but it is a form unlikely to change the situation. Folklore, in short, may be a force for *pacification* rather than *resistance*, a prospect that should not come as good news to those inclined to romaticize the folklore of underclasses.[129]

Mechling's argument is problematic in my view because it relies on a notion of social change rigidly defined along oppositional lines between dominant and disempowered groups; I am arguing for a notion of empowerment that does not rely only on "resistance" or opposition but on recreating cultural forms as a way of changing social consciousness.

In 1934, the relationship between politics and cultural production was a pressing consideration as even the publication of the *Negro* anthology illustrates. Within its pages, for example, Cunard's attacks on W.E.B. Du Bois in particular and the National Association for the Advancement of Colored People in general for the strategy adopted in the Scottsboro case indicate differences between the American Communist Party and the traditional Black leadership, differences that had an impact on cultural politics. Using the essay by Du Bois, "Black America" (a history of African-American achievement since the sixteenth century), printed immediately following her article "A Reactionary Negro Organization," Cunard tries to demonstrate why in her view the theory of high achievement among 10 percent of African-Americans promoted by Du Bois as the "Talented Tenth," rather than being an answer to progress, is a reflection of "bourgeois placidity." It is important also to note that the "Talented Tenth" idea is one among various strategies attributable to Du Bois. Part of Cunard's objection to the NAACP, Du Bois, and the *Crisis* which he edited stems from her opinion that white patronage had corrupted the goals and motivations of black leaders.[130] Where does folk culture fit into debates addressing economic and social problems faced by cultural groups outside the mainstream of power? How do conceptions of folk culture impinge on the negative impact social isolation has on a community's capacity to control its economic and social relations with the world at large? These are questions that make it possible to measure whether Hurston's theories of imitation, text production, and staged performances have any impact and if so, how.

PLAYING WITH BOUNDARIES

Emphasis on culture to the exclusion of politics and economics runs the risk of trivializing serious social concerns. In Hurston's essay "Characteristics," one finds numerous examples where the serious is combined with the frivolous, where it is hard to discern whether her intent is satirical. She describes, for example, how a representative African-American "has modified the language, mode of food preparation, practice of medicine, and most certainly the religion of his new country" (*see* Appendix, p. 250). The reference to "his new country" is a conflation of at least two centuries of African-American history, and her statement's rejoinder parodies "scientific" rationality: "just as he adapted to suit himself the Sheik haircut made famous by Rudolph Valentino" (*see* Appendix, p. 250). Hurston's representative African-American crosses boundaries, moving from the folk context into the sphere of popular culture and mass media.

An analogy can be drawn with what Michael Taussig, in *Mimesis and Alterity: A Particular History of the Senses,* calls "the playful exchange of difference," in his explanation of imitation and mimicry in the Tierra Del Fuego. The Fuegians communicated with Charles Darwin and, later, Captain Fitz Roy by mimicking their gestures and actions, stealing and dividing equally among themselves objects, which could not be imitated, like the buttons from a jacket. Mimicry in this context can be described as a type of desire to communicate—one might say, to commune—which reaches across cultural boundaries in an aggressive colonial encounter. Exchange occurs by default in that the explorers also mimic the Fuegians imitating the explorers, and so on.

This playing with boundaries can be read in several ways. Taken literally, the analogy between using language, preparing food, practicing medicine, worshipping and appropriating the hairstyle of a silent-film star sounds absurd; one cannot get past the content of the second portion of the statement without questioning the rules, the limits, the boundaries of the discourse itself. The reader's attention shifts from the image of Valentino's sheik haircut being mimicked (by whom the reader does not know exactly) to Hurston herself and her method.

Susan Willis discusses Hurston's inconsistent use of pronouns in her autobiography *Dust Tracks on a Road*; according to Willis, "the pronoun shifts enable Hurston to be both Southern and not-Southern, black and not-black, inferior and not-inferior. This is not to say that she assumes a Northern, white identity, rather she lifts herself, as a writer, out of any possible inscription in the stigmatized view of Southern blackness."[131] What Willis identifies as Hurston's ungrammatical usage is not an attempt to separate herself from "Southern blackness" but an example of her attempt to write about culture while criticizing the conventions of cultural analysis. The conflict is methodological but not necessarily an identity problem. As previously mentioned, Hurston's notion of the relation between class and race or culture, privileges or romanticizes, rather than denies, the essentialism of "Southern blackness." Questions arise as to why a scientific interpretation is paralleled with a whimsical one, with an example of a person in the cultural group she is trying to prove is "original." Although "the text asserts its powers over the context"—in this instance, the field research context—and succeeds at tricking the reader, through verbal sleight of hand; the "trick" is not a political maneuver, per se.[132] Hurston is testing the limits of the written text, to see what potential it has for representing the drama of everyday life. "The fascination of the trick becomes a fascination with technique, with the formal operations by which the text is made and shattered."[133] The example she uses, also shows in a sense, the continuity between folk and popular culture and reflects the same irreverence evident in her observations omitted from the original edition of her autobiography *Dust Tracks on a Road* when it was published in 1942.[134]

> If you look at a man and mistrust your eyes, do something and see if he will imitate you right away. If he does, that's My People. We love to imitate. We would rather do a good imitation than any amount of something original. Nothing is half so good as something that is just like something else. And no title is so coveted as the "black this or that." (*Dust Tracks* 210)

Boldly, Hurston appropriates assimilationist discourse. The excess, the reveling in a most literal interpretation of how cultural traits are acculturated leads to an excessive accumulation of examples.

> We have Black Patti, Black Yankees, Black Giants. Rose McClendon was referred to time and again as the Black Barrymore. Why we even have a Black Dillinger! . . . Julian, the parachute jumper, risked his life by falling

43

> in the East River pretending he knew how to run an aeroplane like Lindbergh to gain his title of Black Eagle. (*Dust Tracks* 210)

By using popular personalities, she demonstrates that individual style is important when imitating; fame and other recognition that accompany self-exposure lead to extremes of distinction—Difference for the sake of being Other. She practices the art of mimicry to illustrate a unique way of going about the same thing that other writers contributing to the *Negro* anthology are doing: interpreting black culture for the world at large.[135] The audience for her work in 1934 was conditioned to accept essentialist arguments on black cultures, alongside serious social, political, and cultural criticism. Since mimicry can be "a model for opposition," Hurston's paradoxes underscore, to readers then and now, discomforts concerning race and culture and more important to Hurston, the language used to discuss racial, cultural, and artistic "originality."[136] She directly addresses some paradoxes, as I will show further along with her class analysis, while others she exposes through the unique interpretive style I call "playing with boundaries."

Her playing with boundaries draws attention to the way her text is permeated with nonsensical analogies, jokes presented as if they were serious conclusions based on empirical evidence. She crosses boundaries in the way Erving Goffman identifies with a lecturer whose topic is jokes, who tells them so frequently "examples are constantly slipping out of their frame status as mere examples"; like Goffman's hypothetical lecturer, Hurston's verbal play obtains for her the same reputation "that real tellings would ordinarily earn."[137] But Hurston does not differentiate between translating everyday-life performances she observed into words and analyzing or interpreting her observations; therefore, the text and the metatext she constructs are combined into one.

If metaphors and similes, as Hurston argues, are among African-Americans' main contributions to the English language, her text, again, demonstrates the theory. The text of everyday life becomes a metaphor for a critical outlook on the world, with meanings structurally embedded in actions—gestures, expressions, and verbal arts.[138] The simile concerning Valentino is ironic as a description of a person, because Hurston neither claims to display the hairstyle herself nor does she present a picture of a flesh-and-bones person wearing the style.[139] By pretending to "quote"—that is, by representing someone who saw it or wore it—she indirectly comments on the possibility that the style itself has a meaning that cannot be interpreted literally, or scientifically, and perhaps, is a fabrication. Although quotation marks can be used to produce irony by suggesting the "quoted words" mean their opposite, when quotes are omitted in situations ordinarily requiring attribution, as when reporting someone else's words, then another type of irony occurs, what Roland Barthes calls "transgression of ownership," a method of appropriating.[140] "Ordinary" irony, when words are quoted to mean their opposite, gets cancelled out when quotation marks are omitted. The words then parody the way quotation marks are used to assign "authority" to sources.

> A multivalent text can carry out its basic duplicity only if it subverts the opposition between true and false, if it fails to attribute quotations (even when seeking to discredit them) to explicit authorities, if it flouts all respect for origin, paternity, propriety, if it destroys the voice which could give the text its ("organic") unity, in short, if it coldly and fraudulently abolishes quotation marks which must, as we say, in all honesty, enclose a quotation and juridically distribute the ownership of the sentences to their respective proprietors, like subdivisions of a field.[141]

Within the boundaries of the text itself, Hurston's simile using the sheik haircut can be read as a parody with at least three possible meanings. It can be read as a parody of a mass-media icon, intended to condemn the making of an actor into what Andre Bazin calls a "socioreligious" film persona such as Rudolph Valentino.[142] Or it can be seen as Hurston's parody of an African-American emulating or praising a mass-media figure's style. If it is neither, if Hurston is earnestly trying to show how an African-American literally imitates what appears before him, which I believe she is not, then the simile is a parody of itself. In any case, the key to establishing a parodic meaning is the intertextual reference to either the dubiousness of film-star worship or the desirability of film-star heroism. It also can be read as an intertextual discourse on the revision of folk culture through dissemination of cultural forms found in mass media. The fourth possible meaning is a product of the contrast between the scientific language of the statement's opening and the artificial representation of a "real" person. What is more, the image reconstructs a discourse on stereotypes and thus draws parodic meaning from its reference to yet another text, a subtext of minstrelsy and conventions of masking associated with it.[143] Sorting out parodic references in "Characteristics" is a prickly pursuit, because Hurston's experiments with form remain tempered by her conservative typology. I do not think it is fair to say that her work operates as the kind of social critique ordinarily attributed to parody. The work's parodic dimension derives from her use of folk humor, always replete with mockery, including self-mockery. Parody must necessarily sting and bite the would-be targets. When critical remarks are not aimed at the folk, as in "Characteristics" of Negro Expression, but at an intellectual elite controlling the discourse used to talk about and speak on behalf of the folk, any attempt at parody may be cancelled out or recede into careful manipulating of language and manners, something akin to what Homi Bhaba calls "sly civility."[144]

Presenting "ironic" folklore by erasing the frame that enables readers to differentiate between quoted references and the author's interpretations raises questions about the collector's reliability and the material's accuracy. Robert Hemenway, through his reading of Hurston's correspondence with Langston Hughes, speculates about her reasons for revising her field notes used to produce "Characteristics" and other publications that postdate her fieldwork during the late 1920s, including *Mules and Men*. "Her rewriting grew out of her desire to emphasize the esthetic significance of the folklore performance," according to Hemenway.[145] Indeed, Hemenway's discussion of the revising Hurston describes to Hughes seems to apply primarily to notes on behavior she observed rather than to narratives, although Hemenway equates the different genres when he remarks that "Hurston's rewriting and tampering with material, even done solely for purposes of clarity, would be anathema to most modern folklorists, although the requirements for accurate, authentic transcriptions of folk narratives were not always as exacting in 1929 as they are today."[146]

In her letter to Hughes, Hurston specifically states that for the most part, she is not altering the "story material," whereas she admits extensively rewriting descriptive material despite her concerns about appeasing scientific readers. At this time, according to Hemenway, Hurston is grappling with a "two-fold purpose," a conflict caused by wanting to succeed in two disciplines. "On the one hand, she was trying to represent the artistic content of black folklore; on the other, she was trying to suggest the behavioral significance of folklore."[147]

Hemenway builds his argument toward the conclusion that Hurston had a "dual consciousness" and could not resolve a conflict between scientific and artistic methods. What he attributes to Hurston could be considered endemic to the period, even an extension of a broad dilemma fueling modern aesthetics since Nietzsche's lamentations concerning the way Apollonian translucence paradoxically obscures Dionysian reverie. Hemenway describes a highly conventional polarity "which emerges from her creative effort during the thirties—her five books, her fiction, her plays, her essays," stressing "that eventually immediate experience takes precedence over analysis, emotion over reason, the personal over the theoretical."[148] His argument establishes opposition between emotional and subjective versus rational and objective biases and relies on classifications conventionalized according to race, as well illustrated in his claim that:

> She learned that scientific objectivity is not enough for a black writer in America, and she went on to expose the excessive rationality behind the materialism of American life, the inadequacy of sterile reason to deal with the phenomena of living. She forcefully affirmed the humanistic values of black life, contrasting them with the rationalized inhumanity of white society; she asserted early arguments for black nationalism.[149]

Hemenway sees Hurston's work in terms of a dichotomy, but it seems that she often disavowed the humanism he attributes to her, even while she appropriated scientific rationality, without conforming to the rules of either camp.[150]

One has to speculate about the extent to which Hurston was self-conscious in using oral storytelling and fictional techniques in producing "Characteristics." Is her method an attempt to come to terms with observations she makes "as someone *different*, formed by the experience of loss and loneliness and by the *consciousness* of the difference of the city in the North and the rural community in the South"?[151] Does she attempt to recoup what she senses to be a lost part of her heritage, by appropriating some aspects of expressive forms she observes? One can see the elements of parody without knowing what she consciously intended to parody or whether parody is a symptom of irresolution.[152] Hurston's humor, though lucid, at times stops short of caricature, as she concretely illustrates the process of dissemination across cultures. In this interpretive frame, she explains, for example, "everyone is familiar with the Negro's modification of the whites' musical instruments, so that his interpretation has been adopted by the white man himself and then reinterpreted" (43). The idea that "until the late 1940s folklore was thought of as the product of folk performance" is presented by Hurston as a normalized experience, something "everyone" knows.[153]

Being confused about origins of performance styles, however, would have been easy for "anyone," considering that during the 1920s even the well-known black performers Eubie Blake and Ethel Waters had to be escorted to the Cotton Club in Harlem by "the King of Jazz," Paul Whiteman, before they could be admitted to hear Duke Ellington play.[154] Since Paul Whiteman, according to Hurston was "in so many words . . . giving an imitation of a Negro orchestra making use of white-invented musical instruments in a Negro way" (*see* Appendix, p. 251), questions of originality could only be meaningful when the performance style itself became the focus.

Constraints imposed by racial segregation did not, after all, prevent Hurston's acknowledging the substance of Boas's notion of diffusion: "Thus has our so-called civilization come. The exchange and re-exchange of ideas between groups" (*see* Appendix, p. 251). Although she vacillates between seeing culture as a process of dissemination across cultures and embracing a concept of originality based on a notion of American identity, rooted in American soil, her wavering is counterbalanced by a process Roger Abrahams and Susan Kalcik describe as deciphering perceptions, when "one knew intuitively which specific items were traditional and which were not because one had worked with the materials long enough to feel the difference immediately."[155] But her shifting the frames of reference suggests a difficulty in defining tradition. Terence Ranger and Eric Hobsbawm's idea of invented traditions arising as a consequence of the industrial revolution can substitute for some attempts to define originality in an American context. Invented traditions allude to the past without quite being part of it. In the absence of old, "specific and strongly binding social practices," invented traditions constitute communities within a changing historical, political, and economic context.[156]

IMITATION

In her discussion of "Imitation," Hurston further develops her idea of mimicry as everyday-life drama but in this portion of "Characteristics," she primarily is concerned with refuting the idea that African-Americans are acculturated. To "prove" her point, she presents a class analysis meant to show an ideal or "authentic" cultural knowledge is given form and meaning in the everyday-life behavior of prototypical African-Americans. "The Negro the world over is famous as a mimic," a blatantly pejorative statement, establishes her notion of imitation and the "privileged" position of one endowed with the special knowledge required for authenticating one's identity as a prototype. Caught, again, in the quagmire of ambivalence undergirding her discussion of originality, she shifts between two extremes, cautioning that being a mimic "in no way damages [her] standing as an original" (*see* Appendix, p. 251). But the apparent contradiction is no more than a convention, a frame completed by the unifying idea that "mimicry is an art in itself" (*see* Appendix, p. 251). Is this the inverse of what we really mean by "originality is the modification of ideas"? As E.H. Gombrich argues, "the convention of the frame" enables an artist to create in a way that virtually requires a spectator to participate in constructing the meaning of the work; thus the artist "relies on our readiness to take hints, to read contexts, and to call up our conceptual image."[157] In this way, Hurston contrives a notion of mimicry as originality by evoking a classical concept of mimesis, resembling the dramatic concept articulated in Aristotle's *Poetics*.

Mimicry, originality, and art become the focus of her cultural analysis, leading the reader away from the contested term "Negro," with its racialist agendas and political associations, toward a notion of imitation similar to Aristotle's. Her emphasis on aesthetics becomes clear when she argues that if mimicry is not art, "then all art must fall by the same blow that strikes it down. When sculpture, painting, acting, dancing, literature neither reflect nor suggest anything in nature or human experience we turn away with a dull wonder in our heart at why the thing was done" (*see* Appendix, p. 251). Her similarity to Aristotle also is evident in the value she places on imitating nature and on the pleasure a spectator receives from observing. According to Aristotle, "the habit of imitating is congenital to human beings from childhood."[158] He further argues that imitation has more power over humans than animals because of its importance in early-childhood learning, which is suggested in Hurston's example of "a group of small Negro boys imitating a cat defecating and the subsequent toilet of the cat" (*see* Appendix, p. 252). She heralds the mimic above all other artists because imitation is best achieved through action, and as pointed out previously, action is the basis for African-American verbal art.

Part of her reason for writing on imitation is to disprove what she considers misconceptions about why African-Americans acculturate American "norms" of behavior. "Moreover, the contention that the

Negro imitates from a feeling of inferiority is incorrect," she writes, "He mimics for the love of it" (*see* Appendix, p. 251). Again, she brings to mind Aristotle, who argues that not only is the proclivity to imitate inborn but "so is the pleasure that all men take in works of imitation."[159] As has already been stated, Hurston's essay in part provides a counterpoint to notions of assimilation which imply that African-Americans possessed no customs distinguishable from their white American counterparts. Although major thinkers of the period who influenced Hurston, for the most part, accepted an assimilationist view, Hurston seems never to have been entirely comfortable with the idea, perhaps because she had spent most of her childhood in a historically black town in a remote area of Florida—the site for some of her early field research and the source of tales and beliefs she recollected.[160]

Moreover, her resistance to the notion of assimilation was nurtured during an early stage of the development of Black Studies, particularly African and African-American Studies, under the leadership of Melville Herskovits at Northwestern University, where Hurston considered pursuing graduate work.[161] It is important to note that Herskovits gradually revised his ideas about African-American acculturation, as he had articulated them in "The Negro's Americanism," which appeared in *The New Negro* in 1925. Whereas he argues unreservedly in 1925 that Negroes have assumed every aspect of American culture, without difference, by 1941 his views had radically changed to a theory of continuities between African-American and West African cultural forms.[162] Because of her interest in African and Caribbean cultures, Hurston was strongly motivated to study and work with Herskovits, also a former student of Boas.[163]

Against this background, her opening paragraphs in the section on "Imitation" can be considered an attempt to dispel erroneous notions about similarities among blacks and whites. She is responding to what Gates calls the "racist subtext," particularly because as Ralph Ellison remarks, "the white American has charged the Negro American with being without past or tradition (something which strikes the white man with a nameless horror)."[164] Hurston was apparently aware that white Americans also have been criticized for lacking cultural traditions, and she addresses herself to the disparity, in her critiques of whites imitating blacks.[165]

> Without exception I wonder why the black-face comedians *are* black-face; it is a puzzle—good comedians, but darn poor niggers. Gershwin and the other 'Negro' rhapsodists come under this same axe. Just about as Negro

as caviar or Ann Pennington's athletic Black Bottom. . . . And God only knows what the world has suffered from the white damsels who try to sing Blues. (*See* Appendix, pp. 256–7.)

She practices the sort of masking that enables her to maintain a distance from potential controversy, "for out of the counterfeiting of the black American's identity there arises a profound doubt in the white man's mind as to the authenticity of his own image of himself."[166] Thus, she appears to pander to stereotypes, including denigrating terminology, but "the Negro's masking is motivated not so much by fear as by a profound rejection of the image created to usurp his identity," according to Ralph Ellison.[167] In his explication of the reasons, he could be describing Hurston's technique: "Sometimes it is for the sheer joy of the joke; sometimes to challenge those who presume, across the psychological distance created by race manners to know his identity."[168] Masking becomes a metaphor for the mimicry Hurston practices in her writing, through bitterly humorous stabs at assimilationist rhetoric which can be interpreted as satire. I am suggesting that it is necessary to decode Hurston's writing to expose her parodic references to "master texts" and her satire of assimilationist discourse. Her masking in the published text must be seen as part of a process which began as a search for distinctive features of African-American culture, features which to the fledgling field researcher were not so obvious.[169]

"The group of Negroes who slavishly imitate is small," she observes in reference to middle-class African-Americans and adds: "The average Negro glories in his ways" and "The highly educated Negro the same" (*see* Appendix, p. 251). Hurston's class analysis fixes her definition of black culture. The categories in her hierarchy roughly parallel the distinctions used to classify high-, low-, and middle-brow art.[170] Following deprecating remarks on the minority of "slavish" imitators and their middle-class "self-despisement," she differentiates between attitudes other African-Americans have toward their middle-class counterparts: "The truly cultured Negro scorns him, and the Negro 'farthest down' is too busy 'spreading his junk' in his own way to see or care" (*see* Appendix, p. 251). She also notes that "even the group who are not Negroes but belong to the 'sixth race' " take pleasure in popular blues and sermons of black preachers, although "wild horses could drag no such admission from them" (*see* Appendix, p. 251). As clear as these distinctions may be, she does leave some confusion as to whether only middle-class slavish imitators or, also, members of the "sixth race" criticize black artists such as the musician Roland Hayes. According to Hurston, he "was thoroughly denounced for singing spirituals until he was accepted by white audiences" and the poet Langston Hughes, who "is not considered a poet by this group because he writes of the man in the ditch, who is more numerous and real among us than any other" (*see* Appendix, p. 251). This confusion does not vanish when she categorically asserts, "But, this group aside, let us say that the art of mimicry is better developed in the Negro than in other racial groups" (*see* Appendix, 251).

She ends her section on "Imitation" with examples of performance styles in popular dances, describing various animal imitations, but, again, as with the imitation of Valentino's hairstyle one cannot be sure she is describing behavior she observed. The result is a text that flaunts common stereotypes while attempting to advance an agenda Hurston believed would resolve audience-related problems ever present when writing for the public at large. Since according to Hurston, every occasion that involves any action whatsoever has an aesthetic meaning in black culture and can be seen as a dramatic enactment, a scene, or a full drama, she establishes a point of reference from which to begin measuring whether life imitates performances or vice versa. Known for her close affinity with the folk who appear in her lore and literature, Hurston had very specific ideas about how to create a written language—including plays and performance texts—for the verbal and nonverbal drama she observed and how that drama should or should not, would or would not be enacted in social situations as well as on stage.

DRAMA

In a fundamental way, Hurston's writing is a rehearsal for the form of expression she considered most worthy as a vehicle for presenting cultural knowledge—"and that thing is Drama." Plays, theatrical revues of folk music and dance, sermons, and storytelling, varieties of staged productions, to Hurston, are superior to written texts for conveying African-American folkways. Upon closer examination, however, it becomes clear that she is not simply talking about drama in a classical sense but ceremony and ritual, as well. Again, her multigenre conception of cultural forms becomes evident, and close examination also makes clear why Hurston devoted considerable time during the 1930s to pursuing a theatrical career. The dramas of everyday life she observed and describes and her commitment to producing plays dramatizing that drama can be seen, together, as an aesthetic imperative, motivated by a strong sense of what constitutes a convincing action, whether staged or occurring in an everyday-life situation.

In her section "The Jook" ("a Negro pleasure house"), she sums up some performance-related concerns stemming directly from her involvement with her own and other staged productions during the early 1930s. When she writes "to those who want to institute the Negro theater, let me say it is already established," she addresses herself to Locke and others who considered the time for a black folk theater overdue. Also, however, she characteristically mocks her own theatrical ambitions, noting that the Negro theater "is lacking in wealth, so it is not seen in high places." Yet high places, including the Broadway stage is exactly where Hurston's aspirations were pointing, in part because she was responding to what she considered the major critical problem—that black expression has been appropriated and despite "the use of Negro material by white performers," she had "never seen one yet entirely realistic" (*see* Appendix, p. 256). Thus, she disparages all modifications of black art forms.

> A creature with a white head and Negro feet struts the Metropolitan boards. The real Negro theatre is in the Jooks and the cabarets. Self-conscious individuals may turn away the eye and say, "Let us search elsewhere for our dramatic art." Let 'em search. They certainly won't find it. Butter Beans and Susie, Bo-Jangles and Snake Hips are the only performers of the real Negro school it has ever been my pleasure to behold in New York. (*See* Appendix, p. 257.)

When Hurston took charge of a drama program at North Carolina Central, a black college in Durham, North Carolina, in 1939,[171] rather than content herself with teaching drama to uninitiated students, she pressed the president of the college, Dr. James Shepard, to let her train students in play writing, directing, and production. Unable to convince him, however, she never staged a production during her semester there. Being a faculty member at the small black college temporarily provided some financial stability and, therefore, addressed one of her professional needs, but institutional support, she found, had its limits. Thus, she sought a wider audience which in the racially segregated social cli-

mate meant a white audience and did so through two professional organizations, the Carolina Playmakers and the Carolina Dramatic
Association. Her affiliation with the Carolina Dramatic Association led
to the beginning of a collaboration with Paul Green, author of the
Pulitzer-Prize-winning play *In Abraham's Bosom* (1926) and one of the
few Euro-American playwrights of the period whose work included folk
dramas about African-American folk life.[172]

What Hurston in part hoped to gain by being in North Carolina were
benefits of an environment where folk arts and professional theater
both had high priority. One of Green's former teachers, his mentor and
colleague Frederick H. Koch, who in 1918 founded the Carolina
Playmakers at the Chapel Hill campus of the University of North
Carolina, had done social scientific field research in the western moun-
tains of North Carolina for the Federal Emergency Relief Administration in 1934, which led to his "Smoky Mountain" comedies. Like
Hurston's work, Koch's plays drew upon his observations and experiences in a community where everyday activities seemed far removed
from high art but were just as, if not more, culturally rich. Through his
studies in English literature at Harvard, Koch had been introduced to a
form of dramatic writing rooted in native American subjects similar to
American Scene art, a style emphasizing imagery drawn from everyday-
life situations. The movement among dramatists, to develop an indigenous American theater, a folk drama "of the conflict of man with the
forces of nature," depicting "man's desperate fight for existence,"[173] ran
parallel during the early part of the century with the direction of visual
artists working in the American Scene style. Alain Locke promoted
American Scene painting for black artists, even more adamantly than he
supported white artists' use of "black" imagery: "Locke felt that the
black artist had even more to gain than other American artists from the
desire to create a native art independent from European influences and
rooted in themes of the American scene."[174] The impetus for a similar
initiative in theater was motivated, according to Koch, because "for
many years our American playwrights were imitative, content with reproducing the outlived formulas of the Old World. There was nothing
really native about them. Whenever they did write of American life the
treatment was superficial and innocuous."[175]

The events at North Carolina Central and Hurston's potential collaborations with Green together signify a central dilemma in Hurston's
life and work which exemplifies a dilemma that artists, performers, and

scholars continue struggling to resolve. Her ambition to create theater during her brief tenure at North Carolina Central harkens back to an earlier period, in 1928, when she was studiously engaged in ethnographic research while speculating with Langston Hughes about collaborating on a folk opera. If "her hope to write an opera with Hughes represents her intellectual struggle with the colonizing influence of Western European culture," as Hemenway speculates, when she says to her North Carolina (white) audience, "We are going to try to make plays out of Negro life in the Negro manner," she is initiating what on the surface appears to be a straightforward mission but what beneath the surface could be seen as an expurgation of misconceptions and a revision of dominant approaches to cultural production and representation.[176] Her critical powers were, simultaneously, circumscribed from without and culturally proscribed from within.

Hurston's commitment to creating black theater, if seen as ideological, if seen as a motivating philosophy, exposes a desire for a world where the mundane meanings of communication in everyday life aspire to an elaborated system of meaning like "high art"; thus, ordinary understanding is inverted. In her contrast between white and black dance, instead of using irony, she defies common misconceptions, arguing that "the white dancer attempts to express fully," whereas "the Negro is restrained, but succeeds in gripping the beholder by forcing him to finish the action the performer suggests" (*see* Appendix, p. 248). To explain the meaning and form of abstraction in African-American expressive culture, she attempts to elevate the everyday, to aestheticize it. "Since no art can ever express all the variations conceivable" (*see* Appendix, p. 248), since everyday-life performance is as elaborate as any art, she can find the characteristics, the patterns, in the forms of expression she observes. Her objective is to reify not only an essentialist view of the culture or the race but mimetic performance as a paradigm for the culture and the race. "The Negro must be considered the greater artist, his dancing is realistic suggestion, and that is about all a great artist can do" (*see* Appendix, p. 248). The contested definitions of race and culture now become a debate over who is the greater artist—the most original, the best imitator.

Hurston thought staged productions would contribute more to the world at large's understanding of African-Americans than would written texts. Texts based on ethnographic research often are not accessible to the people who contribute to them—the folk who embody the idioms, who make the texts possible. Hurston was to discover, however, that the resources required to produce theater to a large extent determine not only the venue and, therefore, who the audience will be, but what forms of expression reach the public.[177] Nevertheless, the relationship of artist to audience is crucial to the ritual aspect of performance underlying Hurston's theory of imitation with a difference.

— Preface —

This is the life story of Cudjo Lewis, as told by himself. It makes no attempt to be a scientific document, but on the whole he is rather accurate. If he is a little hazy as to detail after sixty seven years, he is certainly to be pardoned. The quotations from the works of travellers in Dahomey are set down, not to make this appear a thoroughly documented biography, but to emphasize his remarkable memory. Three spellings of his Nation are found, Attacco, Taccou, and Taccow. But his pronunciation is probably correct. Therefore I have used Takkoi all through the work.

I was sent by a woman of tremendous understanding of primitive peoples to get this story. The thought back of the act was to set down essential truth rather that fact of detail which is so often misleading. Therefore he has been permitted to tell his story in his own way without the intrusion of interpretation.

For historical data I am indebted to the Journal of Negro History, and to the records of the Mobile Historical Society

Zora Neale Hurston
April 17, 1931.

6. *Preface to* Barracoon. *(Credit: Zora Neale Hurston Papers, Moorland-Spingarn Research Center, Howard University.)*

7. Hurston collecting children's songs and lore. (Reproduced from the collections of the Library of Congress.)

8. *Gabrielle Brown and Rochelle Harris.*

National Exhibition of Skills
New Auditorium, Orlando, Florida
January 16 - February 6, 1939

THE FIRE DANCE
January 25, 1939 - 8 P.M.

The Federal Writers in Florida invites you to attend this program
that is being presented in connection with the new national folklore studies of the Federal Writers' Project, Works Progress Administration.

Dance Director: Zora Neale Hurston

The Players! Florida troupe of Negro singers and dancers

The Fire Dance, a celebration honoring the arrival of spring, is a
folk dance that originated in Africa. It was brought to Florida by
immigrant Negro workers from the Bahama Islands. The dance has three
parts! The Jumping Dance; Ring Play; The Crow Dance.

Jumping Dance! When a certain tree puts out new leaf, the priest,
or houngan, called the tribe to a celebration. Dancing about a fire-
heated drum of goat-hide, each dancer "moves" according to the drum
rhythm and tone, which is extremely varied. The dance keeps up until
the drum grows cold.

Ring Play: This is African rhythm with European borrowings. One
dancer in center begins to sing and circle the ring seeking a partner
as the verse is being sung. This keeps up until the dancers exhaust
their repertoire of steps and verses.

Crow Dance: This is a rhythmic imitation of a buzzard (African crow)
flying and seeking food. The dancers are costumed to represent human beings, birds, animals and trees. In short, it is symbolic of
all nature taking part in the procreation of life that comes with
spring.

Concerning the dance and its director: Zora Neale Hurston is a
native of Florida. An authority on the folklore of Southern Negroes,
she is currently editing a volume on the Florida Negro for the
Federal Writers' Project of Florida. The dance has been presented
at the John Golden Theatre, New York, the 1934 National Folklore
Festival, St. Louis, and before audiences in Chicago, Winter Park,
Daytona Beach, Sanford, and Lake Wales.

9. *"The Fire Dance" program.*

CHAPTER THREE

Negotiating the Field

❖

THE "LAST AFRICAN" OF "BARRACOON"

In 1944, Hurston published "The Last Slave Ship," an essay summarizing the life story of Cudgo Lewis, "whose tribal name was Kossula—O-Lo-Loo-Ay," in *The American Mercury*.[178] The article's publication seventeen years after Hurston's introduction of Kossula's story to the public in "Cudjo's Own Story of the Last African Slaver," which appeared in *The Journal of Negro History* (October 1927), makes a statement about her determination to present her own views on acculturation and, further, illustrates the essentialist notion of "negroness" she developed as a result of her experiences as a field researcher. Hurston's encounter with Kossula influenced her perceptions of herself. The episode epitomizes various conflicts, often preconscious, involved when no public language for private experiences exists, even when the latter have a bearing on one's intellectual and professional development. Hemenway speaks of the 1940s as a period when Hurston found that the options available for presenting her ideas to the public fell short of her "private motives."[179] Problems arising in conjunction with Kossula's story help to clarify some of the frustrations Hurston faced in trying to find distinctive features of "the Negro," when she believed "his negroness is being rubbed off by close contact with white culture."[180] Since Kossula was sought because of his African past and his status as a survivor in the United States, he personifies the traits against which other African-Americans are hypothetically measured in assessments of their acculturated "characteristics." The African-American folklorist Arthur Huff Fauset had interviewed Kossula and published one of his tales in *The New Negro* (1925), and as Hemenway points out, Kossula's identity is part of historical record.[181]

Hurston's approach to the interviews with Kossula, what she might or might not have expected to achieve when she met him on her first trip and on subsequent visits, influence formal aspects of her written recreations of his narrative, including the manuscript "Barracoon." More important, however, are the exchanges she had with Kossula, as reproduced in "Barracoon"; they illustrate the way professional and personal politics converge.

Her interviews with Kossula were initiated during her first research expedition in 1927. As a result of her initial interviews with Kossula, she produced her first scholarly publication, "Cudjo's Own Story of the Last African Slaver."[182] Long after Hurston had published the article, however, and even after her death, the essay's authenticity has been questioned.[183] Hemenway alludes to a dilemma she must have faced in writing her essay, since "of the sixty-seven paragraphs in Hurston's essay, only eighteen are exclusively her own prose."[184] She copies the larger portion from a book that is not cited in her article, making only minor revisions in the wording, according to Hemenway's discussion. He concludes that her "plagiarism may be an unconscious attempt at academic suicide."[185] He further speculates that her being "caught" would have relieved her from the pressures associated with field research, not only because being "caught" by Boas and Carter G. Woodson, editor of the journal, would have ended her scholarly career, but also because

> She also would never have had to worry again about capturing exactly the dialect in which the tale was told, the precise notations of the folksinger's music, or the nuances of style in the tale-teller's performance. She would be free of admonitions from Boas, scholarly demands from Woodson, and the frustration of interviewing a man like Cudjo Lewis. Folklore collecting had turned out to be tiresome, difficult, decidedly unglamorous labour.[186]

As I mentioned in Chapter One, on this same initial field trip Hurston had found communicating with people in Florida too difficult to produce the results either she or Boas wanted.

She explains in her introduction to "Barracoon," which she produced in 1931 based on subsequent interviews with Kossula, that she "was sent by Dr. Franz Boas to get a first-hand report of the raid that had brought him [Kossula] to America and bondage, for Dr. Carter G. Woodson of the *Journal of Negro History*" (2).[187] In his analysis of what might have occurred on her first field trip, Hemenway does not explicitly detail what he calls the "difficulties" she probably encountered in trying to interview Kossula, simultaneously for Boas and Woodson. Hemenway interprets her actions based on an assumption that her professional priorities primarily entailed pleasing her sponsors and publishing. It is possible to infer from his analysis that the expectations her senior colleagues had for her work would inevitably determine the outcome of her texts, for better or, in this instance, worse. Could the "difficulties" she encountered, signified by her "borrowing" portions of the article's historical content, nonetheless, have been related to personal choices she made based on her face-to-face interaction with Kossula?[188]

How significant is it, for example, that in producing the text Hurston must account for intraracial tensions Kossula's narrative exposes? She describes in her autobiography the reaction she had when she learned from Kossula about the circumstances surrounding his captivity:

> One thing impressed me strongly from this three months of association with Cudjo Lewis. The white people had held my people in slavery here in America. They had bought us, it is true and exploited us. But the inescapable fact that stuck in my craw, was: my people had *sold* me and the white people had bought me. That did away with the folklore I had been brought up on—that the white people had gone to Africa, waved a red handkerchief at the Africans and lured them aboard a ship and sailed away. I know that civilized money stirred up African greed. That wars between tribes were often stirred up by white traders to provide more slaves in the barracoons and all that. But, if the African princes had been as pure and innocent as I would like to think, it could not have happened. No, my own people had butchered and killed, exterminated whole nations and torn families apart, for a profit before the strangers got their chance at a cut. It was a sobering thought. (*Dust Tracks* 145)

Also significant is Kossula's description of how he and his family were considered "savages" by African-Americans, how while enslaved in the United States, he and the others who had come with him on the ship from the continent danced on Sundays, only to be met with scorn. "De American colored folks, you unnerstand me, dey say we savage and den dey laugh at us and doan come say nothin' to us," he told Hurston (65). His statement corroborates what Herskovits wrote in 1925 concerning African-Americans' assimilation "in the days after the liberation of the Negroes from slavery"[189] and what Hurston attributes to middle-class blacks as "their ready-made expression," which is that " 'we done got away from all that now' " (*see* Appendix, p. 251). Herskovits goes so far as to say that "schools sprang up in which they might learn, not the language and technique of their African ancestors, but that of this country, where they lived."[190] Hurston's specific reaction to the knowledge that this pattern began during the antebellum period is evident in her attempt to shape his narrative as an epic, through its historical scope and poetry, and a tragedy—a combination of at least two genres, two narrative traditions, an attempt to capture Kossula's "tragic sense of loss," his "yearning for blood and cultural ties," his "sense of mutilation" (*Dust Tracks* 204), and her own shock and disappointment at learning firsthand of "the universal nature of greed and glory" (*Dust Tracks* 145). While trying to account for differences in "negroness" based on adaptive behavior, Hurston also has to confront that Kossula's presence gives her "something to feel about" (*Dust Tracks* 148). The encounter not only makes it impossible for her to be objective, it shows how personal concerns can outweigh professional demands. In writing her first essay on Cudjo, Hurston might have been too moved and too uncertain how to manage her subjective response, rather than too frustrated with the rigors of scientific analysis, to produce an authentic text. Although justifying plagiarism is impossible, the reasons for it should be scrutinized in light of its being, to date, a one-time occurrence in the long, productive career of a prolific and widely published author.[191] The incident along with the findings subsequently documented in "Barracoon" together show that Hurston reacted to disparities based on social status by displacing her explicit "intrusion of interpretation," as she explains in "Barracoon's" preface: "The thought back of the act was to set down essential truth rather than fact of detail which is so often misleading." (*See* Figure 6) Thus, through a deliberate act of suppression, she resists presenting her own point of view in a natural, or naturalistic, way and allows Kossula "to tell his story in his own way" (author's preface).

Illustrating the problem of cultural understanding between Africans and African descendants in Alabama, Kossula's narrative as told to Hurston shows the problem of ethnographic authenticity on several levels. First, the ethnographer faces the problem of gaining the informant's confidence, which Hurston shows was not automatic. She tells of how she brought food offerings to tempt him to talk about painful parts of his past he had difficulty revealing, but she also shows how his idea of ordering events in his narrative is based on a culturally rooted sense of self. She insists that Kossula speak about himself and his way of life, when Kossula seems to be spending, in her view, too much time talking about his father and grandfather. With what she perceives as scorn and pity, Kossula looks at Hurston, she says, only to question her in a way that reveals his adherence to family hierarchy. "Where is de house where de mouse is de leader?" he asks (19) and then explains that he must give the story in order, from grandfather to father to son, himself. In conjunction with Hurston's gentle prodding Kossula, this passage illustrates how Hurston and Kossula have two different notions of individuality. Kossula's sense of self is based on his connection to a community defined by genealogy, whereas Hurston's apparently corresponds with a concept of a separate and distinct identity. Furthermore, it indicates differences in subjective points of view primarily attributable to custom and Kossula's versus Hurston's sense of allegiance to social protocol rooted "in African soil." How Hurston does or does not reconcile a "scientific," or objective approach with her subjective perspective has a bearing not only on the text and the understanding to be gained from it but also on the formulations, generalities, and conclusions found in her later published work such as "Characteristics" and *Mules and Men.*

It is important to keep in mind the predominant paradigms available for the type of cultural analysis she is undertaking, since at the time of the interviews, she is in the process of learning while collecting information on distinctive characteristics of black culture. Again, Boas's notion of variability of traits in cultural groups and Mason's romantic view of a "primitive" ideal are the key models directing her. The two perspectives diverge, however, and as already indicated, the different ideologies surface in Hurston's work in complex ways and remain irreconcilable; consequently, the clash gets represented by formal aspects of the text.

Although Hemenway says the manuscript "Barracoon" represents an improvement over Hurston's first article, his evaluation of the manuscript raises more questions than it answers. He describes the text as "a highly dramatic, semifictionalized narrative intended for the popular reader," which "skillfully weaves together the scholarship and Hurston's own memories of Cudjo" without acknowledging sources—"the type of book that [Franz] Boas would have repudiated."[192] More provocative is his statement that "the book purports to be solely the words of Cudjo; in fact, it is Hurston's imaginative recreation of his experience," which he says Hurston does because she is interested in presenting a former slave's version of history.[193] As she wrote: "All these words from the seller, but not one word from the sold."[194]

Some of the questions Hemenway's analysis raises are related to Hurston's methods of research and text production. Although he argues that she recreates the slave's experience "as an artist rather than as a folklorist or historian," his argument avoids addressing how distinctions among the genres associated with fiction, folklore, and history must be reexamined because of the alleged orality of the text.[195] The manuscript illustrates Hurston's interest in reproducing speech patterns in writing, providing an example of the Pidgin English many Africans knew before arriving in the United States.[196] Transcribing Kossula's words, she writes, " 'I want you everywhere you go to tell everybody whut Cudjo say, and how come I in Americky soil since de 1859 and never see my people no mo'" (18). Based on Kossula's spoken responses to her inquiries, Hurston recreates the cultural history and context for Kossula's story and structures a narrative of his tragic life—from his capture and his life as a youth through his period of bondage in the United States, his marriage, the births and deaths of his children, and the death of his wife. It would be hard to make the case that she entirely invented Kossula's language and, consequently, his emerging persona; however, it is the interplay between invention and transcription (or reproduction) that demystifies suspicions surrounding Hurston's methods, in particular, and experimental ethnography, in general.[197]

Whether the manuscript in any way represents Hurston's ongoing efforts to come to terms with theories on cultural diffusion or acculturation is worth exploring in light of the comment in her handwritten preface that her text "makes no attempt to be a scientific document, but as a whole is rather accurate." The text supplies sufficient examples of Kossula's describing adaptive behavior, as when shortly after arriving, while in captivity, he is first shown the nature of the work he is forced to do. The newly arrived Africans are not immediately assigned work because they do not understand either the instructions being given in American English or the work being performed. When shown how to plant crops, Kossula reports, the newcomers are surprised to see the mule behind the plow. Despite its difficulty, the labor itself causes no grief. They mourn being enslaved and lament having no explanation for being brought to a foreign country to work. Free-floating irrationality seems to be the source of an unbearable dislocation, separating past from present. Having presented Kossula's description of the Dahomean raid led by King Gelele against Kossula's tribe, the Takkoi, a raid that led to his enslavement, Hurston underscores the sense of loss and detachment pervading Kossula's consciousness. She chooses to include his remarks on the alienation he felt because people in the United States stared with odd expressions. Compounding the sense of strangeness were the futile attempts at talking with American blacks, who could not understand the languages people from West Africa brought with them. Moreover, ridicule accompanied misunderstanding and heightened the pain. When freed from enslavement, Kossula notes a change in his perceptions of work; he remarks that the Africans had become quite hard-working. The men were employed in saw-mill and powder-mill camps as well as on railroads, while the women worked at gardening and sold their food in Mobile. Basket-making among the men also kept the women busy at the nearby market center. All of this Kossula reports to Hurston to stress that self-sufficiency was crucial in forming a community among the last generation of blacks transported from Africa. In writing his story, Hurston does not romanticize or in any way imply that ideals such as self-fulfillment or fully realized self-expression could emerge from such suffering as Kossula has known. Hurston does not interpret his comments, except when she builds a transition from one interview to the next, in her footnotes, and at the end when she summarizes.

Her two months "with Kossula, who is called Cudjo," suggest that she had learned some alternatives to interviewing or question-and-answer approaches as a method of probing into an individual's life. Implicitly, to learn Kossula's history is to discover the variety of events, relationships, and ritualistic behaviors that linked Kossula to a community, that made his speech represent more than a personal remembrance. In short, Hurston was finding out firsthand that classifying Kossula's life story as an example of characteristic Negro expression would be inadequate. Details surrounding his story were as crucial to the telling as the words themselves. Taking Kossula "cling-stone peaches," watermelons, and crabs alternately on different visits, and taking the time to eat with him, whether they talk or not, plays as important a part in her learning about his way of life as the words themselves. Not only facts but also ordinary activities help to establish a sense of camaraderie and contribute to the story. The story, therefore, is more than the sum of its parts, more than a life, more than an account, more than a representation of Negro "essence." Even when no dialogue is possible because Kossula prefers gardening, repairing fences, or being alone—when probing into the past is in conflict with his present priorities—Hurston learns the sensibilities required for her to collect an "authentic" oral history. Being able to perceive that Kossula for the most part welcomed her presence grants Hurston the license needed to attempt writing an holistic life history rather than a strict, factual account.

She notes, with some remorse, having to deny Kossula's request to accompany her to New York. Such a strong bond of friendship had formed between them, she remarks, "It was a very sad morning in October when I said Good bye, and looked back the last time at the lonely figure that stood on the edge of the cliff that fronts the highway" (94). These are not the concluding remarks an anthropologist uses to establish an authoritative voice. Nor does the passage suggest that Hurston had crossed a line onto a terrain where her sympathies would make her one with her surroundings, where familiarity would replace her calculated effort to experiment with the means available to her for giving a member of her own "race" an identity to (in) the outside world. Knowing that she had come to occupy a place among Kossula's fond memories, Hurston must, nevertheless, depart. Bidding her new friend farewell becomes an occasion for her to reflect on the meaning of their friendship, particularly to Kossula, whose life history is rendered as a sequence of separations from familiar settings, losses of beloved family members. In her effort to capture the tenderness surrounding yet another separation Kossula must endure, Hurston draws the reader's attention to a bridge somewhere off in the distance (the same one she crosses on her way out of town). Named after the Cochrane Highway beneath Kossula's home, the bridge becomes an image connecting Kossula to the larger world. The two peaches he offers Hurston, which she tells us are the only ones left on his tree, suggest a beginning. Putting aside the reference to Eden and Genesis, with its precautionary overtones, I would argue that the peaches promise a continuation of the bountiful exchanges upon which their friendship has thrived. Through (this) exchange, Kossula guarantees the continuation of his legacy. Hurston crosses the bridge and, upon doing so, gains assurance that Kossula has passed his story on to her and effectively returns to his place of origin, "*to his memories*" (95) (my emphasis added). She leaves us with images invoking, as in *Jonah's Gourd Vine*, a remote but reverberating, generalized but vivid Africa—"his memories of fat girls with ringing golden bracelets, his drums that speak the minds of men, to palm-nut cakes and bull-roarers, to his parables" (95). In the end, Hurston decides that Kossula has no fear of death, but she attributes his lack of fear to his being a "pagan" rather than to his Christianity. Indeed, she argues his fearlessness as a "pagan" persists in spite of his being a Christian convert. This peculiar interpretation of the Christian need to be reconciled with God before death, serves as a transition to a point Hurston finds more compelling: the past, with its horrors and tragedy, inspires more reverence and awe than the uncertain future. Whereas any potential hazards held in escrow by the future's uncertainty can be explained away as an inevitable destiny all men share in common, the past can never be explained, much less understood, with its string of irrational events piled on one after another seeming only add up to endless reasons for continuing to reflect.

Hurston's concluding remarks, far from being analytic, build upon the sentimental tone set throughout the narrative, illustrated, for example, in Kossula's changing moods and Hurston's responses: as when Kossula so urgently wants to talk that he hardly has patience for her to light the insect repellant; or when he would try to discourage her from staying by offering her peaches as a sign of his hospitality but without being "too cordial." Her persistence—as in one instance when Kossula says he told her not to disturb him on Saturday, wins through charm and generosity. Hurston reminds Kossula that she has come to help him and that he only has to talk to her when and if he wants. The sentimental combines with the tragic, in a narrative told predominantly in the first-person but structured also as a dialogue that goes beyond dialogue as such, and becomes on the surface a story of how two strangers become friends. The text uses fictional devices such as personification of the author, dialogue, and impressionistic descriptions. Simultaneously, the parts of "Barracoon" narrated by Kossula follow the conventions of other slave narratives, including a portion devoted to Christian conversion. The text differs from traditional slave narratives in two key ways: it is not structured around events leading toward escape, although the transition from slavery to freedom is given prominence; and it contains no argument for abolition, enfranchisement, women's rights, or any other political agenda. It does, however, offer a heroic spin on repatriation, a theme surviving in "The Last Slave Ship," where Hurston writes: "Upon gaining their freedom with Emancipation, Kossula and the rest resolved to return to Africa. They worked in mills and shipyards, made baskets and grew vegetables, and saved every possible penny. But their plan proved impractical, and after a year or two they gave up their dream of going home."[198]

"Barracoon" can be paralleled with a variety of slave narratives, "the autobiographies that ex-slaves wrote after emancipation," which according to William L. Andrews, "have been almost entirely ignored or condescendingly dismissed from serious scholarly consideration."[199]

Their omission can be attributed to the ideology they reflect—"their optimism about the future and charity toward the past."[200] Hurston's manuscript, indeed, helps to "fill the gap in our awareness of what was happening to black American autobiography from 1865 through the 1920s."[201] In that the text's autobiographical content is presented in the form of an as-told-to narrative—"the life story of Cudjo Lewis as told by himself" (*see* Figure 6)—it bears some resemblance to the life histories collected from former slaves through the FWP of the WPA, during the mid- to late 1930s. Having been completed in 1931 based on Hurston's earlier work, "Barracoon" foreshadows the forthcoming WPA efforts to document the oral accounts of former slaves.[202] Moreover, it reflects a "significant revision" of what Andrews identifies as "some of the defining parameters of Afro-American autobiography [between 1865 and 1930]."[203] These include "the image of slavery and the idea of the heroic selfhood."[204] Although Kossula's narrative does depict an "image of slavery," it covers a brief period, from 1859 to 1865. Since the *Clotilde*, the ship Kossula arrived on, was the last one known to have been brought to the United States, his story lacks "the image of slavery" that dominates the narratives of slaves recalling their captivity from birth until freedom. It lacks the trajectory of a narrative based on a personal history and concept of selfhood, as Andrews argues, ordered through the movement from darkness under enslavement to light in freedom symbolized by the trope of the North Star well-known from Frederick Douglass's narrative. If the heroic concept of selfhood can be found in the narrative, it is in Hurston's recreation of Kossula's story as a symbol of cultural survival.

Beneath the surface, the sentimentality, Hurston's friendship with Kossula is clearly defined by the requirements of field research. She contributes to his everyday needs by providing transportation, bringing gifts of food, and establishing Kossula's link with Mason—a primary benefactor of the project. Referring to Mason, Hurston states in her preface that she "was sent by a woman of tremendous understanding of primitive peoples to get this story." Although everyday-life drama and expressive forms are Hurston's primary concern, power relations based on differences in social status, the history of enslavement, and economics intrude into the situation. Over the years, Hurston and Mason kept in touch with Kossula. Mason aided him financially and gained his trust as a friend, while he complimented Mason, as Hurston did, for being a sincerely concerned human being.[205] The relationship between

Hurston and Mason has been examined for signs of deception on Hurston's part. Was she pretending to be a devoted subservient, flattering her benefactor to gratify material needs? Was Hurston, as some critics have suggested, a virtual worshipper at Mason's financial altar who was willing to perform "darky" roles to win approval?[206] Their relationship, in my view, was more complex than the notion of performance or masking suggests, although Hurston, indeed, knew all too well what smile to wear for which occasion. Worth noting is the analogy between Hurston and her patron, on the one hand, and Hurston's "informants" and Hurston the field researcher, on the other. Other configurations also pertain: for example, Hurston was at times an informant and, like her own informants, had skills enabling her to communicate with various audiences. Such variations become significant in trying to understand the limited extent to which a simple opposition can explain cross-cultural communication, as well as situations involving differences in "race," status, sex, or age. As one researcher notes, the performance of a "darky" role for "white interlocutors" may be "for the entertainment of other Blacks," but even when the gesture is critical, the performance "is intended to be read correctly by the interlocutor."[207] Following this model, the costs of disclosure (ridicule, for example) being high, the "victim" complies in silence, thus making it difficult to draw conclusions about where the exchange might otherwise have gone. As Hemenway documents, Hurston was unwilling on at least two occasions during the latter part of her career to feign satisfaction with writing jobs when the employers' perspectives did not mesh with hers.[208] It seems she was not so different during the early phase of her career, though as Hemenway argues, Mason's patronage caused debilitating stress for Hurston, which probably accounts for her being less productive during the Mason years than subsequently.[209] Hurston no doubt endured because she felt an affinity with Mason's grandiose good will toward African and Native Americans; they both saw themselves as being on a mission to enlighten the larger world as to the treasures "primitive" cultures manifested.[210] Nevertheless, like Mrs. Ellsworth's concern for Oceola's finances in Hughes's story "The Blues I'm Playing," Mason's controlling, proprietary scrupulousness determined the demise of her power to hold the substance of her treasures.[211] In an effort to exercise proprietary rights over Hurston's work, Mason had counseled Kossula not to let other white people read his life story.[212] Apparently, he had a copy of Hurston's work and had attempted to use it to get money by allowing it to be published in a newspaper.²¹³ Although it is unclear how Mason learned that his story had been made public, she had taken the time to assert herself as a "protector." Furthermore, Mason prodded Hurston to intervene, to "write Kossula and his daughter and tell them they must not give their material to anyone who is white," because the ethnographer Paul Radin had expressed his interest in collecting some "Negro material" from Kossula.²¹⁴ Her reaction to Radin's curiosity shows Mason was not self-critical about the concept of property rights guiding her philanthropy. "It seems to me it is growing more and more a mania with white people, who have no more interesting things to investigate among themselves to grab in every direction material that by right belongs entirely to another race," she intoned. A slightly complicated twist in the story arises when Hurston learns, through an investigation she undertakes at Mason's urging, that Kossula has not received money that Mason has been sending him, probably because his daughter-in-law and granddaughter kept it for themselves.²¹⁵

Part of Mason's private collection, the manuscript of Kossula's story was considered either too controversial or too valuable as a representation of "primitive" culture to have been published at the time. Its value as a document illustrating African cultural survival in the United States is historically significant, however. More important, since the WPA period, increasing interest in the oral narratives of former slaves and their contribution to American cultural history, opens up new possibilities for reexamining the postbellum period, a significant moment in the development of African-American narrative traditions.

Another manuscript in Mason's collection, "Black Death," also reveals in some detail similar qualities of the dual point of view used in Kossula's story. In "Black Death," however, no narrator nor even an informant is clearly delineated. "We Negroes in Eatonville know a number of things that the hustling, bustling white man never dreams of," the tale begins. The opening line establishes a frame corresponding with what John Dollard, in his discussion of "Negro aggression against whites," describes as "a form of local revenge which has to be used carefully and sparingly," which is "the telling of gossipy tales about white people."²¹⁶ Continuing the framing device with the statement that the white man "is a materialist with little ears for overtones," the story shifts into a narrative about Hoodoo:

> They have only eyes and ears; we hear and see with the skin. . . . For instance, if a white person were halted on the streets of Orlando and told that

Old Man Morgan, the excessively black Negro hoodoo man can kill any person indicated and paid for, without ever leaving his house or even seeing his victim, he'd laugh in your face and walk away, wondering how long the Negro will continue to wallow in ignorance and superstition. But no black person in a radius of twenty miles will smile, not much. They know.[217]

Whereas the opening lines suggest the story will focus on a tale that explicitly addresses a social disparity between blacks and whites, what follows is a tale which, like a joke that "conceals its aggressive intent behind the facade of the little story, . . . takes a bit of analysis to make it clear."[218] In the opening sentence, a narrator representing the "we," collectively representing a certain way of knowing—a third sense (beyond sight and hearing)—speaks. That voice, however, also understands its audience as being broader than people within "a radius of twenty miles." The statement "they know" positions the narrator as an arbiter between two points of view, between two distinct if not opposed perspectives.

According to Hemenway, the tale, which was originally submitted for publication as a short story and later appeared as part of an ethnographic essay, is "20 percent fiction" and "80 percent folklore," originating within Hurston's memory and personal repertoire of folktales.[219] The 80 percent folklore content, however, contains a larger portion of invention from Hurston's imagination, combined with local lore and mythical references rooted in African-American traditional religious practices.[220] Remaining unanswered, however, is the question of how to characterize the perspective of an ethnographer whose cultural roots and ethnic background are the same as the culture and ethnicity of her interlocutors.

Ironically, in this instance, the fictional portion of the story mimics Hurston's narrative voice, structure, and style, and the characters have fictional names. Also, her particular telling of the story, which includes inserting herself as a narrator-character, accounts for the effective transition from fictional story to ethnographic text. In other words, the creative talents of the traditional storyteller and the literary artist overlap and converge. According to Larry Neal, "she approached her subject with the engaged sensibility of the artist; she left the 'comprehensive' scientific approach to culture to men like her former teacher, Franz Boas, and to Melville Herskovits."[221] Whether this meant that "her approach to folklore research was essentially freewheeling and activist in style," as Neal puts it, is an issue here.[222] For an ethnographer who is also a practitioner of the folk arts she is studying, "the collector should be a willing participant in the myth-ritual process."[223] On another level, the poetics of traditional storytelling and the skills of the writer, when they merged for Hurston meant that she "transferred part of her [traditional] repertoire to the typed page."[224]

As previously discussed, Hurston did experience some difficulties communicating with residents of Eatonville the first time she returned there to collect tales, primarily because of the educational difference but also because she still was seen in her hometown in her role as John and Lucy Hurston's daughter. Also, her and the community's expectations for behavior according to roles defined by gender differed and had an impact on the dynamics of communicating in the field. In *Mules and Men*, she shows the consequences of her overlapping roles as ethnographer, woman, member of the community.[225] Being of the same or opposite sex enables or impedes exchanges, depending on the information sought. Describing how Cliffert Ulmer, one of the lumbermill workers in Polk County, befriended her, she writes: "The fellow that wants to broach a young woman doesn't come himself to ask. He sends his friend" (*Mules and Men* 70). Because Ulmer's suggestion that she would get more material "by going out with the swamp gang" (*Mules and Men* 71), Hurston finds herself in the position of "going out to the swamp with the boys," where she learns that the men "can hurl their axes great distances and behead moccasins or sink the blade into an alligator's skull" (71), that at the saw-mill camp "men are not supposed to oversleep" (72). In the midst of such factual details, Hurston presents tales as if they are told by the men themselves as they go about their daily routine. Identifying with, and being skilled in the traditional practices of, the group being studied influences the research method as well as the form of the text. By following the customs for male-female social relations, waiting for a mediator to approach her before directly interacting with a man, Hurston shows her willingness and ability to adapt to local expectations for behavior. Her text, in turn, shows readers seeking a literary interpretation the relationship between social context and narrative technique. Through the text, she demonstrates how she adapts a form of expression when, as with traditional forms of expression emerging in a performative context, innovation entails actively reshaping events in the present.

At a time when "primitivist" ideas were arousing interest in black art and culture, among white bourgeois patrons, artists, and intellectuals, Hurston was busy interpreting everyday life observed in the ethnographic present, through her first-hand knowledge enhanced by practical work in the field and translating her interpretations into "primitivist" aesthetics. Much of the work Hurston pursued during this time, however, under her agreement with Mason, restricted Hurston's artistic, professional, and economic freedom to use the material solely as she pleased in fiction and theater. Mason wrote to Hurston, for example, granting permission for her to use specific material she had collected in *The Great Day*, a production at the John Golden Theater in New York, but forbade her to use

> the other data and material which you have collected on the mission for which I sent you ... for any purpose ... without further permission ... particularly that dealing the Conjure Ceremony and rituals which, though printed in the concert program of January 10, 1932, was not performed.[226]

Criticizing the interplay of freedom and restriction implicit in forms of art that appeal to audiences interested in folk culture, Harold Peerce noted in 1936 that "those who profit from Negro primitivism have an obvious interest in preserving that primitivism."[227] Hurston has been rebuked for her willingness to exploit cravings for "the artificial peculiarities of a group kept in systematic impoverishment and ignorance."[228] Although her multigenre texts contribute to furthering the humanistic agenda to broaden cross-cultural understanding, her work never escapes criticism for not addressing directly the questions indirectly raised by her mysterious methods, even if they are viewed as an extension of traditional practices. Explaining the resentment Hurston's contemporaries felt toward her because she "describes her race with such a servile term as 'Mules and Men,' " Peerce, suspicious of Hurston's literary aspirations, says:

> When one surveys the development of the Negro culture, he realizes that it is has been one of evasion whatever its intrinsic beauty. The educational and economic limitations of a dominantly white society have forced the Negro to express himself in ambiguous terms. Thus the folk-hero, *John*, always outwits his master through cunning; thus, Negro songs often satirize the white man without the latter's being aware of any mockery. And while this quality is highly admirable for protective purposes, it obviously impedes further cultural development.[230]

Despite Neal's assessment that Hurston "made her most significant contribution to black literature in the field of folkloristic research," he also concedes that "she was not above commercial popularization of black culture"; and he notes that "many of her contemporaries considered her a pseudofolksy exhibitionist."[231] The question remains, then, as to whether Hurston's conscious pursuit of multiple agendas must necessarily lead her to produce a multigenre text. According to Christopher D. Felker, "The celebration of the primitive was a 'vocational strategy' for Hurston, an occupational prism that enabled her to integrate the different class, educational, and regional backgrounds that she encountered in herself, her sources, and her intended audiences."[232]

THE FLORIDA FOLKLORE PROJECT

As a folklore collector and member of the Florida Federal Writers' Project of the WPA, Hurston's skills as a fieldworker stood out in contrast with the new trainees. Many of the recruits to the project were local housewives who were good writers and had a strong commitment to the work. Stetson Kennedy points out in his introduction to the *Florida Project Guide*: "Unlike many an academic collector, they did not have to relate to their informants; they *were related*: by class, culture, and sometimes kinship. All they had to do was knock on any door, and the *rapport* was there."[233] Although Hurston also shared the culture of her informants, at the time when she returned to collect for the Florida Project her class status, measured not simply in economic terms, had changed. She had a career and had gained so much notoriety for her work that she was exempted from some of the social conventions imposed on blacks. As Kennedy notes in his introduction, because she was a famous New York literary figure, he and his co-workers were counseled that she "put on airs" which included smoking cigarettes in front of whites. "And so Zora came, and Zora smoked, and we made allowances," he writes.[234]

Being made an exception, however, can only partially account for the way Hurston's class and status differed from that of her informants. In many ways, she had the same affinity and rapport with "the folk" that other local collectors had. The major difference, which had to do with Hurston's perception of herself, was her ability to observe others from more than one position, but especially, to observe as an artist. She was aware "that the work of art is itself the product of a negotiation between a creator or a class of creators (equipped with a complex, communally shared repertoire of conventions) and the institutions and practices of society."[235] She could endear herself to people, and she learned early in her fieldwork experience that her academic training would not serve her well in the field unless it was coupled with the attitude of an insider's familiarity and knowledge. According to Neal, "she would have been very uncomfortable as a scholar committed to 'pure research' " and not only had she "learned from experience that the folk collector must in some manner identify with her subject," but her texts "indicate that she had nothing against assuming a persona whenever it was necessary."[236] The quality of her work in the field is best measured by the extent to which her texts represent a way of interpreting culture through an aesthetic response to everyday life. This position is consistent with views on folklore appearing in the *Florida Guide*, stressing "that folk art arises out of community necessity and is replicated because it satisfies a community aesthetic."[237] Nevertheless, her manuscripts stand out in contrast with much work produced by the Federal Writers' Project, given the wide disparity in training among workers on the Project.[238] Hurston's prose style invariably belies that she "was a profoundly professional writer in that she came to see her craft predominantly as a product of technical expertise rather than inspiration, viewed the market as the primary arbiter of literary value, and was guided by an internal sense of responsibility to [the] public."[239]

Revisiting issues she had begun to sort out in the early 1930s, Hurston composed several drafts of an essay initially titled simply "Folklore." Along with other items extending her previous folklore writing which had appeared in her two *Journal of American Folklore* articles, the *Negro* anthology, and *Mules and Men*, essays on folklore she wrote for the Florida Folklore Project were to be included with contributions from other collectors in a book, *The Florida Negro*. Not published until 1993, *The Florida Negro*, like the FWP State Guides, synthesized information on all aspects of local life, with folklore being one category. The Florida Folklore Project researched twenty-eight cultural groups, and the largest collection was on African-Americans; about three hundred informants participated. In total, some sixty-three collectors amassed a huge body of manuscripts, on biography, ethnography, history, beliefs and customs, dances, folk literature (including legends, tales, jokes, riddles, and other forms), speech, material culture, and music; also, songs and oral histories were collected. Hurston's essay on folklore reaches for a comprehensive definition; she refines some terms with reference to formal qualities. She begins her first version of the essay with a searching tone, referring to folklore as "a world and an ageless thing." In its revised form, titled "Go Gator, and Muddy the Water," she is more definite in her universalism: "Folklore is the boiled-down juice of human living," she writes. "It does not belong to any special time, place nor people. No country is so primitive that is has no lore, and no country has yet become so civilized that no folklore is being made within its boundaries" (1).

The first version of "Folklore" shows Hurston's ideas about culture had matured to a considerable degree since she had composed "Characteristics of Negro Expression." By the time she had joined the Florida Folklore Project, she had reached a peace with the analytic requirements of field research. Though she launches into a cosmic meditation on art and culture, the essay's clever structure illustrates her knowledge of folklore taxonomy and research methods as she crafts her own language to define concepts she had been examining for more than ten years. Her wording in the essay suggests that she had grown aware of "culture" as something imposed on ordinary living, "a forced march on the near and the obvious" (1). She shows how fully conscious she is that part of a social scientist's role is to determine what terminology people use to order their environment, to structure their society—this being the language that binds them together and to particular ways of thinking and acting, however fragile the bonds may be. "How many natural laws of things have been recognized, classified and utilized by these people?" she asks. Familiarity, not only being intimate with but also being able to comprehend the environment, precludes adaptation to it and control, she argues. These, furthermore, correspond with a generally accepted idea called civilization—"an accumulation of recognitions and regulations of the obvious" (1). In elaborate language, she intones the same statement she makes in *Mules and Men* about wearing culture like a tight chemise—so close to the skin that it is impossible to see it in objective terms. Intelligence, she argues, consists of trying over the better part of a lifetime to make sense of that which is apparent but complex and, consequently, elusive. Citing Isaac Newton, who discovered gravity, as an example, she insists that something like a scientific law must occur to a gifted person before an entire generation can progress.

Like "culture," the human pastime of manufacturing "art" makes ordinary life something to be revered. But Hurston does not make this claim to disparage or to over-simplify the artist's work. The effort to capture ordinary movements or moments when major changes are observable—one might say rites of passage ("at the moment of the kill or at the bath . . . in the prime of his strength . . . at the blow of her beauty"

[1])—cannot be viewed only as mimesis. More is involved than visible copying. The type of "breakthrough into performance" that the linguist Dell Hymes attributes to verbal presentations occurs with visual representations, particularly when images invoke temporal and spatial referents. Suggested movements and hints of past and future times are keys to the processional quality images need to make plain the progression from mimesis to poesis. Here, according to Hurston, is where culture proceeds with subtlety from a bague knowledge of the environment into lyricism, or the articulation of meaning through song.

Proceeding, she explains sound as the evidence of something shared in common among all creatures in the natural world, as the basis for naming, for lyrical articulations, for tones and rhythms. In and out of synchrony with drum rhythms, the voice is a source of another tradition—literature, which "grew out of sound." She writes that "songs for sound-singing" eventually became separate from "songs for story-telling." The simple twanging of the lyre was enough to accompany mood-singing, but more latitude was necessary for the telling of epics (2). This is a conventional approach to defining the relation between oral forms and literature, as a progression from raw sound to lyric to epic. The Blues becomes the lyric form around which she centers her analysis of sound's movement through stages toward literary language.

> The Negro blues songs belong in the class of moods set to strings which the ancients called lyric because they were sung to the lyre. The form is a line indicating the mood of the singer repeated three times. It betrays the mood of the singer and it walks with rhythm. Contrast and embellishment is [*sic*] obtained by stress and accent in the tune rather than a change of words. (2)

After proceeding with an analysis of songs, which have long been part of her repertoire, most of which appear in *Mules and Men*, she then offers an explanation of how black musical styles and their accompanying lyric forms have developed into lore, from blues to ballads.

The ballad attracts people simply because it is a story told in song form, according to Hurston. With music as a medium, "the ability of the group to create and transmit a story is increased" ("Folklore" 5). The thoughts producing the story correspond with the musical form. Through this correspondence, a near-perfect balance between content and form, the storyteller acquires the liberty to create anew—to add words intended to stimulate audiences' imaginations, as they become

79

"more interested in characterization and action than rhythm as such" ("Folklore" 5). The progression from sound to lyricism is complete when "the music has become the servant of the words" ("Folklore" 5).

Here her analysis, more detailed than in the opening passages, reaches toward a resolution with the scientific terminology she earlier viewed as an interference, to be chagrined. To explain how "the ballad is the prelude to prose," (5) she uses a biological comparison with the process of childhood development, whereby children learn to combine rhythms and rhymes without reason, where rhyming "for the sake of sound is evidence of the youth of his literature" (5). Providing examples of rhymes consisting of "sense" lines and sound lines, she demonstrates the necessity of both sound and sense for the appreciation of the next phase of literary development, prose.

Hurston's ideas about African-American folktales remain consistent from the beginning of her field research in the late 1920s to the FWP period. Writing to Boas in "The Florida Expedition," she had not only mentioned the difficulty of finding tales resembling the animal lore of bygone days but also noted that tales were "usually quite brief, sometimes no more than four or five sentences in length." In the first draft of "Folklore," she examines her previous perception in more depth. She writes, "In some of the tales of the American Negro it is plain that the story makers have no idea of what constitutes a tale. An incident or even a vivid description is offered as a story" (6). Her observations, further, lead her to conclude that African-American folk-tales have features distinguishing black humor in the United States from black humor in the British West Indies and Haiti. Indeed, she considers the humor of African-Americans to be indigenous to North America. But when she goes so far as to say that "there are no sad stories in American Negro folklore," once again, her analysis omits any accounting for the double-edged poignancy so crucial to unmining the deeply suggestive pathos informing tales that emerge as part of vernacular (to be read strife-filled or "agonistic") tradition. She does, however, allow that the laughter pervasive in African-American lore includes inwardly directed humor. She then goes on to examine some tales ranging from the single-statement type to the well-built story with characterization and plot. From whence do stories emerge full blown, as in *Mules and Men*, if they have been repeated to her in fragments? Her observations about humor are quite revealing, considering she leads into the discussion of lore by showing how musical forms precede literature with her focus on the blues as the first stage in this evolution. The blues, however, are not always considered humorous; according to Paul Oliver, it is an error to think of the blues as humorous. Where double-edged humor pierces with laughter-producing words, the response is to defer crying.[239] It seems that Hurston shies away from a direct confrontation with the painful undertone of either self-deprecating or aggressively hostile jokes repeated throughout her storytellers' yarns.

The section of the essay exploring the diversity of black culture in Florida delineates Cuban, American, and Bahamian expressive forms, along with their English and Spanish influences. She includes two Bahamian songs which appeared in her 1930 *Journal of American Folklore* piece and were included in her theater productions, sometimes also referred to as concerts. Getting back to some of the ideas she saw as cause for revelry in 1934, she writes: "In folklore as in all other forms of human behavior, the world is a great big old serving-platter and all the localities are like eatin-plates. All of the plates get helped with food from the platter, but each plate seasons to suit itself on the plate, and that is what is known as originality" ("Folklore" 13). In this passage she shows that the cultural wealth thriving in Florida brings the state in tandem with culture-rich centers all about the globe. Her summary evinces the orientation FWP workers on the Florida Folklore Project sought for the State Guide as well as for their planned volume of "The Florida Negro." She argues that stories composed of specific "Florida elements," though suggesting a certain local "flavor," reflect a quality of folk culture that is universal—not only found among blacks but among "all the races of the globe." Although she seems to contradict her previous point concerning the unique character of African-American humor, she explains the universality of Florida Negro folklore as a product of the state's diverse population, "because Florida has the great conglomeration of people hardly equalled anywhere in America" ("Folklore" 13). In what gives the impression of a major inconsistency, several phrases summarize a universalist idea about experience not only being the source of patterns but also not varying "too widely, class for class." As in "Characteristics of Negro Expression," but with much less sense of irony, she brings the reader in for a close-up view of the apparent sameness underlying difference, the similitude from whence originality emerges. Only Florida's magnetic attraction for workers explains the wealth of the lore found there, where "the lore and lushness of other states and countries have been heaped" ("Folklore" 13).

She ends with a Florida-flavored exclamation—"GO GATOR AND MUDDY THE WATER!!!"—which becomes the title of the revised version of the essay. In this revised draft, with the language ever so slightly refined, the local-flavor theme arising at the end of draft one, is more prominent: As in the first version of "Folklore," she uses the serving-platter metaphor to specify a source for local lore. Apportioned out to various local settings (called "eating-plates") the food analogy brings us to a central dynamic of culture. Why food? Simply because it stands for nourishment, sustenance, and growth, as well as taste? Because it is something we cannot imagine living without? Because it is something that can be presented at one extreme in a pleasing even enticing manner or at the other extreme in a mundane, unimaginative way? When taken as merely utilitarian, food can be equated with chores—the hard work associated with farming or the boredom of consuming unappetizing meals (as many people were obliged to do during the Depression of the 1930s), simply to stay alive. In other words, the routine of daily living is invoked. At the same time, all the potential variety people bring to their meals, as to their daily routines, turns a bland serving-platter into bounty: "Each plate has a flavor of its own because the people take the universal stuff and season it to suit themselves" ("Go Gator" 1).

Describing Florida as a culminating point, where people from diverse backgrounds seek employment in the many industries the state has to offer (unskilled workers, although she directs the reader's attention away from class considerations), Hurston declares the state a "culture delta," rich for the incubator-like effect it has on the newly emerging creative forms she sees. Her vision of Florida harkens to a primeval moment or consciousness. She finds the Floridian, though far from belonging to a leisure class, freed at times "beyond the necessity of making a living" ("Go Gator" 1) and, consequently, poised to grapple with a type of creation. Making a contribution to "the group mind," the newly emergent Floridian, perhaps in a preternatural fog, as if transfixed, in a dreamlike state, begins "to ask infinity some questions about what is going on around its own doorsteps" ("Go Gator" 1). Whether the group is deemed "civilized" depends upon the extent to which its members manipulate the events on this doorstep, she argues. The terms "repetition" and "regulation" are called upon to reproduce the effect of tradition, possibly without having to utter the word. Is it not much more poetic, after, all, for Hurston to employ scientific-sounding jargon while pounding hard, once again, at the main point articulated in the first version of

"Folklore"? The social scientist's or the student of culture's concern remains primarily with the extent to which a group of people have devised a system (or systems) for identifying and classifying patterns ("natural laws") in their environment. Hurston inclines, like the anthropologist Claude Levi Strauss does in his effort to demystify the distinction between Western "science" and "primitive (non-Western) "magic," to interpret elaborate naming systems—such as the metaphorical uses of words Hurston describes in "Characteristics of Negro Expression"—as being as equally scientific as they are artistic.*

The balance of the essay is nearly identical to the first draft of "Folklore," although she invokes the preliterature period, before sound had become music, as she argues, with humorous reference to the romantic innocence attached to "primitive" society: "Way back there when Hell wasnt no bigger than Maitland, people found out something about the laws of sound" (2). If Hell had grown, by the late 1930s, larger than the town adjacent to her beloved Eatonville the potency of humorous anecdotes to be collected in a region where gators animate swampy landscapes was, likewise, increasing.

Also imbued with a sense of humor, two versions of the legend about the same "Uncle Monday" Hurston wrote of in the *Negro* anthology are in the Florida Project collection. As I discuss in a subsequent chapter, "Uncle Monday" shows evidence of genre-combining, which makes it possible to speak of a mythos giving African-American oral literature Hurston collected in Florida its ritualistic significance. A version of the same story written by an FWP worker other than Hurston describes Uncle Monday as a medicine man born in Africa. He is specifically identified with "the powerful crocodile cult of men who claimed brotherhood with the savage saurians."** Although enslaved and transported to the United States, Uncle Monday resisted his captivity in South Carolina and fled to Florida where he joined with some Seminole Indians and marooned blacks. Among them, he gained a reputation as a medicine man and warrior, fighting against whites. Defeated, he and his co-fighters retreated "into the dense woods around Blue Sink Lake." Divine knowledge made Uncle Monday see futility in resistance, but rather

*See Claude Levi-Strauss, "The Science of the Concrete," *The Savage Mind* (Chicago: The University of Chicago Press, 1962) 1–33.
**Anonymous, "Uncle Monday," Florida Folklore Project, Bureau of Florida Folklife Programs, p. 1. All the quotes from this version of "Uncle Monday" appearing in this paragraph have the same citation.

than slavery or death, he opted to "change himself into an alligator, and join his brother saurians in the Blue Sink until the wars were over," after which "he would come forth from the lake and walk the land in peace."

Through performance, Uncle Monday transforms into a gator, in a scene resembling a Fire Dance Hurston staged under the auspices of the Florida FWP:

> So the tribe held a ceremony on the banks of the Blue Sink. As the men beat savage African and Indian rhythms on their drums, Uncle Monday danced. As he danced his face grew long and terrible, his arms and legs grew shorter, his skin grew thick and scaly, and his voice changed to thunder. From the Blue Sink came an answering roar of deep-throated bellows, and a thousand gators swept up from the lake in a double column. Uncle Monday was the biggest gator of them all, and he marched majestically between their ranks and slid into the Blue Sink. With a mighty roar all the other gators plunged after him.*

This passage describing Uncle Monday's passage from human to animal form, his changing guises, is a prelude to the conflict a female conjure doctor has with him. Monday's transformation is the key episode in the two long Florida Project versions as well as in a condensed version, collected in Orange County. Here, where Eatonville is specified as the source, Monday is identified as "an old Negro sorcerer who lived among the Seminoles just before they were sent to the West."** Through "perfecting his sorcery," he achieves his transformation into an alligator and remains as such, except every now and then he takes human form. People in Eatonville say "the old one's gone back," when he resubmerges and the other gators make a racket.

On Negro legends, Hurston writes: "There is a legend that has grown up about the huge alligator which inhabits Lake Belle at Eatonville. He is said to be an ex-slave who escaped from a Georgia plantation during the Indian wars in Florida" ("Negro Legends" 1). Again, though the central figure is not named, he is a medicine man from Africa who resists enslavement and, by working magic, transforms "into the American counterpart of his clan god, the crocodile" ("Negro Legends" 1). The historical theme of the legend is rendered:

> It had been a sad period for the Indian forces that ended with the alligator incarnation of the former African priest. Osceola had been tricked

*Ibid. 1–2.
**Anonymous, "Orange County, Florida, Folklore: Negro Legend. Florida Folklore Project, Florida Bureau of Folklife Programs.

into captivity, Bill Bowlegs had been slain, their ragged forces had been driven south and east before the conquering arms of the white man at last. Some had been removed to Oklahoma and the more relentless had been forced to seek refuge in the trackless wilds of the Everglades. The African priest saw no hope for himself in following further the fortunes of war. He announced his intentions to his brothers in arms, made his nine-days preparation before the day of his big medicine, stood before his sacred fire with his supplication and entered the lake to wait the coming of his kind as he predicted. ("Negro Legends" 1–2)

Hurston's version of Uncle Monday provides a basis for comparison to assess the extent of repetition and variation. The essay also establishes a point of reference for my subsequent discussion of the ways magic and ritual action are suggested through her use of pictorial language.

She describes Uncle Monday as "not a man"—not simply a non-human, but "the big alligator that lives in Lake Belle" (FWP "Uncle Monday" 1). Because his presence agitates the other alligators, he causes them, in their restlessness, to respond with a deafening din that can be heard through the night, when Uncle Monday "goes back to join waters" (1). Their raucousness, Hurston tells us, is a kind of praise-singing, declaring him the ruler and giving him his due. His reign extends from the time when "that haughty Osceola" was overthrown. This war, between female and male sovereignty, has pertinence to my discussion of the decline of Voodoo, in Chapter Five, and, consequently, the rise of Hoodoo in the United States. For now, what matters is the equating of rulers and conjurers or healers, as we learn that "Uncle Monday was a great African medicine man" (1). He was captured and enslaved, then independently found his way to Florida at a time when "Indians" were the the dominant population there. Along with escaped slaves, Uncle Monday gets involved with some traditional medicine, presumably rituals designed to empower him, because Hurston credits him with fierce resistance in confrontations with armed whites.

The narrative shifts to a different, nonspecific time when Monday "lived in a tiny hovel on the shore of Blue Sink." Blue Sink is the lake mentioned in the unnamed folklorist's version, which is located on a site similar to Lake Belle when it was sequestered in a more densely wooded area. In Hurston's version, the woman conjure doctor Judy Bronson's story of conflict with Monday is attributed to "pangs of professional jealousy."

Despite the conscious artistry Hurston used in writing the ethnographies discussed so far in this chapter, a stark contrast may be drawn from field research in which she presents only factual details or interprets in a calm and sober fashion. At times, she stands aside and allows the voices to speak for themselves. Examining a transcript of her interview with workers at a Turpentine Camp in Cross City, Florida, listening to her voice on a tape recording of songs she collected, and watching a video of films she made in the 1920s, a very different sense of her agenda comes across than can be gleaned from her published texts, where the articulated playfulness of the artist prevails.²⁴² These "documents" show the lucidity with which Hurston was able to understand what to emphasize, such as the hammer rhythms of the men laying lines on the railroad as they sing "Gonna See My Long-Haired Gal." As Hurston sings the song and makes the knocking sound of the hammer, she describes the exact movements of the men in the line, and the role of the singing liner who always starts the song and who has to be paid even though his task consists only in keeping the song going to provide the work rhythm— without it, the other men will not work. Through her explanations and her singing, she demonstrates the aesthetics of everyday life.²⁴³

In Hurston's work, the collecting, as one part of a process, should be distinguished from recording, filming, and transcribing as another part, and those two parts are distinctly separate activities from creating a text for the public. She conducts her research as if she is a student or apprentice of the culture. Recognizing that "the genuine thing, largely overlooked and limited compared to 'popularized' versions, is changed into something substantially different when artists like herself adapt the source for different ends,"²⁴⁴ she participates by performing, for example, songs she learns from specific people, singing them in field situations (as described in *Mules and Men* in the passage concerning how learning verses to the song "John Henry" helps to establish her as a competent insider). On field recordings, she performs songs, and narratives about the songs, as an informant for other collectors. With warmth and confidence her speaking voice presents a knowledgeable woman deeply immersed in her subject. Her high-pitched singing, with the hint of a gentle vibrato, precisely intones the un-self-conscious artistry she considers inherent in African-American folk expression. It is clear that she wants to be convincing about the depth of her knowledge and to some extent claim authority as an expert.

The collecting that led to the field recordings housed with the FWP Florida Folklore occurred at a time when it was unprecedented for a black woman to be engaged as a professional folklorist. As mentioned previously, Kennedy has explained that Hurston, because of her status, was excluded from certain customary rules; however, he also tells the story of how Alan Lomax "blackened his hands and face, according to Zora's instructions, in order not to attract undue attention to the black/white, male/female make-up of the team."[245] Race and class were significant factors influencing the collectors' work on the Folklore Project. Hirsch points out the disparity between the perspective of national administrators of the FWP and local collectors; in the south, this disparity had a strong impact, particularly on oral narratives collected from African-Americans. According to Hirsch, white southern collectors "formulated their questions and the commentary they included in their interviews . . . within the conventions of the plantation tradition familiar to them through folklore, literature, and popular culture."[246] Moreover, it is possible to see how the conventions would have an effect on the climate surrounding all collecting done in the south, reflecting "the white southern view that paternalism and a caste system were a new way of continuing the allegedly benevolent race relations of the antebellum era in the New South."[247] Although Hurston's work has been criticized for not challenging social conventions, she does not, in my view, merely adhere to the "norms" by reproducing stereotypes.

Rather than including interpretations showing the kind of biases Hirsch points out and also in contrast with the highly rhetorical interpretive statements she espouses in "Characteristics," Hurston, in her field reports, leaves open possibilities for subtle interpretations. She begins her account of work routines and life in a turpentine camp, for example, "Well, I put on my shoes and I started going up some roads and down some others to see what Negroes do for a living," and continues: "Going down one road I smelt hot rosin and looked and saw a 'gum patch.' That's a turpentine still to the outsider, but gum patch to those who work them."[248] Mimicking "objectivity," she affects a tone one would not presume of a person who identifies herself with the "Negroes" being observed. Further building on this dynamic, she defines the terminology by using an insider-outsider dichotomy. While doing so, however, she appropriates the "insider" knowledge, and to "insiders" the world is likely to have an entirely different lexicon. Differences in point of view are not only linguistic but social and economic. Although some critics have castigated Hurston for neglecting to discuss social, economic, and political conditions and although Kennedy has justified her position on the basis of conventional attitudes in the south at the time, some evidence supports the proposition that subtle differences in language are not merely a derivative dialect but also a social code, an aesthetic point of view, and a survivor's ideology. One could construe the formal aspects of the text as having ideological underpinnings revealed through what is left out as much as what is included. Facts may be presented, as they are in the turpentine camp report: "No school house. Church used for school. 250 pupils with 8 teachers. . . . To 9th grade. No high school in Dixie County. School in Putnam Quarters. None in Cross City."[249] The selection of details and the voices tell all. As Ethel Robinson, a woman in the camp, told Hurston: "Pay women $2.50–$3.00 per week. I wouldn't work for that. I could beg up that in the course of a week. I'd see many a hungry day before I'd work for that."[250] Kennedy has noted an instance when he and a colleague arrived at the turpentine camp and encountered Hurston. He remarks:

> It was unusual that she had not departed prior to our arrival, and unusual that she had turned in a page of cryptic handwritten notes such as "a hand tried to run away last week, and the sheriff had all the roads guarded" . . . "there is a grave not far from here of a hand they beat to death" . . . "a woman told me she cooks, cleans, washes and irons all for $2.25 per week."[251]

Commenting in the footnote, "This may well be the nearest thing to social criticism Zora ever wrote," Kennedy reflects a widely held view.

Although apparently reticent about bringing politics into her work, Hurston, nevertheless, seems to have been a person all too capable of understanding the poverty and racial antagonism she confronted without choosing to centralize the issues. Jim Byrd, a man in the camp, tells her, for example, that he "voted once in Georgia," and continues, "I just remember who I voted for," adding that blacks in the area generally do not vote because of its futility.[252] Simply by reporting the facts as told to her, Hurston illustrates how language not only can offer commentaries on social relations but also implies ways that survival skills can be the basis for a complex system of knowledge that gives meaning to various cultural forms—including gestures as well as inventive forms of expression such as storytelling and songs.

Survival skills are implicit in the expressive forms and in Hurston's method. They are encoded with double meanings—knowledge useful to people within the group and with meanings to be interpreted by observers. Forms of expression survive in part because they are flexible, adaptable to situations in which people who may not be sympathetic are present. This knowledge of how to be flexible, adaptable, and survive in a sense constitutes the sum of the traditional skills Hurston embodies. She practices, for example, varying forms of songs, such as when she sings "Long-Haired Gal"—noting that "Babe" may be substituted, depending on the singer; this is a railroad song she learned in a context to which she, as a woman, would not ordinarily be privy. Singing the male song, she varies the words, as she has heard it done for other songs, as well, such as "Mule on the Mount," which she says has so many variations in so many verses in different states that it is the longest song ever composed. Although varying the words is part of folk tradition, making the male song her own, as she does when she performs the song as an informant for Alan Lomax, is a significant departure from the tradition—a departure that exemplifies the imperative Hurston connected with her survival in the situation, being an ethnographer, being interviewed by a white researcher.

As an informant, she uses her knowledge of how to vary the forms and appropriates this knowledge by demonstrating her ability to reinvent the forms, thus validating her reliability as an informant. As the ethnographer who interprets the meaning of specific signs, such as the hammering rhythms, she appropriates the survival imperative by inventing a method. The pressures of social relations that make survival such a subtle communication skill have required folklorists generally to be aware of how they are perceived by the people they interview, for example. Underscoring this point in her introduction to *Mules and Men*, Hurston confesses that "folklore is not as easy to collect as it sounds" from her recollections of a childhood spent surrounded by "material" she thought she could get years later "without hurt, harm or danger" (4).

> The best source is where there are the least outside influences and these people, being usually under-privileged, are the shyest. They are more reluctant at times to reveal that which the soul lives by. And the Negro, in spite of his open-faced laughter, his seeming acquiescence, is particularly evasive. (4)

When using a participant-observer method, how does the person observed change into or become an active subject in the text produced? What does Hurston, in particular, do to make the people she observes "real" and how is the term "real" in this context to be understood?

Behind this question is a question of the field researcher's responsibil-ity. "The real" now, in a postmodern context, has taken on ironic sig-nificance which presents a problem for anyone attempting to reconcile the relationship between representation and the field researcher's so-cial role. Moreover, in the current decade, no way exists to read some of Hurston's passages, without being put on guard by her essentialist position and without, therefore, speculating as to how readers per-ceived her work in its own period. Have dramatic changes taken place since then in the concerns of a reading public interested in the study of culture?

Broadening the general public's knowledge about black culture is not only a goal Hurston shared with some of her contemporaries; it also bears a strong relationship with late-twentieth century efforts to enhance our understanding of U.S. cultural history. When Herskovits wrote to Boas in 1928 to ask him if he would be attending a conference on racial difference in Washington, D.C., it was a gesture that contin-ues to have significance in cultural studies. Similarly, in 1929 Boas and Klineberg were involved in a study of "Racial and Social Differences in Intelligence," work with which Hurston also became involved. Other anthropologists directly or indirectly linked with Hurston, including Margaret Mead, Herskovits, Frank Tannenbaum, and noted black in-tellectuals such as Ralph Bunche and Charles Johnson participated in an Institute on Race Relations at Swarthmore College. These activi-ties demonstrate the extent to which concern with studying culture was seen as a basis for advancing cultural understanding among the public.[253]

Hurston's ethnographic point of view entails seeing the aesthetics of everyday life as paramount, while tempering her observations with her own artistic sensibility. This "method" finds its equivalent in the style she brings to her texts and other forms of documentation. Furthermore, she tests the limits of her traditional knowledge by challenging the people she observes to reveal more of themselves than they would to a white re-searcher. Thus, she draws attention to what it means to be a member of a racial or ethnic group while engaged in research on cultures with which one closely identifies. Among African-Americans, the issue of identifica-tion is nuanced by the diversity within what often is construed as one monolithic culture; thus, a field researcher's affinity and position changes from one context within African-American culture to another. Hurston attempts to take into account her informants' consciousness of themselves as subjects being studied, their awareness of being viewed as disempowered, and she attempts to recreate that margin between how one is seen versus how one sees oneself through a variety of textual practices.

One example is her report of the near-fatal encounters she had in Polk County, which not only illustrates the possible consequences of fierce rivalry within the community but show how precarious her position is as a researcher—hence, how hazardous it is to cross boundaries. Her collecting meant that she had to spend quite a bit of time with the men in the camp, and she inadvertently became the target of a woman's jealous rage. "Why not look around for an easy victim and become a hero, too?" (*Dust Tracks* 130) She attributes this philosophy to people who are the subjects of her research, as if to make a point about railroad workers' proclivity for violence, but her reflexive point of view—always a crucial dimension of her work—leaves open an additional possibility: "I was nominated like that once [to be killed] in Polk County, Florida, and the only reason that I was not elected, was because a friend got in there and staved off old club-footed Death." (*Dust Tracks* 130) Although it appears that she withholds criticism, she holds up a mirror to her audience as if to show a picture of intragroup tensions and the mirror reflects back upon the voyeuristic observer. Just as putting herself in the position of researching people almost leads to her catastrophic end, the world at large stands to meet its Nemesis by keeping the apparently self-contained conflicts of a group of poor rural workers at bay.

> The very next pay-night when I went to a dance at the Pine Mill, Lucy tried to steal me. That is the local term for an attack by stealth. Big Sweet saved me and urged me to stay on, assuring me that she could always defend me, but I shivered at the thought of dying with a knife in my back, or having my face mutilated. At any rate, I had made a very fine and full collection on the Saw-Mill Camp, so I felt no regrets at shoving off. (*Mules and Men* 163–64)

Hurston is not a naive observer but cognizant of social schisms and the possible fatalities they may cause. There are no small and large conflicts; "club-footed" Death has one general form. She also is offering a critique of her own position, because the conflict nearly leading to her death arises from a sexual rivalry, therefore illustrating the added pressure of being a social scientist having to sort out one's social role. She has to account for herself as a woman doing what conventionally is considered a man's work, just as she has to make manageable whatever conflicts arise because she, too, is an informant.

CONVERSION AND THE BEAUFORT EXPEDITION

Hurston studied a sanctified church in Beaufort, South Carolina, in 1940. Her transcribed interviews document the experiences of individual members of the church, in their own words. Hurston, along with her white colleague and friend Jane Belo, who had organized the project, were present at the interviews, which were conducted after the two women had attended some of the church meetings. The monologues include converts' descriptions of their visions, which are memories of dreamlike episodes that preceded the actual moment of conversion. In the fifth vision of Bishop R.A.R. Johnson of the Holy Church of the Living, the narrative begins:

> *Thursday night behind the garden under a peachtree I went to pray. I fell prostrate. My clothes left my body. I travelled in a white path about as wide as the palm of my hand. It seemed that I went hundreds of miles. . . . One small man was ahead of me, crying "Come and follow me." On every side of the path there was all kinds of threatening beasts, such as panthers, bears, lions, oxens, cows, dogs, snakes and many other different kinds. . . . and they would come roaring and stamping. The Lord said to me, "Fear not, none can do thee any harm as long as thou stay in the path." We came to a river garden. Across it was a strong rope and I had to cross that great river on rope. On the right side of the rope was belching water. On the left were angry flames, fire shooting out forked tongues as though they would sweep me off the rope. . . . The path led on. . . . I came to a mountain. . . . and my God that was leading me ascended the mountain top and stood beckoning me with his hands to come up to him. I said, "Lord, I cannot walk this mountain, it is too straight up." A storm sounded to me: "Just believe, just believe, just believe and you can come up to where I am." Faith revived and lifted me on arms of love to where God stood. . . .[251]*

These are Johnson's words, as he spoke them to Hurston on April 8, 1940. It is the final vision recounted in a series that led to Johnson's religious conversion. When Johnson's account of his vision ends, Belo re-enters the room, and Hurston's note is included in the text of the transcription: "He was just about to speak of his conversion when JB came back again."[255] Hurston perceives that Belo's presence causes Johnson to change his style of presentation.

This is a reminder that Hurston understands such changes in the behavior of her informant as a difference in the level of communication occurring because of differences in "race" and status of the observers. As she says in her introduction to *Mules and Men*:

> The Negro, in spite of his open-faced laughter, his seeming acquiescence, is particularly evasive. You see we are a polite people and we do not say to our questioner, "Get out of here!" We smile and tell him or her something that satisfies the white person because, knowing so little about us, he doesn't know what he is missing. (*Mules and Men* 4)

Johnson's short speech following Belo's entrance proceeds:

> *I was a little boy running, turning somersaults in the sand before my father and mother on the way to church. I began praying in my way. I was not quite four years old. I began preaching. I was converted under a vision. I saw many wonderful things. Revelations strong were speaking to me. Many things that I did not know were in the Scriptures. After becoming acquainted with the Scriptures I found all the Revelations to be true, and encouched in the Scriptures.*[256]

Johnson's description of his vision noticeably differs from his account of his conversion. Hurston's mediating comment influences the reader's interpretation of the text. She alerts the reader to the dynamics of communication within the social situation. Her interpretation directs attention to the form and content of Johnson's language, for evidence of how social circumstances alter the way meaning is produced.

The two passages, along with Hurston's commentary, offer an insight into why Hurston, while pursuing scientific research, maintained that her primary objective was to create theater based on the forms of folk expression she was researching. An insight may also be gained concerning the complicated relations between a researcher and her informants, between the researcher and her colleagues, and their accountability to an academic institution. Although Hurston saw theater as an alternative to academic work and as a viable medium for African-American expression, she effectively labors in the field using skills ethnographers are expected to know. One gets the sense, from reading the field notes, of a structured situation mediated by the ethnographer's presence. When Hurston makes her comment about Belo's entrance and, consequently, the reader is able to observe a change in the convert's narrative, it is important to remember Hurston probably expected the notes to be read only by Belo and the person to whom she was accountable, Margaret Mead.[257] Hurston, as a field researcher, must conform to the requirements established by senior colleagues. She minimizes her analysis but includes enough commentary and interpretation to show her conformity with the methods.

She observes that the Seventh Day Church of God "is a revolt against the white man's view of religion which has been so generally accepted by the literate Negro, and is therefore a version to the more African form of expression."* The transcribed events of a church "meeting" appear on the page in poetical form, showing that the ritualistic aspect of the service's "keynote is rhythm."

> *My spirit goes to Bermuda*
> *Haiti*
> *The Gold West Coast of Africa*
> *Ask the spirit where it's been*
> *My body lies there like dead***

The text of the service is followed by a report of Madame Veronica's "readings"—visions and predictions concerning illnesses ("some one in her house blind, groping around to set fire to the house"["Sanctified Church," Field Notes]). Hurston in her notes makes associations, as with Hoodoo, in relation to the preceding quote in parentheses, or as to specific references in a prediction given to a young woman who is told to "make up your mind, because anyway in 3 weeks you will be alone," which Hurston interprets to mean as the woman will be deserted by a man who "will take action in 3 weeks." Hurston even attempts to become involved in a healing rite when Madame Veronica announces that someone has a pain piercing from chest to back. "Zora tries to rise and claim this pain but another woman behind has stood up and she is the one MMe V. is 'in touch with'—meanwhile frantic gestures on the part of two different women to keep Zora from standing up" ensure that she is thwarted, because as Hurston is informed, "when MMe V. is in the spirit 'you would *throw* her—she'd fall like beef—you'll hurt her if you bring her out of the spirit suddenly' " ("Sanctified Church," Field Notes).

Interspersed among interviews with communicants, including Bishop Johnson, Hurston's notes invoke scientific analysis without quite being detached. In fact, she combines analytic and poetic techniques, producing a metaphorical rendition of the ritualistic expression:

*"Ritualistic Expression," unnumbered page.
**"Sanctified Church," Field notes.

The unanimous prayer is one in which every member of the church prays at the same time but prays his own prayer aloud, which consists of exotic sentences, liquefied by intermittent changing so that the words are partly submerged in the flowing rising and falling chant. The form of prayer is like the limbs of a tree, glimpsed now and then through the smothered leaves. It is a thing of wondrous beauty, drenched in harmony and rhythm.*

Hurston followed the field research methods she learned from Boas, Mead, Herskovits, Benedict, and from the FWP guides. She, nevertheless, remained loyal to her own agenda, which often ran counter to the expectations others had for what her work ought or ought not to be. Nowhere is this fissure between stated goals and finished products more apparent than in the constant references Hurston makes to her theatrical pursuits, even though she was known primarily for her folklore and fiction. Moreover, the movement from goal to product led her through the intricate field research projects, from the first Florida Expedition to New Orleans and Alabama, back to Florida, to the Bahamas, Haiti, and Jamaica, and to Florida again in 1938 for the FWP when she collected music, beliefs, stories, games, information on work, life histories. Fieldwork was at times the mainstay of her livelihood, from the Mason contract beginning in 1927 through the FWP research. By the time of the Sanctified Church project, however, her reliance on income from field research had begun to diminish.

When weighing Hurston's idea of everyday-life drama in black culture and her theater ambitions against the top-heavy institutional support she relied on for her research, events surrounding the Sanctified Church Project illustrate how her professional choices led to an irresolvable conflict of interest. The Sanctified Church project depended on professional supervision from Mead and funds in part donated by Belo, administered by Klineberg at Columbia University.[258] The $300 for two months of work Hurston was to receive for organizing the collecting, interviewing, and reporting in Beaufort, was not enough to make the project worth her while. She needed to find a way to retain part of the work as her own, not merely in the commercial sense, but in terms of the credit she would expect to receive for her contribution. Part of Hurston's responsibility as a member of the research team organized by Belo—the team included a psychologist, sound-recording specialist and filmmaker named Norman Charfin, and a film assistant—was "to han-

---

*"Ritualistic Expression," unnumbered page note.

dle the personal end."[259] She was to imbue the enterprise with human interest, to devote her attention to the subtleties of interacting with people disinclined to reveal information crucial to understanding their actions in any depth. Her understanding of unique features of black life made it possible for her to learn from her interlocutors a communication skill useful also as a survival skill in situations of unequally balanced power. She could observe, for example, nearly imperceptible changes in conversation such as Bishop Johnson's shift from the vivid language used to describe his vision to the prosaic description of his conversion. As in the *Mules and Men* comment quoted previously in this discussion, silence or unspoken meanings can take on greater significance than what is said. She was paid to coordinate meetings with people, apply her knowledge of personal human values and traits to the day-to-day activities in the field, and to interpret what she saw. Her personal goal was to create theater. On the day she received her letter from Belo describing the project and discussing the intentions of the two filmmakers who were to accompany Hurston in the field to make a sound film of the church proceedings, Hurston wrote to Paul Green about the problem of working in the field with men interested in collecting material, particularly gospel music, for commercial purposes.[260] She was interested in using the music in a play she and Green had discussed writing together.

ANOTHER AGENDA

The proposed play, *John de Conqueror*, never materialized, and the unrealized effort is indicative of the direction her theatrical career had begun to take since 1935. The diminution of Hurston's theatrical career should be seen in the context of economic developments impinging on the theater as a whole. In writing about the pressure "Democratic Theater" faced during the 1930s, theater historian Ronald Ross points out that the growing popularity of radio and film entertainment threatened the theater. "With the advent of the depression in 1929, the already tottering position of the theater worsened considerably," he writes. "Largely because of its status as a 'luxury item,' this industry was among the first to feel the economic shockwaves, suffering staggering setbacks in the areas of production, employment, and patronage."[261] During 1935 and 1936, Hurston worked for about six months as a drama coach for the Negro Unit of the Federal Theater Project in New

York. According to John Houseman, the well-known white director who had charge of the Negro Unit, Hurston and other artists who were not relief workers joined the project "certainly not for the thirty dollars a week, nor primarily out of friendship for me, but because they saw in the project a wide-open field for those creative activities which they were denied within the narrow limits of the commercial theater; also, perhaps out of a vague, undefined feeling that, as cooperating members of the Negro Theater Unit, they were helping to start something new and significant in the cultural life of their country."[262] Houseman reports that Hurston, whom he considered more talented than the other writers on the project, wrote a play, *Lysistrata,* her adaptation of the Aristophanes comedy. Although he considered it a likely production, it was never staged because it was too risque and "scandalized both the Left and Right in its saltiness"; Houseman's remarks, from his autobiography, suggest that the play was set in a Florida fishing village and that both its theme as well as its sexual content were responsible for its being censored.[263] The only extant play titled *Lysistrata* included among Federal Theater Project records, however, is the Seattle Negro Unit's version, adapted by the black playwright Theodore Browne. His revision of the classic closed immediately after it opened, ostensibly for its sexual content; however, Ross attributes the play's closing to the controversial political tone it arouses because it is set in Ethiopia.[264]

As mentioned previously, under the auspices of the Florida Folklore Project, Hurston presented Fire Dances; she also proposed staging a "Voodoo Ritual" at the National Folk Festival, along with a one-act folk play, a prayer and chants, and some instrumental selections. Her enthusiasm for theatrical displays of black cultures had not waned. Writing to Sarah Gertrude Knott, the Festival Director, Hurston explained that the Voodoo ritual would illustrate the "African background for American Voodoo."[265] Knott, who in turn wrote to James Weldon Johnson for his opinion as to whether African Voodoo rituals had "influenced the American Negro," raised the question as to whether the ritual would fit into the Festival's program.[266] Johnson's response offers the assurance that because of her research in Haiti, Hurston is well informed about the subject and states that his concern is "the artistry with which Miss Hurston might develop and present her theme . . . whether or not she isolates its setting and its history."[267] His words of caution raise one of the most important problems facing theater artists trying to recreate cultural performances outside the context in which they ordi-

97

narily occur. The degree of artificiality involved in placing cultures on display is complicated when people perform as "authentic" members of the culture and are, thus, placed on exhibit.[268] Johnson had expressed similar concerns in 1934, when "Real Plantation Negroes from Florida" were advertised to perform "in African voodoo rites and fire dances"—Hurston productions. He noted then "that such a demonstration would not be an expression of Negro folk-art, but that if it was put on purely as a *theatrical feature* it would be a different matter."[269]

It seems Hurston's inability to maintain a theatrical career, rather than being a personal shortcoming, though symptomatic of larger issues surrounding the conflicts she encountered during field-research, more important, indicates the difficulty of finding an authentic medium for African-American expressive forms. Because live performance might make it possible to recreate a traditional performance context, or at least to try, theater seemed more viable to her than written texts. Ritualization was necessary to make "real" the type of performance she saw as crucial to understanding the aesthetics of everyday life in African-American folk culture. Problems of authenticating texts, complicated by methods used to transcribe music, for example, not to mention translating dance and other gestures into written forms, could more readily be addressed in a live performance. But as I will show in the following chapter, the idea of "authenticity" itself resists definition.

CHAPTER FOUR
The Authenticity Debate

Ham, in Hurston's 1927 play *The First One*, strums a "rude stringed in-strument," laughs aloud, and dances onto the stage with his wife and son, as the stage directions read. Adorned with a wreath of bay leaves, wearing a white goat string, Ham accompanies his wife and son as the triad "caper and prance to the altar" to join in a "burnt offering before Jehovah." Mrs. Ham (Eve) dons a blue frock decorated with shells and has wreaths of red flowers around her head, wrists, and ankles. She, along with their son who is nude but for the leaves and flowers about his waist, bear bouquets of flowers as they approach Noah. When the wife of Ham's brother Shem criticizes the Hams for failing to bring what she considers a proper offering, Ham replies, with sprite: "We bring flowers and music to offer up. I shall dance before Jehovah and sing joyfully upon the harp that I made of thews of rams."[270]

Though never staged, *The First One* demonstrates the performative idea Hurston uses to ground the argument on black culture she later presents in "Characteristics of Negro Expression." *The First One*, an early ex-ample of her fascination with recreating Old Testament stories, precedes two novels which similarly recast biblical legends (*Jonah's Gourd Vine* and *Moses, Man of the Mountain*) in an African-American context. A remnant of her biography *Herod the Great*, in progress at the end of her life, was posthumously published as "Herod on Trial." Tales involving Noah (also called Nora) appear in her staged productions (*All De Live Long Day*, for example), in *Mules and Men* and elsewhere. Here, Noah's story—his curs-ing Ham to be black—revises the story slave masters deployed to ratio-nalize slavery. In Hurston's version, Noah, while intoxicated, unwittingly curses his favored son Ham. Actually, the wives of Ham's siblings Shem and Japheth maneuver the brothers into misleading Noah. Mrs. Shem dislikes Mrs. Ham (Eve) because she takes after her mother, "a seeker after beauty of raiment and laughter." Mrs. Shem, further, objects, "Noah would make him [Ham] lord of the earth because he sings and capers."[271] To ensure Ham does not inherit Noah's vineyards, Mrs. Shem seizes the opportunity to reverse the situation when Ham sees Noah naked and responds by frolicking, making a joke of his father's reckless pose. Mrs. Shem implores her husband to "stand up and regain thy birthright from that dancer who plays on his harp of ram thews, and decks his brow with bay leaves."[272] Meanwhile, the Hams (pun intended) continue to dance and romp. "And why must Jehovah hate beauty?" Mrs. Ham asks, as if through her words Hurston mocks the common saying "God don't like ugly!" Alarmed at the extremity of Noah's curse, Mrs. Shem laments and all become quite horrified that the consequences far exceed what they had reckoned. Japheth begs Noah to recant: "Our father, and lord of all under Heaven, you cursed away his vineyards, but we do not desire them. You cursed him to be black—he and his seed forever, and that his seed shall be our servants forever, but we desire not their service. Unsay it all." Indeed, Noah regrets what he has done, when he finally realizes it, but because the transformation has already occurred, he banishes the Hams. While Noah and his wife remain behind, "to covet, to sweat, to die and know no peace," as Ham reminds them, he follows the Hurstonesque adage to "jump at the sun": "I go to the sun," he announces. Whereas tragedy folds in around Noah, humor and resilience are with Ham in the end, as "his eyes light on the harp and he smilingly picks it up and takes his place beside Eve."[273] Hurston's stage directions further inflect his "lightly cynical" final speech, before he happily exits, singing "I am young as a ram in spring" and strumming all the while.

Although the work of a novice playwright, *The First One* illustrates the biblical tale's flexibility. Borrowing from the Old Testament to create a tale with local significance, Hurston follows a creation-story convention. According to Lawrence Levine, some African-American creation stories in the antebellum period were "influenced by the ubiquitous Anglo-American myths which insisted that blackness resulted from God's curse on Cain or Ham."[274] Rather than borrowing the story of why and how blacks came to be black to repeat the self-denigrating implications Levine discerns as a pattern in such stories, Hurston revises the story to demonstrate what she means by performativity preceding racial classification. Ham was a performer first and black, incidentally. Moreover, she clarifies her idea of originality as "the exchange and re-exchange of ideas between groups," by casting the story in the form of a tale whites told to rationalize slavery, thus magnifying the dubious significance of positing cultural origins. Finally, crafting the tale into a one-act play suggests its potential for translation to the stage—the overriding test of its authenticity as an expressive folk form, having the capacity to expand into a full-blown "enlargement of life."

Enlarged for the stage, Ham's story mocks the "identity politics" Hurston has been charged with engaging.[275] By using the biblical tale historically appropriated for discourses on enslavement in America, Hurston appears to adopt a conventional frame while illuminating a space where questions pertaining to identity can be examined in full view of the many ambiguities American identity poses. The relationship between the play's formal attributes—its use of ritual, dance, and song—and its pithy examination of "race" and identity make it a clever example of the way Hurston uses humor to show how identity cannot be pinned down to one essence, even (or especially) if it is performance, [for one arbitrary event can alter the appearance]. Ham's being a "ham" is part of the reason his father favors him, and despite his banishment, the trait is a comfort to Ham in the end because he stands outside the family tragedy. The emerging theme of disaster befalling a clan unable to tolerate the playful antics of a "ham," also is a commentary on dramatic form, with its high and low categories for tragic and comic characters. The twist echoes Hurston's famous quip about not being tragically colored and sets a frame for not being tragically dramatic, as well.

Defining identity in America has informed discussions related to race and culture since the eighteenth century, when Michel-Guillame Saint-Jean de Crevecoeur queried "What Is an American?" in *Letters from an American Farmer*. The answer has remained elusive. Crevecoeur, a French immigrant to colonial America, in response to his own question, epitomizes the newly forming identity he observes in the colonies as a blend of European strains; though English traits are emulated, the ideal American is a blend. Crevecoeur received credit for initiating the idea of assimilation which has come to be equated with the "melting pot" view of American society. The new breed of humanity he saw emerging had left behind a way of life so filled with strife, so lacking in promise that homesickness was alien. On North American soil, emigrants are regenerated by "new laws, a new mode of living, a new social system."[276] Crevecoeur's argument relies on descriptive examples he takes from observations he made while traveling around the colonies and the frontier. This descriptive style gives his book the flavor of an ethnography more so than a travelogue. His efforts to classify, analyze, and draw inferences with broad implications—in short, to explain the American character to a European audience—make Crevecoeur's work a progenitor of twentieth century ideas on cultural assimilation. For it can be argued that Crevecoeur's vision idealizes Americanness as a synthesized culture not only because it predates the arrival of emigrants from the Mediterranean and Eastern Europe—to say nothing of Asia and Latin American—but also because Native Americans and African-Americans complicate the question "What Is an American?" beyond the society's capacity to resolve paradoxical identity questions coded in racial terms. Whereas Native Americans were outside Crevecoeur's conception of Americanness, African slaves he observed in Charlestown, South Carolina, had the marks of American institutions literally and figuratively imprinted on them and, therefore, presented a dilemma for American society.

The authenticity debate as it pertains to African-Americans begins with the earliest writing in English by enslaved blacks—from the eighteenth century poetry of Phillis Wheatley and the narratives of James Gronniosaw, John Marrant, Ottobah Cugoano, and Ouladah Equiano. Their works' authenticity was challenged because according to the dominant ideology, as Gates rhetorically puts it, "Blacks and other people of color could not write."[277] Texts written in English by blacks meant "that the African was indeed a human being and should not be enslaved."[278] The authenticity debate is based on the question of whether written texts produced by African descendants (or other signs of acculturation, such as artistic forms more broadly defined) reinforce or undermine notions of "difference." According to Gates, "the sense of difference defined in popular usages of the term 'race' has both described and *inscribed* differences of language, belief system, artistic tradition, and gene pool, as well as all sorts of supposedly natural attributes such as rhythm, athletic ability, cerebration, usury, fidelity, and so forth."[279] Hurston engaged in debates over authenticity given that "race," the use of language, and definitions of culture influenced her artistic choices. In *The First One*, she gives a frontal illustration of the connection between identity and expressive form, where cultural performance is explicit.

Identity questions cannot be separated from issues pertaining to authenticity or from aesthetic judgments (or values). As the philosopher Charles Taylor argues, individuals proffering definitions of themselves to establish their differences from others have historically been crucial in debates over what constitutes authentic identity. Although originality, implicit in the notion of authenticity, "demands a revolt against convention," a larger, unifying theme undergirds individualized approaches to self-definition. Dating back to Enlightenment thinking from Rousseau to Hegel, focusing on social inequality, such thinking problematizes the individual's relationship to the world at large. Taylor ties this shift in with a movement away from mimesis (imitating) toward poesis (making)—that is, from copying to creation as a means of self-expression and self-definition. "If we become ourselves by expressing what we're about, and if what we become is by hypothesis original, not based on the pre-existing, then what we express is not an imitation of the pre-existing either, but a new creation."[280] Hence, Taylor argues, "the demands of authenticity are closely bound up with the aesthetic."[281] He proposes a move toward clarifying what authenticity means and its importance in ongoing debates. Relativist views are all too often polarized against totalizing norms which hold up an idealized picture of what all individuals in society ought to be, as Crevecoeur does. On the other hand, people who argue for definite criteria as to what represents morally sound judgments find fault with relativists for insisting on tolerance of diverse perspectives. Taylor argues that being concerned with authenticity necessarily involves an ethical stance which means one need not shrink away from the responsibilities that go along with owning up to the priority authenticity has had in American intellectual history. Trying to define it needs to be a goal in itself.

During the 1920s and 1930s, the pressure to define American identity and to create authentic American art had a certain intensity as a relativist notion of American culture broadened the possible forms and styles such art might take. Cultural pluralism, an anti-assimilationist theory of heterogeneity in American culture, first articulated by Horace Kallen in 1915, established a powerful counterpoint to the assimilationist idea which came to be known as "the melting pot," after Israel Zangwill's 1908 play *The Melting Pot*.[282] Werner Sollors identifies direct links between modernist writing emerging in the 1930s and gradual emphasis during the early twentieth century on ethnic identity as a desirable attribute rather than a hindrance. Not only did the exploration of ethnic themes expand in the variety of subjects (Yiddish, Irish, and African-American arts providing numerous examples), forms of representation in drama and fiction were visibly altered due to "double audi-

ences." According to Sollors, "ethnic writers in general confront an actual or imagined double audience, composed of 'insiders' and of readers, listeners, or spectators who are not familiar with the writer's ethnic
group," where "the opportunity presents itself for the writer to play a variety of roles."[283] The role of mediator or translator being crucial, writing with ethnic flavor often includes glossaries and dialect, according to
Sollors, which become signs not only of a text's ethnicity but its modernity. Hence, the questions of authenticity challenging African-American
writers to "prove" their identity through the nineteenth century, in the
twentieth century provokes them to challenge the terms used to define
their identity.

A breakthrough for black and white artists occurs in the 1920s, two
generations removed from the Civil War, much less tempered by
Reconstruction's ordeals than by World War I's international schism.
For blacks with an eye toward the stage, the past and the present were
separated by minstrelsy's legacy. According to the theater historian
James Hatch, minstrel performances had been gradually fading from
the stage since the 1880s. Black musicals, in particular musical comedies, were abundant during the first two decades of the twentieth century. The advent of ragtime inspired the first wave in the 1910s, whereas
jazz brought in the second wave of the twenties. While endowed with
the dynamism and inventiveness associated with these new musical
styles, the early black musicals broadened the scope of characterizations
theretofore seen on commercial stages. Indeed, according to Allen
Woll, "reviewers often criticized black writers, composers, and performers, for what might be considered 'ambition,' any effort to break or alter
the white conventions that governed black theater on Broadway."[284]
Although *Shuffle Along* (1921), with music composed by Noble Sissle
and Eubie Blake, included romance and therefore broke, as Woll notes,
"the love taboo" restricting blacks from being seen in a serious light, the
show was a close relative of minstrel entertainment. "Its comedy of ma-
lapropisms and black chicanery tended to reinforce existing stereotypes
rather than change them," Woll explains, and though the show "became the model for all black musicals of the 1920s, it also set certain
boundaries."[285] This, in part explains, what Hatch observes is "a peculiar
phenomenon—the relative absence of comedy in black drama."[286] The
pervasiveness of comedy in early black entertainment, with its close
affinities to minstrelsy, has driven black dramatists away from comedy as
a medium for presenting black culture on commercial stages. Hurston

and Hughes are two of the exceptions. Hurston's play *The First One* is one of her early efforts to stretch the boundaries of conventions such as the appropriated biblical tale with its reflection on the close relation between legend and cliché, with its parodic twist on stereotyping. As Baker explains in *Modernism and the Harlem Renaissance*, assuming conventional frames offered by minstrelsy ("darky" jokes, for example) and its customary masking techniques (such as dissembling) can be seen as a dynamic in verbal performances of the late nineteenth and early twentieth centuries. In finding ways to appropriate the forms constraining them, black artists gave expression to a modernist sensibility specific to their historical moment. Baker contributes a great deal to our understanding the historical circumstances surrounding the creative output of the Harlem Renaissance. By rereading previous critiques of the Renaissance, which stress black artists' tendency to assert their identity either too much or too little, Baker shows, rather, that the content and tone of what they voiced resonate through much of what we take for granted in contemporary verbal arts derived from music. For example, the paradoxical humor of the blues developed during that generation and has been transmuted in a variety of forms.

Like Booker T. Washington, Bert Williams, and Charles Chesnutt, who are, respectively, exemplars of oration, popular performance, and fiction writing, Hurston, too, "demonstrates in [her] manipulations of form that there *are* rhetorical possibilities for crafting a voice out of tight places."[87] She recognizes the paradox at the center of the culture she studies, as well as her definition of it, where originality stems from an ability to observe well and to adopt conventional forms as one's own. As I discussed previously, she exploits the double meaning of borrowing within and across cultural boundaries. Although Hurston considers mimicry a universal skill among blacks, writing to Mason, Hurston attributes her talent for observing to her patron: "But of course it is due to you in my case, because you sent me to look and see." It would seem that she concedes to an idea of "universality" as inclusive and not simply attributable to one discrete group. It would seem also that, according to Hurston, the continuous influence of one culture on another supersedes the influence that individuals within a culture have on one another. The exchange across groups generates something previously unknown and, by implication, desirable. But there are consequences. The quest for originality can lead to the kind of conflict prompting Hurston to write to Mason criticizing the black musician, singer, and songwriter J. Rosamond Johnson for being unoriginal and opportunis- tic—perhaps because of his training in both popular and classical music and his aggressive pursuit, along with his partner Bob Cole, of a career in mainstream commercial musical theater. The team was, nevertheless, credited with moving black musical theater during the 1910s away from the "coon show" variety which had been the mainstay of early black pop- ular entertainment, an offshoot of the minstrel show.

Hurston's objections to Johnson and others who were producing shows for white musical theater brought her into direct conflict with prevailing trends in commercial theater. At the same time, the increas- ing popularity of black folk arts presented a dilemma for her, a dilemma that would take on more significance long after she had ceased working in the commercial theater world. Black folklife had become the focus of black theater written by white playwrights, such as Ridgeley Torrence in his 1917 play *Granny Maumee*, and reached a climax in the 1920s with Eugene O'Neill's *The Emperor Jones*, Marc Connelly's *Green Pastures*, and Dubose and Dorothy Heyward's *Porgy*. In black musical theater, black folk culture as a source for comic representations made it difficult to compromise with commercial demands on the one hand and aesthetic preferences, on the other. The conflict had to do with a more general question of how the increasing popularity of folk forms, along with their exposure to broader audiences, influences the folk arts themselves and how folk forms change when they become accessible for wider con- sumption. For Hurston, this question took the form of a distinction she drew between "the folk" and the black middle class.

Hurston respected and admired black culture as lived among ordi- nary hard-working men and women. Conversely, she disdained and crit- icized black intellectuals who "get on the band wagon . . . the backs of the poor Negro and ride his misery to glory."[288] Writing to Mason, Hurston goes into quite a bit of detail about her distaste for the domi- nant, old-guard black intellectuals of her time, excluding Alain Locke (who favored art over politics). Her discussion resembles discussions in the 1980s and 1990s about the failures versus the merits of Affirmative Action. She argues, for example, that "the things our 'leaders' are fight- ing for are privileges for the intellectuals and not benefits for the hum- ble."[289] In a passage about the social movement toward equal rights, she questions the value of a struggle aimed at the class of black Americans who already are relatively privileged compared with their brethren who are least in control of the political agenda.

> We have had black, inky battles for pullman reservations, hotel privileges, white neighborhood residences, white wives for Negro doctors, appointment of Negro lawyers to federal jobs etc. But oh so little to improve the lot of the man in the street. And nobody is going to waste time and golden syllables telling the bottom black what to do to help himself. Unctuous syllables are reserved for tea-table conferences where the leaders secretly boast "no other Negro was present besides me."[290]

Beyond social and political gains being sought, the question of how to create art, how to foster an arts movement reflecting progressive attitudes about black culture had become part of a politicized agenda. Hurston could in no way avoid being at the center of such a controversy, given that her views about how and how not to represent black culture directed her life's work. Thus, in seeking to distinguish herself from the black mainstream, she at times became vitriolic, as when she wrote to Mason: "Complain in lyric verse about the fate of the black man, but kick him in the face if you meet him. He is supposed to be a figment of the printed page at so much per line. He must not walk in daylight and disturb the cogitations of our intellectuals."[291] Although her statement shows she was not insensitive to travails of poor "folk" who reaped no benefits from the commercialization of black folk art forms, her outspokenness stops short of articulating an answer to the question: how does one bridge the gap between "folk" represented and artists doing the representing. This problem refers back to issues I raised earlier, concerning the type of essentialism Hurston practiced, where a parallel can be drawn with questions Gayatri Spivak poses as to whether privileged intellectuals can ever speak from an authentic point of view in speaking on behalf of silenced classes, or even the masses.[292]

Showing her high regard for "the folk" by mocking the intellectuals, Hurston criticized the political altruism the privileged practiced, as nothing more than a failure of originality, which is to say a failure on the part of intellectuals to practice effective politics. She wrote: "They have done enough for the poor brute when they plead for a seat for him in a pullman—where he'll never have enough money to go anyway—and when they let him furnish them a gangplank to board the publicity ship."[293] In place of false political representation and pretentious artistic representations, Hurston wanted to see an untainted picture of black folklife exposed to the world at large. Toward that end, she practiced political compromise behind closed doors, in negotiations with people who had the power to fund her vision. When Mason restricted Hurston's

freedom of choice and expression in using folklore she collected on expeditions to the South in her production of *The Great Day*, she had no
critical response. Her idealism did not allow her to question overtly the
underlying conditions of power; it is fair to say she was in line with the
general thinking at the time, at least within the boundaries assumed
under the FWP's folklore collecting during the 1930s. "The white/black
relationship was generally regarded as a fixed one and therefore not a
fit subject for commentary," according to Stetson Kennedy.[294]

AUTHENTICITY AND THE CONVERGENCE
OF COLOR, "RACE," AND CLASS

Personal conflicts based on color consciousness, in the creative works of
African-American artists, have historically been the converging point
for class and "race" issues. Hurston's one-act play *Color Struck* (1925) is
one example. The term "color struck," according to the anthropologist
John Gwaltney, means "accepting Euro-American aesthetic and racial
values."[295] The drama of a dark-skinned woman, Emmaline (called
Emma throughout the play), who because of her color torments herself
so much she destroys her relationship with John, the man who loves her,
Color Struck ironically ends with Emmaline having given birth to a white-
skinned baby—presumably because of an interracial liaison, when John
unexpectedly returns to see her and discovers the "truth."

Color Struck dramatizes the havoc Euro-American beauty standards
wreak in Emma, who suffers devastation because she is unable to recognize her own positive traits. The play focuses on Emma's internal conflict, an inferiority complex. Hemenway's analysis of Hurston's last
published novel *Seraph on the Suwanee* aids in interpreting *Color Struck*.
He provides evidence of Hurston's compulsion to recreate a character
whose inferiority complex makes loving her impossible. Hemenway
cites Hurston's personal struggle first to overcome her own lack of confidence about her appearance as a young woman and later to maintain
an intimate relationship with a man having the same problem that
Arvay, the white protagonist, manifests in *Seraph on the Suwanee*. Emma,
in *Color Struck*, cannot believe John, her lover, is sincere in his affection
because he must, in her view, prefer "half white girls." Despite his
protestations and many demonstrations of his love for Emma, she remains unconvinced and reveals the trait that led to Othello's demise—

misguided jealousy. Emma's jealousy leads her to say to John, when he cautions her that he "don't like to be accused o'ever light colored girl in the world" because it hurts his feelings: "Then you don't want my love, John, cause I can't help mahself from being jealous. I loves you so hard, John, and jealous love is the only kind I got. . . . Just for myself alone is the only way I knows how to love."[296] The conflict escalates as Emma convinces herself that John is "carryin on" with Effie. Friendly, attractive, and light-skinned, Effie is possibly a better dancer than Emma, even though Effie thinks John and Emma are "the bestest cakewalkers in dis state" (90). Dancing skills have crucial bearing on the outcome of the play, thematically.

Set at the turn of the twentieth century in a dance hall, the play's central action is a cakewalk competition. Blacks from all over Florida participate. Indeed, John and Emma board a train to go to the dance with the group from Jacksonville, Effie among them. Emma and John nearly miss the train, though, according to John, because, "She says I wuz smiling at Effie in the street car and she had to get off and wait for another one." Here and in other scenes, Hurston presents a thoroughly baffled John: "I never gits a chance tuh smile at nobody," he reminds Emma, "You won't let me." The dialogue and action are structured so it is impossible to tell how much of the discord can be attributed to Emma's imagination. "Jes the same, every time you sees a yaller face, you *takes* a chance," she insists. She almost enters a confrontation with Effie when she offers them some of her blueberry pie. After Emma "freezes up," she rudely rejects Effie's offer. "Youse jus hog-wile ovah her cause she's half-white!" Emma shouts at John because he feels obliged to compensate for her impolite behavior and accepts the pie. "No matter whut Ah say, you keep carryin' on wid her. Act polite? Naw Ah aint gonna be deceitful an' bust mah gizzard fuh nobody!" As Emma grows more hostile, John, ever the consoler, tries to calm her—an impossible task. When she gets to the point that she cannot face participating in the dance, "can't go in there and see all them girls—Effie hanging after you" (96), filled with rage and hatred, Emma abandons the idea of the contest. John goes on to win, with Effie, allowing Emma to confirm her view that "us blacks was made for cobblestones" (97).

The cakewalk—a dance dating back to antebellum plantation life—was heralded by James Weldon Johnson as a major contribution to American performance styles.[297] The dance, developed as a black imitation of the quadrille, was a precursor to chorus-line dancing in musical theater. A high-kicking movement, half strolling, half prancing, the cakewalk has a jocular style, on the one hand, and an air of dignity, on the other. It is performed while dancers maintain an erect posture associated with ballroom formality. An enormous cake is the prize for winning dancers, but as *Color Struck* illustrates, the spotlight is on music (here, an orchestra "of guitar, mandolin, banjo, accordion, church organ and drum") and the spectacular bowing, petticoat flinging, silk hat-tipping, graceful gesturing, precision strutting and parading, singing hand-clapping accompaniment.

Failing to dance, Emma proves herself to be a shadow, self-effacing to an extreme. She shows that the appearances upon which all human worth are valued, for her, are distorted—indeed, turned inside-out. Effie, the "half-white," turns out to be a closer relative of Ham in *The First One* than the visibly black Emma. The final scene, which occurs twenty years after the first two, exploits this idea that appearances are meaningful only for the unseeing. Long separated from John, Emma lives in a shack with her daughter who is ailing. John, now a widower, reappears to renew his love for Emma, whom he still finds "just as bright as a basket of chips." But Emma refuses to permit John to turn on any lights. "Oh, let's we all just sit in the dark awhile" (99). Desperate to see her, John keeps insisting. "Strike a light honey so I can see you—see if you changed much. . . . (99)"

> Emma: "We don't exactly need no light, do we, John, tuh jus' set an talk?"
> John: "Yes, we do, Honey. Gwan, make a light. Ah wanna see you." (99)

When Emma questions John about his wife, suggesting she must have been "some high-yaller dickty-doo," John assures her his deceased wife quite resembled Emma. "Make a light an Ah'll show you her pitcher," he coaxes. Then, "He strikes a match and holds it up between their faces and they look intently at each other over it until it burns out" (99). Though still without lights, John has been encouraged by his glimpse of Emma: "Light dat lamp!" he intones. "He strikes another match and lights the lamp" (99–100). But Emma is unable to bear it and extinguishes the light again. After she finally agrees to marry John and to get a doctor for her daughter, John gains control of the light momentarily. Then Emma reverses his action, leaves and returns as if to ensnare John in another jealous trap. Indeed, she accuses him of coveting her daughter, to which he responds by finally recognizing the futility of a relationship with a woman who "so despises her own skin that she can't believe anyone else could love it!" (102). In the end, Emma's only reason for not getting the doctor's help in time to save her daughter's life is "couldn't see." Blindness and living in the dark are a contrast to the sun at the ending of *The First One.* Whereas Ham revels in his ability to perform, Emma not only denies herself self-expression through dance but excludes herself from a deeper level of existence.

Color becomes a particular kind of question from the perspective of gender because views about race and "racial purity" versus interracial blending prominent during the early part of the twentieth century were influenced by differentiations in the status of black and white women. Hurston's mentor Boas, in his book *Anthropology and Modern Life* (1928), discusses patterns of marriage and procreation based on skin color among African-Americans. He concludes that contrary to common fears about miscegenation, interracial marriage and procreation would be beneficial to the society as a whole. Hurston's play and Boas's discussion underscore one of the major sources of social conflict emerging from postbellum race relations. "Illegitimacy" as a social status, particularly as a consequence of interracial heterosexual relations, not only entails a stigma but also becomes a barrier to social progress on a whole. As Boas writes: "The biological arguments that have been brought forward against race crossing are not convincing. Equally good reasons can be given in favor of crossings of the best elements of various races, and for closely related groups these arguments seem incontrovertible."[298]

The source of conflict for Emma is an internalized social attitude, a lack of self-acceptance which becomes so extreme she cannot escape the fate of being a victim and a pariah. Hurston presents the character in a critical light, by illustrating that her identity problem is self-perpetuated. Thus, she subtly suggests that a concept of racial "purity" presents an alternative to intraracial conflicts rooted in self-destructive attitudes and can foster "positive" self-images. She implies that an Afrocentric point of view can counter the "majority" population's hostilities. The whole notion of "racial purity," however, underscores the ambiguities and paradoxes implicit in defining American identity and does little to aid our understanding of what constitutes distinctive features of a culture, particularly in a nation composed of transplanted cultures. Indeed, the obsession surrounding "this infernal American identity machine thus composes a mosaic of alterities around a mysterious core of hybridity seething with instability," as Taussig has aptly surmised.[299]

"Racial purity" for Hurston seems to be equated with color and close-ness to folk culture, rather than with an ideological concept based on supporting "racial" progress. For example, she seemed to prefer darker skinned performers, rather than "mulattoes," to appear in her concerts and musical revues. Again playing with surfaces, she remarked to Mason about "a fine black girl as contralto soloist, and a lovely black girl as so-prano," as well as a baritone, "a dark brown also"; these were among the performers rehearsing with her for *The Great Day*—"no mulattoes at all," she noted.[300] Her reasoning was tied in with her desire to present an al-ternative to most musical performances played to mainstream audi-ences, which featured fair-skinned performers and which in Hurston's view were for the most part slavish imitations of white musical theater—blacks imitating whites imitating blacks, or, white musical theater mas-querading as black theater. In this case, imitating white culture takes on a literal meaning; it is not simply imitating white behavior but becoming visibly white, embodying "whiteness," and making a display of black cul-ture as an imitative model. Her placing the light-skinned Effie as Emma's rival in *Color Struck* and the white character Arvay in the self-ef-facing role in *Seraph on the Suwanee* nevertheless makes vivid the arbitrary value of color in itself. Rather, individuals' acceptance of society's or oth-ers' standards makes for problems. Imitative behavior is atrophied when one loses control over the performative dynamic and takes oneself too seriously, which is to practice "slavish imitation." Hurston thought of J. Rosamond Johnson in this way, as "either always in the act of imitating someone else or imitating the Rosamond Johnson of 35 years ago."[301] Hurston was virtually alone among the black intelligentsia in the dis-comfort she felt with the status quo in the art world. Of her peers shar-ing similar critical views much could be said about the ironic position they occupied in a highly charged period of awakening artistic agendas.

Making propagandistic art by representing black life in a favorable though realistic light, with its conflicts and contradictions was consid-ered at the time an effective way to raise consciousness among white and black audiences. In 1926, with his founding of the Krigwa Players (from the Crisis Guild of Writers & Artists), W.E.B. Du Bois articulated an agenda for black theater which would reverberate throughout the twen-tieth century and reach a crescendo in the 1960s. According to Du Bois, the need for theater by, for, about, and near blacks required roles and subjects that would provide alternatives to the Broadway stage. Garland Anderson's play *The Appearance* (1925), the first full-length play by a black author to appear on Broadway, and Willis Richardson's *The Chip Woman's Fortune* (1923), the first one-act by a black author on Broadway, are early nonmusical productions to reach the commercial stage in New York. The Lafayette Players, performing for black audiences in Harlem, staged plays by white playwrights, to counter the assumption that blacks were capable of performing only comic roles. Aside from the small black theaters catering to black audiences, few venues were open to present new images. The black artists critical of the direction toward which popular theater seemed to be headed were in an oppositional position; artists and critics on both sides of the art-versus-propaganda debate occupied an oppositional distance from the status quo. Black artists such as Anderson and Richardson, creating for the Broadway stage, challenged the status quo by virtue of the new subjects they brought to the form. The multipronged opposition growing among the black intelligentsia during the 1920s and 1930s set a precedent for the pursuit of a distinctive African-American aesthetic urgently pursued during the 1960s. They were following the lead of the African Grove Theater, founded in 1820. "The company performed Shakespearean dramas before mixed audiences as early as 1821," according to Loften Mitchell, but harassment from the police and disgruntled whites caused the theater to close in 1824.[302] The irony arises when the whole issue of assimilation and integration becomes part of the discussion about aesthetics.

ARBITERS OF THE "REAL"

"You said so often that you had planned an auditorium in connection with [the African Art Museum] so that *real* Negro folk music could be heard in the midst of it all."
—Hurston to Mason, January 6, 1933[303]

"If we give *real* creative urge a push forward here, the world will see a New Negro and justify our efforts."
—Hurston to Mason, January 6, 1933[304]

"The songs should be 'treated' by a *real* musician before he could sing them."
—Hurston to Mason, October 15, 1931[305]

In his book *The Real Thing*, Miles Orvell argues that artists in the United States during the early twentieth century promulgated a "culture of authenticity." In contrast, their counterparts during the late nineteenth century were absorbed in what he calls a "culture of imita-tion."[306] According to Orvell, artists in the late nineteenth century sought to control images through idealized representations. Henry James, for example, insisted on the sanctity of illusion, while objecting to techniques that would draw attention to the artifice used to produce realistic images. For James, "to invite inspection of their artifice, or to exploit the literal was to court sensationalism."[307] Thus, it might some-times be necessary, as in James's story "The Real Thing," for an artist to represent aristocrats, for example, by having lower class models pose for a painting. "For although the [aristocrats] advertise themselves as 'the real thing' and hence would seem to be better than any possible model, the artist finds their very authenticity limits his own powers of plastic ex-pression. He is too bound by their fixity as individuals to use them with the flexibility that art requires."[308]

By 1900, with photography's influence "pushing the conventions and techniques of mimesis to the breaking point," being authentic began to mean somehow being documentary or factual.[309] "The Jamesian illusion of life was giving way to a quality of authenticity that was expressed in terms of the metaphor of the mechanically reproduced image."[310] The shift, and Orvell's using James as an example, cannot be separated from certain assumptions about social class inherent in ideas about realistic representation. As a preeminent example of late-nineteenth century re-alism, James, with his aristocratic characters, stands for a view of society based on a model of gentility—at least, as an ideal subject for artistic representation. Photography, on the other hand, introduced greater possibility for presentation of a broader world, one which might, for ex-ample, include machines, factories, and workers—drawing attention to the power of mechanical reproduction.

Among artists resisting the nineteenth century trend toward idealiz-ing life among the upper social classes was the African-American histo-rian, novelist, dramatist, and abolitionist William Wells Brown whose play *Escape, or a Leap for Freedom* (1858) is an example not only of a work including characters from different circumstances—the house slave, the educated black, etc.—but in its abolitionist agenda it also is an ex-ample of political theater, comparable to agit prop(agitory propa-ganda). Not only the heroic tradition in slave narratives, but also what Errol Hill calls "The Revolutionary Tradition in Black Drama" provide evidence of expressive forms created in part to redefine realistic conventions by using African-American traditional forms such as sermons and spirituals, as well as propaganda.[311]

While Euro-American artists in the early twentieth century, as Orvell documents, began to shift toward naturalistic images—which is to say, images drawn from all social classes—African-American artists were becoming increasingly aware of their unique social status and were attempting to choose terms and visual forms compatible with their sense of aesthetic authenticity. Black artists showcased in the *Crisis* magazine, including playwrights for the Krigwa Theater, were responding to limited portrayals of black life by trying to broaden the range of lifestyles represented. Angelina Weld Grimke's play *Rachel*, for example, appealed to a propagandistic impetus to give a convincing portrayal of middle-class stability, an image of black life that had been denied public exposure. Even when they conformed to the same formal conventions of realistic narrative and other aspects of style that Euro-American artists employed, black artists' depictions of experience could implicitly challenge underlying class assumptions. Ironically, James perceived experience as "the power to guess the unseen from the seen, to trace the implication of things, to judge the whole piece by the pattern, the condition of feeling life in general so completely that you are well on your way to knowing any particular corner of it."[312]

Although "the real" consistently bears some relation to the social context of objects, characters, and situations, efforts to capture in artistic form an exact quality of reality lead back to technical questions about craft—styles, structural traits, references, signs. Roland Barthes's notion of "the real," referring to a text, a formulated idea, or set of ideas can be useful in trying to understand why black and white artists can create realistic works that differ dramatically in the realities portrayed. It is not simply enough to say that reality can be different according to who sees or represents it, when the formal conventions are apparently—which is to say, on the surface—similar. It is necessary to look more deeply into the structural characteristics of specific works and icons to understand how it is that differences in methods used to represent reality are differences in world view. Naturalism can be defined as a style depicting everyday life through concrete references to raw details in the environment. Not only is nature delineated in fine detail, as in Wright's elaborate rendering of the flood in "Down by the Riverside" (1936), but also human life is stripped of all pretense. The grotesque side of life arises amidst nature's tranquil surface, as in Sherwood

Anderson's *Winesburg, Ohio* (1919) or Jean Toomer's *Cane* (1923), where a rural landscape's beauty threatens violence. As in fiction of the 1920s and 1930s, in folk plays of the period, naturalistic representation helped to capture the travails of characters whose lives are marked by devastating circumstances and whose means for coping do not always correspond with what is deemed socially acceptable in bourgeois terms. Realistic representation, in contrast, suggests a moral sense of how things should be in an orderly world. Although naturalism seems to move toward more "authentic" versions of reality, as a style it only goes but so far in distinguishing a unique character of African-American culture within the larger American context.

Epitomizing the growing interest in authenticity in the early twentieth century by the slogan used to describe Coca Cola as "the real thing," Orvell describes the increasing allure surrounding objects or experiences deemed "real." My sense of what Orvell means by a "culture of authenticity" is indelibly linked with the growing need among artists to establish American roots for their work, as American Scene painters sought to do and as Harlem Renaissance artists did in creating images consistent with Locke's vision of indigenous art. The Coca Cola, or "real thing," metaphor extends the vision of originality in American cultural values beyond the ephemeral, imagistic domain molded and inhabited by artists to the concrete world designed by engineers. As mentioned previously in conjunction with changing perspectives in folklore studies during the early part of the century through the 1930s, the idea that "pure" traditions no longer exist is conditioned by a sense of the need to broaden the way "tradition" is defined. Having a fixed notion of culture was inconsistent with a twentieth century perspective of diffusion and acculturation. Ironically, however, it is this notion of change in a scientifically grounded world, which makes it seem ever more urgent to reproduce, in part because of scientific know-how, more factual, more "real," more "authentic" representations of everyday life.

Given the trend toward a "culture of authenticity," Hurston clearly understood the importance of establishing a precedent for signs and symbols to be identified with black culture. She, nevertheless, understood the ironies of such a plight. Although her version of "the real" included a sense of authenticity describing persons and objects, she could also use the term to qualify her actions; thus, a "real" push toward a New Negro must be seen as a criticism of her contemporaries' purported efforts to achieve the same goal. Moreover, she could make an ironic commentary on the way "real" art was assessed by the established patrons of high art, who had their own views—in stark contrast with Hurston's—on how to value African-American forms of expression. She is able to write to Mason of her reservations about a would-be patron for a young baritone she has been nurturing as a protégé to perform in one of her shows; the would-be patron favors further training and a professional arrangement for the music, causing Hurston to remark, facetiously, that "the songs should be 'treated' by a *real* musician."

In her opposition to the elitist prerogative to define culture, Hurston stood apart from other African-Americans making inroads in the commercial theater, most of whom could attribute their success to the involvement of major white playwrights—not to mention producers and directors—in fostering a black theater. Commercial success belonged primarily to musicians, dancers, singers, and actors—in short, to the performing artists whose acclaim was due to collaborations between whites and blacks. As Harold Cruse poignantly notes in *The Crisis of the Negro Intellectual,* black playwrights had much to overcome to reach the prominence of their fellow artists on the performing side of the industry. Because culture had burgeoned into a business during the early part of the century, the black cultural movement of the period known as the Harlem Renaissance held an inherent contradiction. Cruse argues that art as private enterprise, although equally as important as the "spiritual, intellectual, ethical, aesthetic, revolutionary, political" content, cannot—or should not, theoretically—impede artistic expression.[313]

The problem facing Hurston and her peers, particularly writers pursuing careers as dramatists, was economic and political as well as artistic. Although they were to a large extent producing during a time of great interest in their work, they had to strike a balance between pleasing patrons and pleasing an evolving African-American audience and sensibility. According to Nathan Irvin Huggins, it was not inconsistent for a black artist to embrace the benefits of patronage precisely because of being "valued not for what one might become—the benevolent view of uplift—but for what was thought to be one's essential self, one's 'Negro-ness.' "[314]

Not only were Hurston and her peers faced with defining an aesthetic, they confronted institutional powers organized to control theater venues, capital, and profits. Since the artists themselves were for the most part at the whim of the current trend in mainstream American culture, their power resided in their capacity to share with whites eager to support them the "expectation that the America of the machine and philistine could be transcended by men of talent, sensitivity, and art."[315] Even artists such as James Weldon Johnson who, unlike Hurston, belonged to a traditional black bourgeois elite, but who also were in the unprecedented situation of being a cultural commodity, were subject to economic, political, and cultural trends of the time—the "inherited abolitionism, Christian charity and guilt, social manipulation, political eccentricity, and a certain amount of persiflage" that accompanied philanthropy.[316] According to Cruse, "The Negro middle class, being politically, socially, and economically marginal, was both unwilling and unable to play any commanding role in the politics and economics of culture and art, *as either patrons or entrepreneurs.*"[317] Because of their limited economic and political influence, black artists empowered themselves individually and through works produced explicitly to authenticate black identity ("Negroness") at a time when Americans were predisposed to reifying racial differences. Works identified with the Harlem Renaissance are heralded and disparaged, and are still being resurrected from obscurity (as with Hurston's work), because they display in their form, method, and style of opposition the idiosyncrasies of the period's racial politics. Even when they illustrate ambivalent attitudes, as does *Color Struck*, works of the period exemplify the idea that "race has become a trope of ultimate, irreducible difference between cultures, linguistic groups, or adherents of specific belief systems which—more often than not—also have fundamentally opposed economic interests."[318]

Among African-American artists, the need for patronage, primarily as economic support, was strong. The other conditions attached to patronage, having to do with influencing the types of work produced by artists and the aesthetic direction of an arts movement, during the 1920s and 1930s had implications for cultural development within the black community as a whole. As Cruse explains, and as Larry Neal has acknowledged in his work on economic development in Harlem subsequent to the Renaissance period, the economic infrastructure of the community is central to the arts.[319] Black artists could be considered as having a progressive effect on the community as a whole, and on the world at large, because their goals were perceived as compatible with the community's and were "honored and sustained, ironically, by the very commercial apparatus that the *avant garde* traditionally distrusted."[320]

The notion of community is conflated with the term "Harlem Renaissance," however, since being located there was not a precondition to being included in that arts movement. Identifying black artists with a monolithic community as the term "Harlem Renaissance" implies, complicates rather than simplifies the problem of how to specify common social, economic, and artistic goals. The main challenge then, as well as during the Black Arts Movement of the late 1960s and early 1970s, was to reconcile class differences, particularly between artists and intellectuals, on the one hand, and working people, on the other. Middle-class patronage for black artists would not, even if substantial, grant the artists greater liberty to pursue work that would challenge the status quo beyond the limits established by the political power brokers for the middle class. On the other hand, most of the artists themselves have discovered that even if they are products of "the folk" their status and relationship to community social relations changes.

Whereas social change may be an objective for a community and for individual artists, change can only occur if there is autonomy. Autonomy, according to Cruse, would seem to be the main objective of a cultural arts movement; however, cultural autonomy entails institutions, institutions require support, and the basis for institutional support—along with the political power and economic resources to sustain it—must be composed of people whose interests, values, or whose world views, are represented, people in the community. The model described here is for the most part the opposite of what occurred during the Harlem Renaissance. Most of the institutional and individual support for black art originated outside of the community. Even well-established forums such as *Story* magazine, the *Crisis*, and *Opportunity* relied upon the support and contributions of prominent whites.

Hurston, in particular, yearned for economic independence. How, after all, could she (or any other African-American) define a distinctive, "authentic" black culture in the United States if doing so meant adjusting to constraints imposed from outside authorities? She succeeded in defining "authenticity" as originality which incorporates social constraints, even while modifying them. Through understanding and interpreting the art of mimicry in its various forms, she demonstrates how the practice of the art can transform social contexts from which it arises. Her claim has a historical, economic, social, and individual (personal) basis. *What* Hurston says about African-American culture and how she does so is as important as her accomplishment in establishing her voice in spite of the economic constraints. Moving beyond sociological interpretations aimed at influencing the way culture is produced, it is possible to exam-

ine cultural productions for methods possibly useful in influencing sociology—or, better, social relations as played out in theory and practice.

THE FEAR OF IMAGES

Hurston's work suggests that unique characteristics of African-American
culture are implicit in expressive forms and that world view and mythos
are more important than material conditions in shaping works of black
art. Although the economics of her situation precluded any attempts on
her part to stand fully outside the mainstream view of African-American
culture, economic dependence does not exactly translate into an analo-
gous struggle at the aesthetic level. Establishing one's identity and role as
an arbiter of African-American culture means confronting "the real" in a
peculiar and ironic way: the distinctiveness and "authenticity" of African-
American culture and defining oneself as an expert or authority on (or
representative example of) the culture, is integrally tied in with the specific attributes of distinctiveness and "authenticity." Each of her statements about the "real" characteristics of black culture refers, often
ironically, to economic class, social status, color, gender, and male-female
relations. Through the use of irony, she implicitly criticizes the need for
such distinctions. Religion, with its ritualistic accoutrements, offers countless occasions for employing "by-words," infinite opportunities to " 'seek
out de inside meanin' of words' "(*Mules and Men* 134, 135). These meanings reflect something other than an idealistic concept of authentic folk
culture.

Like *The First One*, other of Hurston's texts call into question whether
the blind acceptance of Christianity can be attributed to blacks. She car-
icatures this idea in *The Fiery Chariot*. Ike, who prays for God to take him
away to heaven on His fiery chariot (away, that is, from the plantation),
appears shaken when Ole Massa masquerading as God in a white sheet
arrives at the door. After stalling, Ike convinces Ole Massa to stand clear
of the door. "O Lawd, the radiance of yo' countenance is *So* bright, Ah
can't come out by yuh," says Ike to which Ole Massa responds by taking
"one step backward." Unrelenting, Ike pleads: "O Lawd, heben is SO
high and Ahm so humble in Yo'sight, and Yo' glory cloud is so bright
and Yo' radiance is so compellment be so kind in Yo' tender mercy as to
stand back jes' a lil bit mo!" Arbitary changes of meaning perpetually

upset the image of placidity associated with unquestioning submission to a master's authority, as when a black Noah, called "Ole Nora," appears in "How the Woodpecker Nearly Drowned the Whole World," a story Lonnie Barnes tells in *Mules and Men.* This Nora, who brought no trees on the ark, forbids the woodpecker to use the ark to satisfy his craving for wood. Unable to obey the restriction, the woodpecker finds a secret place to peck. But "Ole Nora" catches the woodpecker, and while remaining silent, smashes the woodpecker's head with a sledge hammer, which explains "why a peckerwood got a red head today." Barnes rationalizes, "Dat's how come Ah feel like shootin' every one of em Ah see," for almost drowning the whole world. Once it is understood that 'peckerwood,' or 'peck,' as Gwaltney lists the term, is "a derogatory term for Southern white men," the story has anything but a folksy tone.[321] The animal character and biblical reference cannot be read simply as part of the story's artifice. The tale's hero, Ole Nora, is able to master primeval desires, like the woodpecker's uncontrollable impulse. In restoring order, Ole Nora metes out punishment with a vengeance equal to or surpassing the judgment of God. In "How the Possum Lost the Hair off His Tail," also in *Mules and Men,* Larkins White tells how Ham made banjo strings, from the opossum's tail which "useter be one of de prettiest sights you ever seen"—a "bushy," "plumey" tail. Ham "loved to be playin' music all de time" and "had a banjo and a fiddle and maybe a guitar too" (112). Unable to bring them aboard the ark, Ham fashions a banjo from a cigar box. This tale, which Hurston presented as a one-act play in *All De Live Long Day,* like *The First One* celebrates the creative powers' triumphing over duress, while lampooning the biblical tale.

The overriding category and, therefore, the most "real" characteristic determining authenticity, for Hurston, is economic class. Herein lies a crucial distinction and an ironic one. The first obstacle to overcome has to do with how she exempts herself, as an arbiter, from her criticism of the middle class. She does so by identifying artists and intellectuals— or at any rate, highly educated and cultured people—as a class distinct from and not subject to the pressures to conform. She did not share the kind of middle-class values many of her counterparts in the black art world embraced, but she had acquired some privileges which changed the conditions of her life. Mainly, her life had changed because her world broadened; greater mobility, access to people, formal education, and professional training assured a measure of freedom from the types of labor required to earn a living without those options. When Hurston worked as a maid for a brief time during 1950, after she had achieved many of her professional goals, she was deeply sensitive to the inconsistency between economic necessity (which pride caused her to deny) and artistic commitment, not to mention prominence.[322]

One other black folklorist to have done research contemporaneously with Hurston, Arthur Huff Fauset, similarly sought to clarify the meaning of authenticity in African-American culture. Likewise, he was critical of intelligent people who pretentiously call themselves "intellectuals" or, more damning, "intelligentsia," in order to set themselves up as arbiters of cultural correctness. "Besides a few big words added to the lexicon and one or two hifalutin' notions about the way the world should be run, the contribution of Intelligentsia to society is as negligible as gin at a Methodist picnic," writes Fauset.[323] He satirizes the class of people who had become powerbrokers of culture, particularly black culture. His critique entitled "Intelligentsia" appeared in the only issue of *Fire!!* magazine ever published—alongside fiction, poetry, drama, and essays by his and Hurston's fellow writers—young artists whose attitudes toward social and artistic conventions challenged the existing standards, including in addition to Hurston and Fauset, Langston Hughes, Gwendolyn Bennet, Richard Bruce (Bruce Nugent), Wallace Thurman, and others. They formed an elite within an elite, distinguished because of their critical stance, their willingness to oppose *Crisis* editor W.E.B. Du Bois's ideological mandates for black art.

The question of what is "real" in African-American culture has not ceased to be an issue for black artists and intellectuals since the 1920s. Significantly, the issue received public attention in 1991 when the play written by Hurston and Hughes, *Mule Bone*, was produced on Broadway. Henry Louis Gates, Jr., who initiated the production when he presented a copy of the script to producer Gregory Mosher, has been at the center of the debate over authenticity in black culture as it exists in its current form. In the 1980s and 1990s, according to Gates, among blacks an inordinate amount of concern, even insecurity, is still in evidence over whether or not black characters and black life are stereotypically represented in film, theater, television, and elsewhere. Gates has argued that the conflict arises because middle-class blacks are uncomfortable with black vernacular culture and do not want to see, hear, or in any way witness black life—but especially black language—as "different" from an assimilated ideal. "Black art in the twentieth century, then, is a piv-

otal arena in which to chart worries about 'political correctness,' "
writes Gates.[324] He sees the black artist as burdened with having to represent "the race" according to "explicitly political programs" and "black
creativity" as, therefore, potentially devastated.[325] Black musicians, he argues, to some extent, except perhaps rap artists, have "escaped this
problem, because so much of what they composed was in nonverbal
forms and because historically black music existed primarily for a black
market."[326] Gates's discussion tends to privilege the verbal over the nonverbal, and that can be misleading, since it can be argued that black
music has not escaped commercial, and by extension controlling political, intervention. For example, the blues singer Ma Rainey, whose
struggle to control the recording rights to her work is portrayed by
August Wilson in his play *Ma Rainey's Black Bottom*, certainly did not escape problems ultimately linked with questions of authenticity. Whether
black music has ever "existed primarily for a black market," other than
in community-based performance arenas is doubtful. Gates argues that
because black music has remained within a black market, "it escaped
the gaze of white Americans who, paradoxically, are the principal concern of those who would police the political effects of black art."[327] This
paradox, however, has had a long-standing history in black cultural
production.

Black artists have historically been outspoken on aesthetic issues,
making strong claims about their preferences, to assert a degree of control over cultural products which affect their livelihood. Questionable
views about "authenticity," "originality," and "real" black culture, rather
than advancing theater and other art forms, merely intensify intraracial
class conflicts. His argument that Hurston and Hughes envisioned
changing the future direction of black theater with their collaboration
on *Mule Bone* overlooks performance-related questions which have
nothing to do with the content of the work but everything to do with its
transformative possibilities. Although many people may enjoy the performance, and although entertainment—especially for comedies—may
be the first priority, to insinuate that representation of vernacular language and styles of performance in itself is enough to transform the theater and to change the direction of black art in the twentieth century is
to overrate the significance of the debate over stereotypes and their alternatives. More important, from theater artists' point of view, is
whether a performance holds enough power to ensure its impact and
continuance. Can audiences be drawn, can the production achieve the

producers' and artists' desired support, participation, and recognition? On some level, the potential impact a production has is of concern not only because of the images presented but also because of live performance's potential significance as ritual. Neal's emphasis, for example, on "separate symbolism, mythology, critique, [and] iconology" in black theater, extends beyond concern over images, particularly how "the race" is represented; he shifts the focus away from expectations established in the past toward a broader conception of African-American culture as rooted in a distinctive, complex cosmology.[328]

To transform the theater and to effect a black theater movement has always been a political issue no matter how inconvenient the tyranny of "politically correct" aesthetics may be. There have been politics of representation—just as there have been politics of education, labor, housing, and other human rights—in the United States, circumscribed by race, ethnicity, and class. Indeed, representation in the twentieth century, intersecting with freedom-of-expression debates, political movements such as African, African-American, Caribbean, and other liberation movements in the 1960s and at other periods in the century, cannot avoid difficult questions which must ultimately go beyond what "images" appear and focus on struggles over power and the control of resources which enable artists to assume productive roles.

As W. T. J. Mitchell (whose statement appears at the opening of this book) observed, when he began working on a theory of images, he found himself investigating the fear of images—a fear often manifested by cultural critics. Moving, like Mitchell, toward an understanding of the ideological dimension of images, of the relationship between iconology and iconography, I attempt to show in subsequent chapters how Hurston's work resolves the unequal power relationship balanced in favor of words over images. Her pursuit of a theatrical answer to problems of cross-cultural misunderstanding, although thwarted, is nevertheless important to consider because of the challenges it presents. Her stage productions had only a moderate impact when measured against the work for which she is well-known—her fiction and folklore.

The Great Day (1932), *From Sun to Sun* (1933), a choral and dramatic "program of Original Negro Folklore," *Singing Steel* (1934), and *All de Live Long Day* were produced by Hurston. She also directed "The Fire Dance," which was described on the invitation as "a folk dance that originated in Africa." Her troupe of Bahamian dancers appeared in the folklore revues, along with performers of folktales, work songs, children's games, sermons, and blues songs. Although considered minor compared with her written productions, Hurston's theatrical productions predate the publication of her folklore books and novel and, as mentioned previously, occupied much of her time and energy. If she had continued producing and directing, her cultural legacy as inherited by subsequent generations of African-Americans would be different not because black theater would have been revolutionized but because the power relations of cultural politics and production would have to have been substantially altered.

The social, political, and economic circumstances which affected Hurston and her peers during the 1930s and black artists historically cannot be dismissed in drawing conclusions about the ongoing debate over black aesthetics. Although, as has been argued, adverse economic circumstances do not necessarily impede artistic creativity, institutional and community support is linked to the continued viability of cultural production. Within that rubric, many assumptions about artistic freedom of expression arise. Hurston's ambitions to do research, publish, and produce theater outweighed the economic pressures she bore, although her theatrical productions themselves did not. That is, the productions became a lesser priority because of the need to support herself through publishing and other, unrelated work. She enjoyed fame and acclaim from her publications, and felt, as she wrote in *Dust Tracks*, gratified later in life. Nevertheless, it would seem that her self-sacrifice—the years of tight budgeting and doing without to please her patron— amounts to retribution, as if Hurston were a ritual agent or a sacrifice.[329] She bears resemblance to the victims of fate in the "dramas of epidemic" Femi Euba describes: "Preoccupied with the fate of their people, they are often lost in their far-sightedness between national interest and personal ambition, on account of which they are satirized by their own fate."[330]

CHAPTER FIVE

Hurston's Hieroglyphics:
The Word Magic of Ritual Action

The idea that black Americans interpret the English language in terms of pictures, what Hurston calls "hieroglyphics," arises from her knowledge of spoken language's many contexts and from her understanding of how words not only signify actions but contain power as performative acts. Her notion of hieroglyphics is important to an understanding of African-American culture and is the key to a riddle at the center of her life and work. The term "hieroglyphics" ("which were believed to be God's writing in natural images rather than a phonetic language")[331] recalls ancient Egypt, where people who apparently did not believe in death spent unlimited time preparing for it, just as Hurston did not believe African-American culture has an essential nature but spent her life characterizing it. Just as Walter Benjamin saw Baroque tragic drama as "modern allegory," I would like to suggest that the drama of everyday life and its counterpart in the spiritual practices Hurston describes in African-American culture, can be considered as modern allegory. The dramatic action Hurston describes as revealed in African-American culture is not focused on individual style for its own sake (as art for art's sake) but on continuity with a collective cultural experience, just as ancient Egyptian rituals were practiced to ensure constancy of the world's order.[332] Hieroglyphics become signs for a cultural code embedded in expressive forms, but the code is not a vehicle for hidden symbolic meanings: it is evidence of cultural knowledge and survival. ("Such a language of images implied there was nothing arbitrary in the connection between sign and referent. Natural images promised to dissolve the universal language through which God communicated the meaning of His creations to human beings.")[333] My purpose is to show how harkening to a distant past hints at an archetypal metaphor for African-American culture. Expressive forms are living evidence of archaic knowledge. The riddle at the center of Hurston's life and work seems to lie in a certain sense in which she excavated the past *as lived in the present* only to be, in turn, excavated and reborn as a living legacy.

Her unique understanding of language and other expressive forms in African-American culture explains why her *writing*, fiction as well as folklore, takes so many forms and stands out in relation to other works on African-American culture. It also explains why her work has been the subject of an increasing number of critical discussions about what it means to "write" from an oral tradition. Through her bold combining of literary techniques and social-scientific concepts, she exemplifies the level of experimentation needed to create texts that are formally congruent with the cultural performances they describe. Her folklore and fiction illustrate the way that words can be pictographic substitutes or signals for actions, representing iconic and emblematic relationships in African-American verbal forms. She demonstrates the intertextual dynamic between verbal and nonverbal expression.

"BLACK DEATH," A TALE OF SYMPATHETIC MAGIC

Hurston shares much of her language in common with her ethnographic subjects. Various sources have discussed the extent to which some of her published fiction corresponds with folktales she would tell to her friends in New York during the 1920s—tales that apparently were based on memories from her youth in Eatonville, Florida.[334] "Black Death," mentioned in Chapter Three, is one such story. What is important for the discussion in this chapter is the way "Black Death" demonstrates the relationship between words and actions through a tale about the practice of sympathetic magic. The tale recounts a number of incidents involving a conjure man named Old Man Morgan, who has put curses on various people. As indicated in Chapter Three, Old Man Morgan's evil power to kill people "without ever leaving his house or even seeing his victim" derives from a mysterious belief held by blacks but not by whites. Included among the people he has cursed, according to the story, are Della Lewis, who received "the loveless curse"; Hiram Lewis, whose curse was to fail as a farmer; Emma Taylor, whose teeth

Morgan caused to fall out; Horace Brown, who became "as the Wandering Jew" because Morgan put a black snake skin in his shoes. Morgan also was able to cause a number of illnesses through devious means. He brought about Lena Merchant's madness by putting a sprig of her hair into a bottle, corking it, and throwing it into a running stream with the neck pointing up stream, and he caused Lillie Wilcox's blood to dry up by burying her fingernails with lizard's feet.

The core of the story is Hurston's rendering of how Morgan murders, in addition to bringing on illnesses and performing various other acts to exert power over people and nature. According to Hurston, "the undoing of Beau Diddely is his [Morgan's] masterpiece." Her choice of words suggests the tension inherent in the kind of act she describes—a tension between two worlds, one mundane and the other decidedly outside of everyday events, both worlds overlapping at a terrifying juncture, where the stability of ordinary occurrences is undermined. Although "masterpiece" connotes artistry and high achievement, the act being re-lived through the words plunges any potential witness—including a spectator who merely sees or hears—into the depths of dark powers, into the unexalted terrain of the "black death."

The event takes place because Docia Boger's daughter has been impregnated by Beau Diddely who refuses to marry her because he already has a wife. When Docia remembers that "folks said Blue Sink the bottomless was Morgan's graveyard. . . . All Africa awoke in her blood." The awakening of Africa not only invokes an ancestral past, it also supplies a crucial link between the present moment in which the story is being told and a moment historically situated, pre-Christian, and mythic because it must be recreated. The action words in the story "Black Death" demonstrate their magical power within the context of the rural southern village where the narrator is situated.

The striking passage of the story entails a shooting. First, at Morgan's direction, Docia chooses a gun rather than "water" or a "knife" as her weapon. Morgan simply tells her to look into "a huge mirror" and says of Beau Diddely, "when he comes, shoot to kill." Then a series of actions leads to the climax. A play on doubling occurs, as "both [Morgan and Mrs. Boger] faced about and gazed hard into the mirror that reached from floor to ceiling." (207) The mirror, given its size, transforms the environment into a simulacrum—a window of shadows and light, which enables Morgan to simulate the presence of another person, the man to be killed. Thus, "Morgan grew misty, darker, near the center, then Mrs.

Boger saw Beau walk to the center of the mirror and stand looking at her, glaring and sneering." (207) This produces an effect on Mrs. Boger, an altered state in which "she all but fainted." Having complete control of the situation, "Morgan thrust the gun into her hand." (207) His transformation signifies his power to rearrange the world, which becomes apparent as the roles of the other characters change, as well. Mrs. Boger, who "saw the expression on Beau Diddely's face change from scorn to fear," (207) suddenly loses her self-righteous innocence when she "found it in herself to laugh." When Morgan instructs her to aim because she only gets one shot, "she leveled the gun at the heart of the apparition in the glass and fired." (207) Because Beau Diddely's double "collapsed," magical effects are visible when "the mirror grew misty again, then cleared." (207)

Whereas a gun is capable of producing dramatic effects, the mirror has greater significance in bringing about magical results. Mirrors, according to the anthropologist James Fernandez, hold a fascination for people in numerous cultures, not only because they reverse images horizontally and create what he calls "the see-through effect," but also because they "create an interesting arousal and state of wonder."[335] Although Fernandez does not discuss Hurston or African-American cultures in his essay "Some Reflections on Looking in Mirrors," which is based on his field research in West Africa, he emphasizes cross-cultural comparisons and the ritual uses of mirrors. Therefore, his discussion has a special light to shed on "Black Death." Fernandez describes the see-through effect as an image's projection as far behind the mirror as the objects visible to the eye are in front of the mirror. This illusion partially accounts for Mrs. Boger's astonishment upon seeing Beau Diddley in the mirror. For is it not her own countenance she expects to greet her vengeful stare? As Fernandez tells us, the mirror is well known for its power to objectify, and this fits neatly with his idea that the mirror has been considered a reflector of a more perfect self in some cultures (Japan, for example) which more broadly, he infers, may "explain why engines of evil such as vampires could not be seen in mirrors."[336] If evil figures "have no perfection," then it follows that the tricks mirrors play can be responsible for reorganizing the social, and by extension, moral disorder upsetting Mrs. Boger's world. "Or it may simply be believed that evil destroys itself in a mirror by being brought to recognize itself," as Fernandez argues.[337] To say that the gun obtains its power from the mirror is to follow a line of persuasion Michael Taussig pursues in his discussion of "His Master's Voice." Cuna Indian women reproduce the RCA Victor logo on molas (colorful fabrics used for clothing), and their mimetic activity thereby suggests that technology relies on magic for its power and credence. This is especially so, he argues, because the notion of fidelity represented in the logo by "the talking dog" draws its credibility from the viewer's awareness that "there is no real master, just the copy of the master's voice."[338] By way of analogy, Old Man Morgan can be substituted for the master, whereas the copy of his voice is the image of Beau Diddley—a metaphor for the choice Morgan offers Mrs. Boger. The metaphor, a projection of Mrs. Boger's vengeance (the evil that "destroys itself in a mirror"), exemplifies the type of mental activity preceding changes in the physical environment (a haunting reminder of the cliché about reality being constructed). The probability that the picture in Mrs. Boger's mind's eye is reflected in the mirror as Beau Diddley's image illustrates what Taussig calls "the power of the copy to influence what it is a copy of."[339] In this instance, the copy is Beau Diddley's mirror image, with Mrs. Boger's passion for retribution being profound enough to do damage. Hence, we see how an apparently simple folktale contains metaphors that condense ritualistic practices associated with magic, "superstition," and other categories of behavior considered unscientific, unorthodox. The elegance of the story's language consists of its economy, its capacity to guide the reader through several sensory levels, from the aural to the visual to the tactile.

Several pieces of information hold interest in the story of how "Black Death" reached a wider audience, first as a fictional story winning honorable mention in a 1925 contest sponsored by *Opportunity* magazine, and later as folklore—part of the essay "Hoodoo in America" published in a 1931 edition of the *Journal of American Folklore*. Hemenway interprets the two versions by way of explaining the special relation Hurston had to her ethnographic material. He implies that her traditional background and methods enabled her to use skills grounded in non-Western religious practices to create a literary work in English. Hemenway's point that the short story was written before Hurston had formally studied folklore and that the 1931 ethnography failed to mention an informant leads him to conclude that "Hurston, a product of a tradition in which narratives were community property rather than any individual's private possession, simply transferred a part of her repertoire to the typed page."[340] The idea that narratives are "community property" presumes more than it is possible to know, however, and goes against the sense of specialization and individual creativity also associated with oral storytelling; tales become known in part because they are associated with a particular teller's unique rendition. To this extent, a certain amount of secrecy surrounds tales about Hoodoo. Furthermore, it is likely that ethnographic skills are as effective as traditional knowledge in constructing a story, in that, as Stephen Tyler notes in his commentary on ethnographers' textual practices:

> Ethnographers project their fragmentary and incomplete experience of exotic cultures into a rhetorical form that creates the illusion of a comprehensive and coherent whole, and readers, by prior acquaintance with this form, fill in the missing parts, creating in their imaginations what is not given but must be there by implications drawn from the form itself.[341]

Hemenway's assessment, while reasonable, does not explain why Hurston was comfortable moving between genres, or how she did so. Under what circumstances would a story be "community property"— which is to say, how and why would a story like "Black Death" have been known and to whom, and how would Hurston have acquired it? Perhaps the more interesting question has to do with the significance of the story in a particular social and cultural context—its meaning and how it represents an important aspect of the everyday-life drama that interested Hurston. "Black Death," like Hurston's stories in "Herbs and Herb Doctors,"[342] in my view, have more of a kinship with myths than with folktales.[343] According to Stith Thompson, "myth has to do with the gods and their actions, with creation, and with the general nature of the universe and of the earth," at minimum.[344] Otherwise, myths and folktales share similar traits. Notably, "They both disseminate, they both take on accretions and are subject to the vicissitudes of memory and forgetting."[345]

Variations from one version of "Black Death" to the next also are important for what they reveal about context. The short story contains elaborated passages that are not part of another version consulted for this chapter, and the version of the story appearing in "Hoodoo in America" includes different people.[346] Variations add to, rather than detract from, the authenticity of the story—as either a myth, a folktale, or a work of fiction—since the tale emerges in the continuous present as a lived event centered in the bodies of particular persons. Like a myth, the tale invokes an ancestral past, elaborates a practical message, and demonstrates a method whereby "language as such has an independent existence and has the power to influence reality."[347] On one level, it prescribes a way to act in certain circumstances—as a guide for women, urging them to be skeptical in their relations with certain men. On another level, it represents a corrective ritual meant to restore order, albeit through a drastically punitive measure. Context, purpose, and effect are the measures for understanding how meaning is created for a specific group of people and what the social implications are on a larger scale. Variations in the story also indicate that Hurston was consistently engaged in an effort to sort out the material she considered to be at the core of authentic black expression, as a way of tying her work in with the trends of the period. The mythic and ritual content of the story are not clearly delineated as such because "Black Death," as well as the stories in "Herbs and Herb Doctors," emerges within a Hoodoo context, which is covert and diffuse. Moreover, Hoodoo, as an African-American folk religion, along with its close relative Voodoo, had yet to be systematized. Hurston, according to the historian Jessie Gaston Mulira, was "the most important eyewitness of voodoo activities in the 1920s."[348] Mulira distinguishes Voodoo from Hoodoo while pointing out the close connection between them. "In many respects the Voodooist and the Hoodooist have much in common," Mulira argues.

> This point is clear if one understands that voodoo connotes the positive religious rites while hoodoo generally connotes the mystic and magical aspects that are usually evoked for negative purposes. There are many instances when voodoo has been evoked to achieve a negative purpose, such as 'the death dance.' Conversely, hoodoo has occasionally been used to protect against evil of impending danger. Many voodooists have also incorporated their knowledge of hoodoo into their practices. For example, Marie Laveau, though a voodoo queen, was also a hoodoo practitioner. To be a good voodoo priest or priestess, in fact, one had to have a working knowledge of hoodoo.[349]

Mulira also notes "that all professional voodooists claim to know various ways of killing people."[350] Thus, formally, Hoodoo and Voodoo differ very little, although Hoodoo became popularized as a commercial version of Voodoo, through the sale of products capitalizing on people's desire for quick solutions to problems. Shortly after Hurston completed her field research, the practices she documented in her *Journal of American Folklore* article "Hoodoo in America" (1931) and in *Mules and Men* were subject to change. As Joan Dayan has observed, terms used for the Haitian religion vodoun, from which Voodoo and Hoodoo are derived, are "most often used by outsiders to signal the backwardness, indolence, and greed that they feel needs correcting."[351] She distinguishes between the various Francophone spellings—Vaudoux, voudoo, vodou—in contrast with the Anglophone Voodoo, ordinarily equated with sorcery.

Hurston's bold approach to the subject of magic indicates she consciously chose to be unconventional in presenting the story through different media. She did not invent "Black Death" or any of her fictional work from an imaginary reality. Inventing without reference to an archetypal model upon which to build characters and events is contrary to her idea of originality and artistry. Her version of originality entails specific revisionary skills—the "mastery of form" or "deformation of mastery," to borrow apt terminology from Houston A. Baker, Jr.[352] If "nothing is half so good as something that is just like something else," as Hurston mockingly argues in her provocative tract "My People, My People," what is the "something else" that "Black Death" imitates? Is it a literal transcription meant to be taken at face value?

What Hurston hoped to gain by retelling the story can, in part, be discerned from a letter she wrote to Boas in 1928, in which she explains that "the subject of sympathetic magic is being looked into."[353] At the time, she was attempting to systematize her knowledge of magic as practiced and reported. Magic is one of the ritualized forms of expression in Hoodoo (healing rituals are another), and "Black Death" is an example of how the practice is passed on as a tradition. Whether presented as fiction or folklore the important point is that the tale is an *account* of a set of actions narrated as if they necessarily must have occurred in the order told; it is not an eyewitness's observation of a specific incident that happened at a particular time in a particular place.

Tales about the supernatural abilities of mythic or legendary "hands" (known conjurers or healers) haunted Hurston's adult life. She had spent her childhood in a closely knit rural community where African descendants had maintained their unique sense of time, linked to ancestors integral to everyday-life order and stability. In their everyday lives, they might regulate some activities as stipulated by an American clock and chronologically order their work routine to correspond with the demands of a capitalist economy. But in the time reserved for self-apprehension, renewal, and grounding in a domain less tangible than day-to-day survival, each allows time for delving into what Toni Cade Bambara calls " 'alternative,' as they say, channels of intelligence and being."[354] Although Hurston presents that world as self-contained and self-sufficient, the gesture can be considered a rhetorical device used to demonstrate social, psychological, spatial, temporal, and above all philosophical distance from the quotidian. Here, again, I would like to refute arguments that accuse Hurston of idealizing "the folk" by ignoring their economic "realities" and presenting people as docile exotics, content with their isolation and simple life. "Black Death" provides a testament to the complexity and conflict inherent in the lives of Hurston's "folk," even to the extent that Docia Boger has to seek retribution through male supernatural power symbolized by a gun. The juxtaposition of a contemporary crisis and an archaic formula for retribution, "Black Death," along with another mythic tale I will discuss further along, shows the revision of a trope, of how a woman's ethics are empowered by a man's superior knowledge, in a world where power and authority can belong to priestesses as well as priests. Here, a woman receives the tone of male authority while donning the mask of a person victimized because of gender. The masking of male power in this magical tale may in part be attributed to a transition from Voodoo (transplanted from the West Indies) to the increasing influence of Hoodoo occurring during the early twentieth century. Although women often maintained positions as strong leaders among Voodoo practitioners in New Orleans, where Hurston conducted the major portion of her research on the topic, men are considered the primary healers and conjurers in Hoodoo, according to Mulira, and by the 1940s had become dominant.[355] Hurston's Hoodoo research supports the idea that the credibility of women's healing and magical powers gradually diminished and became a covert tension (a subtext, as it were) throughout her writing, even though she maintains that both men and women can become Hoodoo doctors. In New Orleans, Hurston was initiated into the secret society of practitioners by Luke Turner, who told her he was a nephew of Leveau, allegedly the last great priestess.

The words in "Black Death" represent events occurring in time and space; they are not a mimetic repetition, an imitation of someone's words as they would be if they were directly quoted.[356] They seem to constitute a tale that would be told only in secret, or for that matter only secretly known, although presented as if a whole community is aware of its substance and implications. The tale invokes the language of ritual, which "appears to be used in ways that violate the communication function."[357] That is, the language of the story appears to be directed at no one; it is attributed to no one. This would explain why Hurston would feel at ease in transferring it from one written context to another, for it is *a representation* of the words of either an initiate or an authoritative practitioner. Or is it, as Bambara says of "Uncle Monday," a similar tale appearing in "Herbs and Herb Doctors," simply "typical of the tales Zora told at boarding school as a kid; tales of people she'd known or heard about traipsing through the stores and homes of Eatonville"?[358] For the sake of my argument here, to consider the story as a tale Hurston heard during her childhood, submitted for a fiction contest while she was a young author, rediscovered as a report of traditional magic being practiced for destructive purposes which she later re-presented as scientific evidence of Hoodoo establishes a social context without, however, the spatial details needed to establish a performative context. Both the fictional and the ethnographic are variations of an oral traditional recollection, suggesting a mythic time, with references to persons, situations, and events familiar within traditional African-American cultural contexts. This mythic dimension is a basis for understanding how the tale operates on other levels, as well.

In the story, Hurston positions herself as an artist and as a social scientist, but she achieves success in both areas because the language she uses is so specific in its description of what happens and in its references to people, places, and objects. What is concrete appears to be objective—hence, the sense that the story is a report. The meaning of "vodoun" as spirit, god, or image is transfered onto objects.[359] According to Alfred Metraux, an object "sometimes becomes an independent *loa*."[360] At the same time, its magical power seems to derive from its ritualistic form; thus, it is not that Hurston provides a story or a report so much as she passes on a vehicle through which traditional views of the world can undergo transformation. As Dayan has so eloquently stated, historical circumstances ensured that spiritual beliefs and practices from the past would be rearticulated in the present and future. "The institution of slavery," she writes,

> in wrenching individuals from their native land and from their names and their origins, produced communities of belief that would ever be distinguished from the mood or character of Western religion. The gods came to the New World. . . . When the gods left Africa, they taught their people how to live the epic of displacement. No longer simply identifiable in terms of parentage or place, they would come into the heads of their peo-

ple and there urge a return to a *thought* of origin, a place as urgent as it was irretrievable.[361]

Although anthropologists and other ethnographers have written analytic texts to discuss sympathetic magic and other traditional religious practices, Hurston introduces a "hybrid" form as a desirable genre. Her success in doing so, in my view, must be attributed to special knowledge and talent other than being a tradition bearer, an initiate or practitioner of Hoodoo, and a sensitive observer. A special quality of her language must be acknowledged, a quality that lies beyond the idiosyncrasies of everyday idiomatic speech. Although no *overt* distinction between secular and sacred usage can be made, close examination exposes a difference that Hurston would have had every reason to disguise, since she was trying to show how magic would appear in its social context. I am not referring to a literary device she is consciously using to try to create an "effect," nor am I pursuing a literary analysis of her text. The text accomplishes multiple goals because she uses performative language. It seems she has found not only a genre but also a method of documenting magical rituals, a method that appears to exclude the need for mediation because it builds upon a semiotic code formally based on expressive behavior, on actions known through their results. Thus, beginning with the death, she shows how words themselves are its cause; they are the medium for events that make sense only because they reflect a way to organize an experience that is occurring in the mundane world but that is anything but mundane. It is not, however, like the other everyday-life dramas Hurston describes.

Doing research on sympathetic magic differs substantially from collecting folktales or life histories. To begin with, meaningful information about magic is entrusted only to the initiated. Although stories about certain events alleged to have happened may be commonly known, the tales defy verification; no fact checking or laboratory experiments can prove or disprove the information that might have become part of Hurston's traditional repertoire, as Hemenway says. The stories do not present ordinary information. On the other hand, the extraordinary seems to preclude interpretation.

"Black Death" derives its power from references to events, with the main event being Docia Boger's gazing into the mirror. Again, an everyday-life event as drama entails reflection. Rather than the mirror showing a picture of the self, it becomes a threshold between the world of images and the world of words—the reflection in the mirror being in a sense a word-picture, words as action, the words being Docia Boger's wish, the action being her wish taking form. Beau Diddely's appearance in the mirror is no mere "image"; rather, it is a tangible result of the imagination, a concrete analogy. Docia's intention, in an Aristotelian concept of drama as tragedy, can be equated with her action. The plot, giving structure to her actions, orders them. Beau Diddely's appearance in the mirror thus establishes the condition necessary for his death. Necessary but not sufficient. Docia Boger's aiming and shooting the gun into the mirror must occur just as certainly as the mirror refracts, even as it doubles.

The woman's gaze, here, is used to discredit the visual medium—seeing only with the eyes—as a way of knowing. The woman, Docia Boger, seeks fair treatment, recourse, power, control over her own and her daughter's body and the ability to change the ordinary course of events. Her overriding intention is to get revenge, and to do so requires an alternative form of action. The alternative can be devised and recreated again and again through the traditional stories, even with structural variations, until language itself becomes a vehicle not merely of thoughts and actions but of a world view, a mythos reenacted.

Despite the criticism that can be made of insisting on a relationship between rituals and myths, it seems reasonable to speculate about the possibility that ritualistic language in "Black Death" suggests that the tale has mythic content and is not simply a story about supernatural events.[362] Myth, it has been argued, may only tangentially give meaning to rituals, if at all.[363] Stanley J. Tambiah argues that the words of a magical ritual draw their authority from their apparent connection to an ancestral past. Debates over the analogy between Western science and "primitive" magic have, furthermore, led Tambiah to conclude that magical rituals are not "failed" scientific methods; rather, they have different goals and meanings in the societies where they are practiced. In opposition to Robin Horton's view of African religion as a "closed system," Tambiah argues, "it is fundamentally mistaken to say that African religion and ritual are concerned with the same intellectual tasks that science in Western society is concerned with."[364] Thus, ritual practices as well as the mythic content of stories associated with them in African-American traditional contexts may be manifested through the ritualization of ancestral knowledge in certain linguistic practices.

Tambiah's argument connects him with a broader discourse on the applicability of Western analytic categories to non-Western cultures.

Placing the argument within an African context makes it particularly relevant when considering Hurston's research on sympathetic magic in relation to Boas's methods. Inasmuch as she meant her work to be representative of African-American culture, presented from a perspective conditioned by membership in the cultural group being researched, the work, finally, can be viewed as Hurston's personal ritual of transformation with significance for African-Americans collectively.

When Hurston was formally researching sympathetic magic in 1927, Boas was presenting her with specific questions cued into larger issues he considered important to the development of the field at the time. He advised her to pay more attention to the form of diction and movements, than to the content of stories, but to emphasize "current superstitions."[365] He expressed interest in comparing superstitions among English-, Spanish-, and French-speaking blacks, as well customs related to marriage, birth, death, and other rites of passage. His focus on form over content was based on the thesis that African culture in America primarily had been retained in mannerisms, whereas much of the lore, for example, had similar content as the surrounding cultural groups in the new environment. I am summarizing Boas's views, here, to place Hurston's formal concerns in context. Some of what to her appeared obvious, was to Boas a subject to be scrutinized in clinical detail. They disagreed on some points. Their exchange, through letters and occasional meetings, brought Hurston in contact with the dominant social scientific methods. Although Boas seems to have had the strongest influence on this area of her work, as previously mentioned, she also worked under the supervision of Herskovits, Klineberg, and Mead, at different junctures. Thus, she is conditioned by the same ideas shaping the work of major American anthropologists, emphasizing forms and patterns as an approach to understanding cultural differences. To the extent that her work is representative of social scientific paradigms emphasizing formal aspects of expressive culture within groups and dissemination across cultures, it suggests possibilities for reexamining the bases upon which boundaries are drawn between different cultures.

Although Hurston introduced her subject in a unique style, written texts, unlike staged productions, make it difficult to ritualize the knowledge one wishes to impart. "Psychologically, Hoodoo empowered all of its adherents; it allowed them to perceive themselves as actors in the world, not the passive reactors the dominant society held them to be," according to Cheryl Wall.[366] Unlike performances, texts on black culture to be read by an academic elite would be inaccessible to the people empowered by Hoodoo, thus denying them the kind of self-apprehension the Nigerian dramatist Wole Soyinka says is a necessary part of rituals rooted in African tradition. If the media through which traditional knowledge is reflected becomes part of a cultural group's means of perpetuating itself, then I would argue that "the aesthetic drama of African deities in their new syncretic mode," on the western side of the Atlantic, is enacted in the rituals Hurston documents.[367]

Hurston is not as interested in "images" and the problems they present in debates over authenticity in black theater, film, and other media as she is in the nonliteral meanings implicit in the languages—including movements and gestures—of people who have had to recreate their world view in English. She understands that above all else, the hieroglyphic, which is to say the pictographic character of language in oral storytelling, multiplies the meanings of words and causes several dimensions of time to overlap. Mythic time, historical time, and the present intersect. In the present, the mirror introduces a spatial and temporal dichotomy; action occurs simultaneously in at least two places.

"HOODOO IN AMERICA" AND
THE HIGH GODS IN SPACE

Hurston's 100-page "Hoodoo in America" is a showcase of her findings from the Bahamas, Louisiana (including New Orleans), Florida, and Alabama. Her brief introduction explains that "Hoodoo" is the only term African-Americans have for "veaudeau" (Voodoo), which she calls "the European term for African magic practices and beliefs" (317). Both terms, she states, are "related to the West African term *juju*" (317). Used interchangeably with "Hoodoo," among African-Americans the terms "conjure" and "roots" ("folk-doctoring by herbs and roots"), respectively, indicate the magic and healing domains. After offering a demographic overview describing Hoodoo's spread in the South and summarizing some variations from one geographical area to another, Hurston offers her distinction between "spiritualism" and "Hoodoo." Her purpose in doing so is to clarify the difference between congregations in which people communicate with the dead versus those where people do so as an adjunct to practicing Hoodoo. She stresses the distinction to make plain to her readers that the larger society considers Hoodoo disreputable and hoodooists, aware of their precarious social status, find ways to shield their activities from public view. This point about concealment harkens back to my point about the partial exposure of clandestine knowledge in "Black Death" and corresponds with a concept of Voodoo as being, at the core, a "cult of the dead," centered on ancestral devotion.[368] Hurston explains in *Mules and Men* that Hoodoo "is not the accepted theology of the Nation and so believers conceal their faith" (195). To be a Hoodoo doctor, one must either inherit the talent, serve an apprenticeship, or receive a "call." Hurston notes that "the most influential doctors seem to be those born to the cult," with the primary example being the legendary priestess of New Orleans, Marie Leveau—a third-generation conjurer known throughout the region during the nineteenth century. The major portion of "Hoodoo in America" is a treasure trove of supernatural tales and data on traditional medicine, organized according to informants' reports idenitified by the name of the intiate and religion (Catholic, Protestant).

Repetition of key references throughout the article indicates that Hoodoo religious and healing practices have an order, one might say, a system. In the Bahamian Obeah (the West Indian term for "Voodoo") section, one doctor's repertoire, for example, the technique for killing an enemy, as in "Black Death," requires use of a mirror, as well as a basin of water and "a sharp knife or dagger." A scripture reading is followed by a description of how the death occurs: "Then the looking glass will show you your enemy, known or unknown. When he appears, chop the water with the blade and it turns to blood in the basin. In two or three hours the enemy is dead" (324). Water is an important medium in the reports and resonates with an occurrence Metraux observes, whereby the dead are said to dwell for a time "at the bottom of a river or lake."[369] Combining a mirror and water in his ritual "to make a marriage," Hurston's informant (who claims to be a grand-nephew of Marie Leveau) Albert Frechard intimates that "if you go to get him from across water to marry—take a brand new tub (big) and fill it with clear water" (365). Getting him from across the water may mean he is an initiate, "for it is the fate of all who have practised Voodoo to spend at least a year and a day in a stream of water," as Metraux tells us.[370] The desire of the dead cult member to return to life among his living kin, if unheeded by responsive relatives, can cause them pain. Hurston's informant Frechard further directs: "Get a three dollar candle. Place candle in the center of the water (tub), take a large mirror, place it in front of the tub and candle. Take your rubber hammer, knock three times to call the spirit to advocate the man's mind to come marry" (365). Again, Fernandez corroborates that mirrors and various bodies of water, along with other "reflective surfaces," are the locations from behind and beneath which ancestral spirits emerge. Furthermore, he remarks, "The mirror, it appears, is par excellence the instrument of paradox."[371] It is the play upon paradoxical qualities of surface appearances Hurston garnered from her studies of hoodoo in the South (and, later, voodoo in Haiti) which she fashioned into a lexicon capable of capturing (to the extent that language alone can capture) the various ingredients of ritualistic expression.

The many problem-solving recipes compiled in "Hoodoo in America" show the extent to which Hoodooists were sources for obtaining the means to cope with challenging situations of every kind—from loneliness and betrayal to legal entanglements and financial disasters. In the section "prescriptions of root doctors," Hurston explains that folk medicine is widespread because "in the sawmill camps, the turpentine stills, mining camps and among the lowly generally, doctors are not generally called to prescribe for illnesses, certainly, not for the social diseases" (414). Nevertheless, she again distinguishes curing from its more elusive relative—the ability to manipulate supernatural forces. "Nearly all of the conjure doctors practice 'roots,' but some of the root doctors are not hoodoo doctors" (414). In this portion of the article, "conjure stories" are set apart from the descriptions of rites that precede them. The rites consist of prayers of supplication and instructions. Some are incredible incantations designed to bring woe upon a person (or persons) thought to be the cause of misfortune, as in "the curse," when the supplicant pleads to the "Lord" to neutralize enemies through paralysis, desolation, pestilence, and death "because they have dragged me in the dust and destroyed my good name, have broken my heart and caused me to curse the day that I was born" (337). These affects proceed, though, from the supplicant's helplessness. "I have been sorely tried by my enemies and have been blasphemed and lied against. My good thoughts and my honest actions have been turned to bad actions and dishonest ideas. My home has been disrespected, my children have been cursed and ill treated. My dear ones have been backbitten and their virtue questioned" (337).

Hoodoo doctors intervene in the moral order and authority of Christian and constitutional codes which apparently are deemed insufficient to reconcile hoodoo believers to their earthly plights. Causes of the misfortunes that overwhelmingly dominate Hurston's evidence are sometimes attributed to enemies, evil spirits or specific forces, such as "spirits of contention and strife," "the spirit of restlessness and envy," whereas in some of the accounts no cause is identified. A supplicant's need for retribution takes priority, with no questioning of the viability his or her request has, as in the situation of "The Lady in the Law Suit." She has been accused of disturbing the peace, attempted murder, burglary. One may wonder whether she committed her alleged crimes. The ritual is directed at confounding the judicial process. As in numerous rituals, the enemy is invoked through substitution, by his or her name being written on a piece of paper. The supplicant is instructed to "do this so that his [the enemy's] testimony will not be believed by the learned judges and the high sheriff, and so that he will become confused when he speaks to the judge" (344). Conversely, a specific incense (used by King Solomon) must be burned on court day, to "give your man of law wisdom in his words so that they will be believed by the judges and high sheriffs and you shall at once be set free" (344). Here the question of similitude—what constitutes a likeness of the person— is far less straightforward than when a doll is meant to substitute for the targeted person; however, in another ritual Hurston documents, a doll as well as the person's name with a piece of paper are enclosed in a coffin to produce fatality.

The fact that names are the only parts of the "Black Death" story Hurston changed in the "Hoodoo in America" version, "The Case of John Wesley Roberts," seems to indicate that in her early career she made little distinction between art (fiction, literature) and science. Old Man Morgan becomes Old Man Massey, a (the same?) South Central Florida hoodoo man; Beau Diddley becomes John Wesley Roberts, and Mrs. Boger's daughter bears the namesake Janie. Might not this unplanned pregnancy have been the fate of Janie Crawford Killicks Starks Woods in *Their Eyes Were Watching God* had she not been "rescued" by her arranged first marriage? Further, might not such an event—being taken advantage of and rejected by a man—been part of Hurston's adolescence, the period of her life about which so little is known? I raise this biographical question to draw attention to the consistency with which this type of tale recurs throughout her work as another indicator of the commonality not only of language but of the everyday-life dramas shaping the stories.

The rejection theme figures prominently in "Hoodoo in America," including a story resembling the aside about Annie Tyler in *Their Eyes Were Watching God*. Rachael Roe, "dry with anger, hate, outraged confidence and desire for revenge" (369) approaches Ruth Mason, who "is a well-known hoodoo doctor of New Orleans, and a Catholic" (368). Hurston makes this story an occasion to explain the difference between a fire dance, done for pleasure, and a hoodoo dance, which is "done for a specific purpose. . . . a case of death-to-the-enemy" (368). The line between observer and participant very nearly disappears here; as an apprentice for Ruth Mason, Hurston explains, she was a subject of debate among other initiates, who questioned whether she had served as a devotee long enough to dance. Permission was granted her when Ruth Mason, "who had a troublesome case of neuritis" needed a surrogate. A frightening scene ensues when "promptly on the stroke of ten Death mounted his black draped throne and assumed his regal crown, Death being represented by a rudely carved wooded [sic] statue, bust length" (369). As the ceremony proceeds, one wonders whether Hurston truly will give herself over to the willful destruction of a human life. "The person danced upon," she reports, "is not supposed to live more than nine days after the dance." Adding to the drama, she startles readers when she admits being "eager to see what would happen in this case," only to report, further (to the reader's immediate relief), that "five days after the dance John Doe deserted his bride for the comforting arms of Rachael and she hurried to Mother Ruth to have the spell removed" (371). Was Hurston anxious to be an accomplice? Did she consider full involvement a necessary component, to authenticate her writing?

Commenting on the Voodoo episodes that Hurston reports in *Tell My Horse*, Wendy Dutton ventures, "even the most complacent reader cannot help noticing Hurston had become much more of a participant than an observer."[372] Dutton examines the work Hurston did while in Haiti and concludes that her struggle to find an effective form for writing about her observations on Voodoo caused her to produce a text unsuccessful in scientific terms. Next to *Tell My Horse* and *Mules and Men*, according to Dutton, "Hoodoo in America" is much more satisfying, mainly because *Mules and Men* reiterates the same information as the earlier piece, while *Tell My Horse* exposes the dilemma Hurston faced when she had become so absorbed in her subject she was no longer able to delineate the boundaries—no longer able to determine whether her objectives as a researcher were in conflict with her duties as an initiate or how to resolve the conflict.[373] Dutton's analysis of the importance invisibility has in Voodoo practices is helpful for an understanding of the tension surfacing in *Tell My Horse*. The Voodoo practice of making oneself invisible, she explains, acquires urgency for Hurston when she begins to feel her position (as an observer who will in turn report on what she has seen) poses a threat. Citing the example Hurston observed of a man zombified as punishment for talking, Dutton speculates that Hurston suspected her own fate was endangered: "Her own work became a warning, and, effectively spooked, she cut off her research and returned to the United States."[374]

Thus, language itself could be used to make oneself or another invisible. This idea is supported repeatedly in her writing, as if she is practicing the sort of word-magic involved when the name of a person targeted by a hoodoo spell is inscribed on a piece of paper. According to Taussig, trying to reproduce a person's spirit through writing does not mean that writing itself is a powerful or magical medium but a measure of "the capacity of the imagination to be lifted through representational media, such as marks on a page, into other worlds."[375] Hurston fully endorsed this "capacity of the imagination" and was ever motivated by the desire to alter ordinary circumstances in accordance with her perceptions. She sought to alter the world not so much into what she thought it ought to be as into how she thought others ought to see it—through fully opened eyes and perhaps, like her, through "the spy glass of Anthropology."

Hurston's understanding of distinctive uses of language in black culture, particularly in relation to oral forms and sympathetic magic, bears upon her personal life. The forms of expression she studied, at times, converged within her private sphere; theory and practice, again, become intertwined. Her personal correspondence reveals how she used various rituals to influence circumstances in the lives of Charlotte Osgood Mason and Jane Belo. When Mason was ill in October of 1931, for example, Hurston wrote to her: "Promptly at twelve oclock last night I set the altar for you and asked the powers invisible for your health in fire. I know that you will improve. The end candle fell at the moment when I uttered the words."[376] And when Belo wrote about her mother's family's objections to her Jewish fiancé, Frank Tannenbaum, in a letter to Hurston, Hurston replied: "I opened a window in my soul and sent out my spirit to help you safely into Frank's arms. It can't be otherwise, darling. You will see. I shall put a Houngan on your mama that shall keep her silent until all is over. I am sending a mouth-gag in a spiritual way."[377] What is intriguing about these references to Hurston's purported power to change circumstances in Mason's and Belo's lives are Hurston's assumptions.

She presumes to know enough about the nature of the problems that Mason and Belo face to resolve those problems by using solutions rooted in African-American healing practices. The articulations of her actions, when they appear in writing, in the letters to Mason and Belo cross a boundary between public and private, between professional and personal. The passages reveal that Hurston either considered methods of sympathetic magic part of her routine or appropriated them to manage her relationships. Confronted with the complexity of her situation as a mediator between cultures, she might have exploited the purported effectiveness of traditional healing practices as a way to empower herself and to exercise control. She does, after all, refer to Mason as "mother of the primitive world" and ingratiates herself to Belo while maintaining another, contrary agenda to supersede their initiatives.

When she calls upon the "High Gods in Space," as she does numerous times in her letters to Mason, Hurston on one level seems to be practicing a kind of conjuring; however, there is also reason to believe that she is creating a metaphor for the complex solutions required to alter the situations presenting obstacles to her work. Obstacles arise especially because of the complexity of social relations related to patronage and control. Mason's illness itself does not signify a problem, but Hurston's personal friendship with Mason does present certain challenges because of the imbalance in power implicit in their economic relationship. The High Gods in Space, for Hurston, can be equated with a force necessary to resolve what she considers a cultural hoax, the exploitation of black culture—"primitivism," practiced by whites and blacks whose aims differ from hers, who are more interested in commercial profit and social prestige than in the integrity of the products they create and promote. Their ideas about social progress, rather than being of any benefit to black and poor people who invent the cultural forms, make it more difficult to develop art works that challenge the popular norms, which then were becoming ever more standardized.

Popular conceptions of black culture as "primitive" had a meaning in the "high art" world, as Hurston well knew. Although "noble savage" characterizations in the theater by playwrights, such as in Eugene O'Neill's *Emperor Jones* (1920), and apparently stock personifications of idealized black characters, such as in DuBose and Dorothy Heyward's *Porgy* (1927), would not satisfy the most critical judges of "authentic" cultural representation, Hurston no less than her vanguard contemporaries attempted versions of an ideal "primitive" and, indeed, idealized the alleged primitive quality in black culture.[378] In her specific sense of "primitive," however, Hurston played with the multiple meanings of the term.

A twentieth century development first identified with modernist art movements in Europe, notably Fauvism and Cubism, "primitivism" has been defined as a Western reaction to or interest in non-Western art forms. I am concerned with the primitivist influence on modernism in the United States in the 1920s and its manifestation in works by African-Americans. In addition to the burgeoning interest in art nègre, among black artists a new outpouring of works redefined literary aesthetics in terms of performance—including oral interpretation of poetry, and neo-African (or "primitivistic") iconography, vernacular culture, and other non-textual qualities which came to bear the burden of communicating a special relation between black culture in the United States and on the African continent. Therefore, for the purposes of my argument, it is necessary to define primitivism beyond the boundaries of art history.

William Rubin, Director of the Museum of Modern Art's "Primitivism" in Twentieth Century Art Exhibition (1984) to some extent broadens the definition of primitivism by acknowledging that in primitivism, as well as in the study of primitive art, the two disciplines of anthropology and art history overlap. First, he notes that anthropologists and art historians share an interest in understanding the work in context. His agenda, however, is to revise that approach because it presumes that modernist artists have knowledge of the "primitive" cultures inspiring their work. "The ethnologists' primary concern—the specific function and significance of each of these objects—is irrelevant to my topic, except insofar as these facts might have been known to the modern artists in question," he writes.[379] (Only the Surrealists, he argues, were to some extent an exception.) Moreover, Rubin concedes that the term "primitivism" is ethnocentric, "for it refers not to the tribal arts in themselves, but to the Western interest in and reaction to them."[380] Thus, Rubin has capitalized the terms "Primitive" and "Primitivism" to account for pejorative connotations that some critics have, according to him, erroneously attributed to the concepts. He argues that they have misunderstood the art-historical significance of the terms. Appreciation and admiration for work difficult to name and classify have been the motivations for modern artists' incorporating non-Western styles in their work—not an inherently disparaging attitude.

Precisely because of the crossover between art and anthropology, Hurston's work is a likely place to begin an investigation of the relationship between primitivism and modernism in African-American performance traditions and literature. The pejorative connotation of the terms "primitive" and "primitivism" makes them controversial and problematic in the context of African-American art forms. One question which automatically arises is why bother at all to call upon these terms and risk repeating the same distorted messages produced in the past, by association? According to Hal Foster, the "Primitivism" in Twentieth Century Art Exhibition at the Museum of Modern Art, which is the basis of Rubin's discussion, appropriated a notion of the "primitive" as part of Western tradition and thereby left unresolved questions concerning imbalances of power implicit in the exchange of cultural products across cultures. Foster examines an essay on Gaugin by Kirk Varnedoe (also in the exhibition catalogue) to draw a contrast with Rubin's art-historical approach and Varnedoe's philosophical one. The philosophical complement, according to Foster, more clearly elucidates a deeply rooted Western rationalist bias inherent even in the progressively reformulated ideology promoted by the exhibit. Varnedoe generalizes primitivism and connects it to a quest for origins and to cultural critique—that is, to a way of reflecting on the direction in which civilization seems to be moving by reflecting on "origins and organic growth," a concern he attributes to thinkers of nearly all scientific and humanistic disciplines. The problem with the exhibition's ideology, according to Foster, is its redefining of primitivism as a benign way of conceptualizing art objects of colonized people. "And the final contradiction or aporia is this," writes Foster, "no anthropological remorse, aesthetic elevation or redemptive exhibition can correct or compensate this loss *because they are all implicated in it.*"[38]

In an effort to move beyond art-historical approaches to primitivism, the literary critic Marianna Torgovnick in her book *Gone Primitive: Savage Intellects, Modern Lives* examines various well-meaning Western intellectuals' efforts to represent in their work cross-cultural encounters from the perspective of one who purports to know what being "primitive" has and does not have in common with being "civilized." The results of their efforts—from Tarzan novels by Edgar Rice Burroughs, to anthropological signposts such as *Tristes Tropique,* by Claude Lèvi-Strauss—according to Torgovnick have only continued to perpetuate an unenlightening discourse of difference. Despite her admission that primitivism "will often be unappealing and oppressive, sometimes even repulsive," she avoids examining whether alternative terms are available and escapes from looking at non-Westerners' perspectives on themselves.[382] Torgovnick raises the question as to whether ethnographic field research necessarily produces a less colonizing perception of non-Western art than an aestheticized, non-contextual approach ostensibly meant to decolonize the work by granting it "art" status. Her point resonates when considering Hurston's struggle to reconcile folklore collecting with theatrical pursuits. By focusing on the inadequacies of ethnographers and their texts, Torgovnick leaves readers to judge whether her sense of non-Western cultures is noticeably different from the views held by the people she criticizes. Examining field research processes, as through Hurston's work, makes clear how unpredictable face-to-face encounters with members of a culture under scrutiny can be. Undervaluing the field researcher's methods because of a skepticism about whether empiricism has viability, however, distances the subject (non-Western cultures) further rather than bringing it into sharper relief.

Torgovnick, for example, discusses "going primitive" as a phenomenon similar to what might be called "going native" for an anthropologist who imitates the behavior of the "natives." For Torgovnick, this idea is related to "getting physical," which she interprets in light of Freud's theories on repressed sexuality. The underbelly of "the primitive" is pulled out of proportion in Torgovnick's sexual interpretation of "getting physical." Without exploring the phrase's meaning based on a broad notion of the tactile dimension of cross-cultural contact in the field, she establishes an opposition between what she perceives as Bronislaw Malinowski's sterile, repressed objectivity versus Margaret Mead's virtual obsessiveness concerning sexual behavior. Not yielding to the compelling evidence that ethnographers' first-hand contact with non-Western cultures provides, Torgovnick concludes her book by warning of the need to rethink and rigorously to criticize attitudes toward non-Western cultures. Because she focuses on the flaws in Western writing about "primitive" cultures, we still do not know, in the end, how her perspective would be dramatically different from Malinowski's or Mead's were she to have attempted a cultural critique while in the field. Torgovnick does not account for nuances of meaning that a performance-centered approach might contribute—an approach incorporating the views of all participants, observers and observed, alike.

Although I agree with Foster's concern for the "denial of difference," insinuated by the apparently benign absorption of "Primitivism" and the "Primitive" into Western art, the whole issue of primitivism is pertinent to Hurston's work as part of the background against which African-American artists have continued to pursue aesthetic self-determination during the twentieth century. Implicit in that pursuit has been the kind of acute awareness exemplified by Hurston's invoking the High Gods in Space to mediate between discontent and acquiescence. Between rejection of the Civilized and acceptance of the Primitive, and vice versa, there is a space where Hurston, and other highly skilled culture bearers and producers of her period, create modernist forms that do not simply reinforce dichotomies.

Between toying with outsiders' perceptions of black culture, on the one hand, and trying to establish guidelines for "authenticity," on the other hand, Hurston managed to produce work that spoke in several languages at once—or, perhaps it is more accurate to say her work represented multiple languages. Speaking and apprehending in ways other than seeing are the actions constituted in her methods of representation; not only does she explicitly refer to the importance of this but also she directs our attention away from the literary conventions of the text and away not so much from seeing the movements and gestures of others but from any reliance we may have on trusting surface clues as final. Instead, she requires us to focus on that which is unseen in order to "read" not simply what the communicator wants us to know but the complete "text" which includes, in addition to a communicator's message, the background, foreground, shades, and tones of everything the person communicates.

"Black Death" has a significance apart from the physical body of the legendary character Beau Diddely, but the significance has only a non-literal meaning if the tale is not interpreted as a quasiliterary story nor even as a traditional folktale but as a traditional folk performance or a theater work, which is to say as a three-dimensional event, a drama occurring in space and time. This is not to say that the important parts of what gets reported can be visualized as occurring in time and space. Indeed, even if one grants a certain priority to the text and all that it represents, the second quality in order of importance may be the voice with its variations in "coloring and intonation."[383] Thus, the tangibility of the story stems from the storyteller's ability to relay the connections between the events in the story and the historical memory evoked by speaking, including the sound of the voice as well as the intimacy with the characters and their fates conveyed. Not only a familiarity but also a satisfaction, even a pleasure, come in repetition of the story, as a way of attuning and re-attuning with the tale's power to transport the listener on a journey beyond words, beyond seeing.

Here is where Hurston's study of sympathetic magic overlaps with her work as a writer, her study of traditional narrative, and her skills as a raconteur. It was through studying sympathetic magic that she came to an understanding of contradictions in everyday life and, therefore, contradictions in the dramas, which is to say the means of enactment, ritualized in black culture. Moreover, considering the ritualistic actions she used to empower herself in her relationships with Mason and Belo, she was aware of the larger stage upon which the drama of everyday life occurs. Using a frame analysis or a world-as-stage model, it is possible to interpret how she could have been at once outspoken, independent, and rebellious, on the one hand, and obsequious, dependent, and ingratiating, on the other.[384] She was enacting the same ritualized form of self-disclosure and concealment which had ensured the continuance of Hoodoo and other practices she believed were embodied in African-Americans. Her everyday-life dramas and those of the people she represents are iconographically documented in the hieroglyphics of African-American cultural performances.

IN THE SENSES

The use of mythic time and reflections on an ancestral past are clues to a system of thought represented in the performative language of Hurston's tales. Identifying the clues, which are implicit, becomes a project to dismantle the spatial and temporal references in written versions of the texts. Because I have already discussed the extent to which Hurston's written tales correspond with literal transcriptions of specific persons' words, I shall move toward a more detailed analysis of how she has excavated a performative language (hieroglyphics) and translated the written equivalents into ritualized forms. For example, the tale "Uncle Monday" begins:

> People talk a whole lot about Uncle Monday, but they take good pains not
> to let him hear none of it. Uncle Monday is an out-and-out conjure doc-

tor. That in itself is enough to make the people handle him carefully, but there is something about him that goes past hoodoo. Nobody knows anything about him, and that's a serious matter in a village of less than three hundred souls, especially when a person has lived there for forty years and more.[385]

"People talk" but Uncle Monday does not hear. Or does he? The ambiguous double negative "not to let him hear none of it" suggests the mystery of knowing the unknown and hearing the unspeakable. In any case, the sound of things ultimately tells of origins. Also, the people take "good pains"—not necessarily a contradiction. Although the phrase is what Hurston calls a double descriptive, the term "pain" draws attention to another sense, touch. Taking pains becomes a way of touching, a feeling that hurts but in a good way; the painful is inverted, and that which is dreaded is elevated—which is to say, it points to a different, higher ethical order.

People "handle" Uncle Monday—again, referring to the significance of "hands," which in itself is another term for conjure doctor. If "there is something about him that goes past Hoodoo," it harkens to a distant (mythic) time and space. He has lived in the village of three hundred residents for forty years, but in a sense he has been absent and unknown beyond all possibility. His presence is illusory, perhaps because his identity is fluid, or perhaps because the stage upon which he enacts his everyday-life drama is not the everyday-life stage known to all. Houston Baker remarks about a character in *Mules and Men*, "that only a set of cultural doctrines that go deeper than the lore of everyday life issuing from culture bearers such as Mr. Allen can compel and regulate this gigantic, vernacular cultural force."[386] Similarly, the far-reaching "cultural doctrines" in Hurston's conjure stories exceed everyday-life boundaries and stretch toward another definition of order—indeed, toward another temporal frame outside the quotidian.

A sense of the story as mythic rather than legendary is reinforced by the lack of specific biographical or historical information (other than a comment about when he appeared forty years earlier, about the late 1880s) which would help to explain Uncle Monday's origins. At the same time, however, the ritual aspect has precedence over the mythic. Hurston's conjure stories underemphasize any symbolic meanings by avoiding vision-related metaphors and seem, rather, to refer to actions. Ritual's priority over the mythic is retained in Hurston's lexicon as powerful historical memories.

One reason her written language recreates actions through analogies based on other senses besides seeing can be derived from accounts of her early childhood visions which she associated with the death of her childhood, with a paralyzing sense of distance from other people ("a cosmic loneliness") and boredom—all of which produces a craving she cannot name at the time. "Without knowing it, I wanted action," she writes, "So I was driven inward. I lived an exciting life unseen."[387] The unseen is associated with action and heightened significance, reenacted in expressive forms, learned in various cultural contexts, relearned through research, and passed on through an evolving critical tradition. What has been ritualized is a metascript elaborating a cultural history deeply rooted in experiences associated with group identity, embodied as well as reconstituted one generation after another. My rereading of Hurston demonstrates how performance is iconographically embedded in her texts and why Baker designates her "the intimate *home*, the imagistic habitation or poetic space of the spirit in which works of mythomanic transmission can take place."[388]

In "Uncle Monday," variants of the myth—which is to say different versions of the plot—are attributed to people such as Joe Lindsay, who was the first to see the mysterious newcomer. Lindsay's version passes as an account of Monday's origins. Significantly, "they said that he had seen no more than several others." The entire story builds upon hearsay, but also, ironically, the naming of specific individuals. Interestingly, Uncle Monday's name follows a tradition considered a West African retention, giving names according to the day of the week on which the person is born.[389]

Thus, as a locus where different versions of stories converge, "Uncle Monday" reinforces the magical power inherent in naming. As Tambiah notes, two contrary postulates of sacred language are that god created the world through naming and that man named things in nature through speech.[390] The recurrence of tales that appear elsewhere in Hurston's work indicates that the story extends far beyond one unified narrative, and, therefore, cannot be historically placed. "Uncle Monday" includes, for example, a version of the story "Black Death," discussed previously. As part of "The Florida Negro" (1938) manuscript, "Uncle Monday" postdates the two previous versions (including John Wesley Roberts in "Hoodoo in America," 1931) and is a noticeable variation. What previously had been a discrete tale now, in "Uncle Monday," has become one piece of evidence in a much larger scheme—a full-blown myth, as it were. The story's expanding proportions, especially considering its supernatural content, again liken it to Mircea Eliade's definition of myth as relating "a primordial event that took place at the beginning of time."[391] The ritual significance, however, again supersedes and emerges from formal qualities in the language—so that hoodoo and voodoo (also mentioned in the story) are associated with powers not rooted in the soil (that is, the United States) or the sky (that is, the Christian heaven or God) but in the river, which is—not coincidentally, in my opinion—the home of a Yoruba female diety Yemoja (or Yemaya) whose presence has been documented in various forms throughout the Americas.[392]

I hope to have made clear in this section how Hoodoo has acquired its power and sustained its presence among African-Americans and how it is a basis for Hurston's refiguring of the English language in her texts. This occurs not simply because of the African retentions or even continuities in the expressive culture she documents, but because certain African descendants in the United States have deliberately sought to connect not just with the historical but also with an ancestral or mythic past, to survive in the present. Their efforts, consequently, have ensured future survival of Africanist world views as exemplified in Hurston's work-as-legacy. This is, furthermore, tied in with a refigured "maroon" ideology such as Baker presents in "Workings of the Spirit."

RETURN TO ORIGINS

> The old man [Uncle Monday] had been seen coming from the direction of the lake. That was the first that the village saw of him, way back in the late eighties, and so far, nobody knows any more about his past than that. (31)

Having explored the concept of origins and originality in relation to concerns about authenticity posed during the crucial period when African-American cultural critique was taking form, I would like to reintroduce here a different sense in which origins have played an empowering role. The example of Uncle Monday emerging from the river and being singled out because he is a stranger about whom nothing can be nor ever has been known, becomes a kind of paradigm for Hurston's suggestion that people have a lot of discomfort about origins. Being a stranger, in this instance, means having special power. As Arnold Van Gennep has argued, in some societies strangers are endowed with either benevolent or malevolent power. Furthermore, that strangers often must undergo rites of integration establishes a basis for any number of provocative actions to be associated with a stranger's presence. What is more, according to Van Gennep's argument, the sacralization of space, or the distinction between profane or secular spaces and persons and the sacred dimension where magico-religious rites are considered necessary, is something that changes according to the different boundaries a person crosses. Thus, when a person ordinarily living in a secular dimension enters a foreign territory, as a stranger she becomes sacred and, therefore, a candidate for ritual transformation. I am suggesting that Uncle Monday can be seen as an archetypal stranger who signifies the status of African-American people in the United States—endowed with mystery and special powers.

Discomfort over origins, the stranger imbued with special powers, and the perceived necessity for ritual transformation are at the root of Hurston's life and work and their continued significance for African-American studies and performance theory. They prompt Hurston's pursuing definitive characteristics of African-American expressive forms and, more generally, for various scholars seeking answers to key questions concerning how to distinguish African-Americans from members of other cultural groups. Her life and work constitute a paradigm for the cultural group as a whole and its movement toward self-realization and self-actualization.

Perhaps the most revealing version of Monday's story appears in Hurston's autobiography *Dust Tracks on a Road*, as part of a story she claims to have invented as a child. Actually the story is not so much a replica of the other two; it has some of the same references. For example, the man in the story can walk on the water and transforms into an alligator: "I saw the early moon laying a shiny track across the water," she writes.

> After that, I could picture the full moon laying a flaming red sword of light across the water. It was a road of yellow-red light made for Mr. Pendir to tread. I could see him crossing the lake down this flaming road wrapped in his awful majesty, with thousands on thousands of his subject-'gators moving silently along beside him and behind him in an awesome and mighty convoy. (80)

Just as Hurston admits that this man who lived "in a one-room house by himself down near Lake Belle" in her fantasy "was the king of 'gators," she reports of Uncle Monday that "everybody knows that the father of all 'gators lives in Belle Lake" (107). Lindsay, one of the people who witnessed Uncle Monday's strange ways, reported hearing "bull 'gators fighting and bellowing all night," just as Hurston says she fantasized as a child: "When I heard the thunder of bull 'gator voices from the lake on dark nights, I used to whisper to myself, 'That's Mr. Pendir!'" (*Dust Tracks* 57) The Uncle Monday tale, in other words, bears as much relation to Hurston's childhood imagination as to community folklore. The alligator imagery draws attention to the interplay between folklore, fiction, and autobiography in Hurston's work:

> But one evening around dusk-dark Sam Merchant and Jim Gooden were on their way home from a squirrel hunt around Lake Belle. They swore that, as they rounded the lake and approached the footpath that leads towards the village, they saw what they thought was the great 'gator that lives in the lake crawl out of the marsh. Merchant wanted to take a shot at him for his hide and teeth, but Gooden reminded him that they were loaded with bird shot, which would not even penetrate a 'gator's hide let alone kill it. They said the thing they took for the 'gator then struggled awhile, pulling off something that looked like a long black glove which had come from his right paw. Then without looking either right or left, he stood upright and walked on towards the village. Everybody saw Uncle Monday come thru the town, but still Merchant's tale was hard to swallow. But, by degrees, people came to believe that Uncle Monday could shed any injured member of his body and grow a new one in its place. At any rate, when he reappeared, his right hand and arm bore no scars. (109)

Hurston reports in *Dust Tracks* that she had such a rich inner life that "animals took on lives and characteristics which nobody knew anything about except myself" and that "little things that people did or said grew into fantastic stories." (57) She, in a sense, describes the method she uses to compose her tales. What, then, can be inferred about the significance of distinctions between genres for Hurston and, consequently, for her scientific observations about patterns of expressive behavior, particularly the verbal art of storytelling? In "Hoodoo in America," one brief rendition of a 'gator tale reads:

> In Florida they work with all kinds of beasts. One man used to work with alligators. Somebody wanted a girl out of the way. One day a big 'gator with a red handkerchief around his neck walked up to her house and called her name. She ran to the front door to see who it was; but she didn't see nobody but the 'gator. He called her again and turned around and went back to the lake. She was dead in three days. (402)

It would seem that unself-conscious mixing of hearsay, research data, and personal gloss, together give meaning to the term "authenticity" in Hurston's lexicon. For this reason, an unpredictable factor must be taken into account when ciphering not only the meaning of her tales in their various incarnations—fiction, folklore, and factlore (autobiography)—but also the meaning of a pivotal person such as Hurston in the shaping of African-American world views and mythic traditions.

In *Myth, Literature and the African World,* Wole Soyinka talks about three major Yoruba deities and the myths surrounding them, all of which have been recreated in drama and literature. It is not just that myths are presented in dramatic form with the deities as characters, but that archetypal crises are enacted for purposes of group as well as individual stability. Thus, rituals practiced in traditional culture may not be translated directly into a modern context but are refigured in cultural productions which, nevertheless, serve a group's needs for stability and for maintaining continuity with the past. Similarly, John Roberts explains, in *From Trickster to Badman: The Black Folk Hero in Slavery and Freedom,* that during the antebellum period in the United States, "intragroup solidarity in the slave community took on a sacred aura in a peculiarly African sense."393 Thus, the gradual revision of traditional archetypes and myths occurred out of necessity during the period of enslavement and, as I am arguing, continues with each successive generation. The importance of an individual's life and circumstances as a microcosm of a group's survival can be seen in light of Soyinka's plays pertaining to Yoruba archetypes and can be seen in Robert's interpretation of how the reliving of an ancestral mythos takes form and acquires significance through identification with collective well-being. "Not only was this view of their situation strikingly similar to that which had influenced African religious worldview and social organization," according to Roberts, "but it also became influential in facilitating the transformation of the ritual and expressive traditions surrounding African religious specialists."394 By "African religious specialists," he means conjurers similar to Hurston's Uncle Monday, also appearing as Old Man Morgan, Old Man Massey, and Mr. Pendir.

Of the paradigms Soyinka discusses, conflicts derived from Sango seem relevant to the aspect of my argument concerning the continuation of African-American mythos rooted in historical memory and recreated in expressive forms. Sango, according to Soyinka, gives meaning to a society's "racial or social origination"; thus, Sango's fate could be seen as metonymically related to the emergence of African-American culture. His "tragic rites," according to Soyinka, "are consequently a deadly conflict on the human and historic plane, charged nonetheless with the passion and terror of superhuman, uncontrollable forces."[395] What I am suggesting is that Sango, whose tragedy dramatizes human weaknesses caused by hubris and whose resolution comes about through moral revenge, provides a model rationalization for how to interpret the presence of mythic paradigms in African-American world views.[396]

Yoruba archetypes cannot be seen as having been overtly transferred into an African-American context. Still, because of the strong influence of Yoruba religion among West African people who were enslaved in the United States, the arguments for vestiges and continuities of certain practices not only seem valid but also can also be viewed from another angle.[397] Taking Hurston as my example, I am proposing that in addition to the possibility that patterns of expressive behavior are culturally learned, individually internalized, and practiced without self-consciousness, certain patterns of expression manifested in traditional and artistic forms are also consciously ordered. The distinction between traditional forms of expression and aesthetic genres, therefore, loses its significance, because the interplay between the two becomes socially, culturally, and perhaps also psychologically imperative in maintaining collective stability and continuity. In other words, what is important is not the continuity of traditional forms, unchanged, but individual and group survival as made possible through recreating traditions. Inasmuch as Soyinka shows the importance of mythic archetypes in reformulating Yoruba world view in modern dramatic and literary forms, it is logical that scholars of African-American, Caribbean, and Latin American cultures have identified a similar pattern on the western side of the Atlantic.

AFRICANIST THEORIES

A brief sketch of some major scholarly discussions tracing the emergence of African-American culture and the significance of African continuities will serve as the basis for analyzing how Hurston's work establishes a trajectory for tracing the conscious realization of an

African world view in African-American cultural productions. It is pertinent to Hurston's work that Herskovits, another student of Boas and a person with and for whom Hurston had worked, had strong views on the extent to which some aspects of black culture in the United States can be attributed to African retentions. Although in his often-cited work *The Myth of the Negro Past* (1941), he attempts to erase any doubts about the distinctive features of black culture being African in origin, he had previously held a contrary view. Although as early as 1930, Herskovits had been questioning the possibility that links might be found between, for example, motor behavior of African people on the continent and African descendants in the United States, Willis Weatherford and Charles Johnson, in 1934 used Herskovits's position to support an argument for acculturation.

> The apparent persistence, in parts of South America and the West Indies, of such Africanisms as 'day names'; certain speech idioms; and the prominence of the mother in the feeling tone of the Negro family in these parts, have suggested to Dr. Herskovits the inevitability of some elements of the culture in North America. Since, however, the historical circumstances under which they were introduced to the respective cultures of North and South America differ considerably, and since practically all of the North American Negro traits observed as possible persistence of African culture can be explained historically, Dr. Herskovits offers the further suggestion that the historical factors may have reinforced the original cultural drives. If there has been such persistence, there is a like possibility that both the American and African cultures have been mutually affected through this contact.[398]

While Herskovits gradually came to the position for which he is well known, at the time when Hurston was interested in studying with him and was herself developing an awareness about the relatedness of expressive patterns among African descendants in the United States as well as the Caribbean, a counter trend toward an understanding of African-American culture as entirely acculturated emerged.

By 1949, E. Franklin Frazier in a critique of Herskovits's argument, had concluded that "Negroes acquired new habits and modes of thought, and whatever elements of African culture were retained lost their original meaning in becoming fused with their experiences in the New World."[399] In trying to enhance his argument for furthering the cause of integration, he frankly states that "the majority of the Negroes have sloughed off completely the African heritage."[400] Again, this position, which starkly contrasts with Hurston's and Herskovits's search for unique cultural patterns among American and Caribbean blacks, serves as a useful background against which to illuminate the ideology of cultural difference that had begun evolving at the time and which has, subsequently, grown rather than diminished in its influence. Further evidence that the integration or acculturation view nurtures thinking such as Hurston's, regarding the peculiar American attitude toward origins and originality, can be found in Frazier's reliance upon N.N. Puckett's work *Folk Beliefs of the Southern Negro* (1926). Frazier notes that Puckett set out, like Herskovits, to discover African retentions among blacks in the United States but finds, instead, that African-Americans assumed many practices from Europeans.[401] Only steadfast curiosity and persistence spurred Hurston and her colleagues to challenge such views.

Not the least of the people raising doubts about the idea that African-Americans adopted European forms was Boas himself, who alerted Hurston to the doubtfulness of such a view. He wrote to Hurston, describing "a very peculiar problem involved in the question of transmission [to non-Europeans] of European tales, proverbs, riddles, games, and songs because the planter certainly did not bring much of it and the question is who the Europeans were from whom all this material was obtained."[402] Although Boas admitted that research methods at the time might make it impossible to solve the problem, he did consider it an important thought to keep in mind.[403] His concern with specific patterns of behavior showing culture as something dynamic which a group of people can share in common, shifted emphasis away from race and integration, toward a closer examination and deeper understanding of folk traditions. This is in striking contrast with Frazier's later view that "the folk Negro has become transformed through education and greater participation in American culture."[404]

Unavoidably, the substance of cultural productions cannot be separated from social and, by extension, historical consequences. Therefore, it is logical that interest in probing African-American expressive culture for a clearer understanding of how traditions have undergone modifications while retaining continuity with an ancestral past estranged through devastating historical and social circumstances has increased since the early part of the twentieth century. As Robert Farris Thompson's research on the iconology of African-American art has documented, African world view appears as a visual language in material culture as well as in gestures. Increasing awareness of a religious lexicon among African-Americans has multiplied the number of forms in which the past has been made present. What is important, again, to keep in mind is that the sense of time informing this bonding with tradition and the past does not correspond with a linear, chronological order.

Sunday Anozie has written about the way that Western structuralist thought can be applied to an understanding of African poetics. He focuses considerable attention on the two concepts of time used by structuralists to distinguish successive ordering (diachrony) and simultaneous occurrence (synchrony) to make the point that African conceptions of time do not easily correspond with either category. In particular, diachrony poses a problem within African linguistic systems, according to Anozie, because the concept of the future is conflated into the immediate present, whereas the past accounts for a greater number of variations in semantic form. Although Anozie does not discuss African-American poetics, per se, his applying Western linguistic method to African languages represents another example of the usefulness a cross-cultural analysis can have in attempting to specify distinctive features of one culture in relation to another. Using comparative analysis is one way to take maximum advantage of methodologies developed outside the context of the culture being studied, while keeping in mind that the primary objective is to further the field—which is to say, further the development of the critical methodology most pertinent to or compatible with the culture.

Since the purpose of this section is to place in perspective the importance of scholarship linking African cultural models with manifestations in the West of congruent forms, it is useful to consider Thompson and Anozie as two contemporary examples that lend themselves to an examination of iconography in Hurston's work. Both Thompson and Anozie have demonstrated the importance of form in relation to dynamic concepts based on movement and gesture. They have also paid attention to aspects of language other than the semantic, stressing tone, for example, as an important contributor to meaning. Among the concepts mentioned in Thompson's work *Flash of the Spirit, ashé* (or life force) receives considerable attention because it contributes much to an understanding not just of religion in itself—as an institution, which it never seems to be in discussions of African religions—but of the source of expressive culture more generally. Thompson, for example, refers to the god Shango's artistic embodiments and to the creation of a particular sculpture of Shango as "the application of a rich inventive mind to

the problems of artistic identity."[405] Another observer of tangible and intangible traits in African art, Robert Plant Armstrong devotes an entire
book, *The Affecting Presence*, to a discussion about relational concepts observable in specific expressive forms that indicate a power approxi-
mately the same as consciousness of a world view—a power he chooses
to identify as presence, described in terms of apprehension. He speculates, "We do not even perceive now all the possibilities of *kinds* of relationships which may obtain. In addition to spatial and temporal
relationships of before and after, contiguity, continuity, greater and less,
faster and slower, are there relationships of entailment, for example?"[406]
He also suggests that there may be "relationships we have not even suspected."[407] Again, I am exploring some key examples which show persis-
tent patterns not that far removed from the patterns sought by Hurston
and her counterparts; this is not to make a simple point about continuities and their importance in interpreting African-American culture.

ICONOCLASM AND ENGENDERED PERFORMANCE

Hurston's insistence on innovating forms to match the distinctiveness
she saw in African-American culture was not merely iconoclasm. "The
iconoclast," writes Mitchell, "prefers to think that he worships no images
of any sort, but when pressed, he is generally content with the rather different claim that his images are purer or truer than those of mere idol-
aters."[408] Rather, she was, along with contemporary critical observers
who have been working since the 1960s, offering a critique of the iconoclasm threatening to inhibit African-American cultural production.
Thus, her work not only introduces archetypal images but also provides
prototypes for critiques of cultural production imbedded in African-
American expressive forms. Hurston herself, as I have already suggested, is a prototype of the ritual agent whose role is not to be a model
but to be a kind of medium for social redress. Here, during what Victor
Turner calls the redressive phase of social drama, performance or ritual
emerges as a possible vehicle for change.

By referring to everyday language and behavior as African-American
hieroglyphics, Hurston makes an analogy between ancient Egyptian culture and black culture in the United States. The analogy suggests a common bond, perhaps in the multiple interpretations of both cultures'
origins. Also, the perceived need to interpret the languages, or the most

obvious expressive forms of both cultures, creates a mystique. Consequently, the ephemeral and the sacred are implied. More important, the association between ancient Egyptian hieroglyphics and a religious world view—which is to say, a ritualized belief system—is transferred to an African-American context.

It is not just that Hurston's interpretations of black culture depend on her special perceptive skills but that her way of seeing has its roots in an enigmatic idiom—less a style of presentation than a cult, less a form of representation than a system of emerging expressions. A statement such as "They say that Uncle Monday has a singing stone, and that is why he knows everything without being told" no longer seems to be line of spoken words from the mouth of an informant but a code for a universe Hurston exposes as outside the physical sciences and even remote from the ordinary social world and the sciences that seek to interpret it. She takes hold of her multiple talents—for listening/hearing, speaking, imagining, and crafting written texts—and empowers the senses through simple graphic display. Her skill bears more in common with the work of the playwright who, like a manual laborer or artisan, coordinates the senses in an effort to make concrete some structure.

More so than a playscript, however, her texts are enactments of "brilliant performances that reflect what Hurston termed the Afro-American's 'will to adorn.' "[409] The social dramas described in the tales become ritualized through intertextual icons. In my reading, the singing stone Uncle Monday is alleged to possess evokes the "small river-worn stones" and the "strong of small glass beads, crystal-clear 'like water,' " identified with Yemaya.[410] As the tale goes, "It is believed that he [Monday] has the singing stone, which is the greatest charm, the most powerful 'hand' in the world. It is a diamond and comes from the mouth of a serpent," living "in the deep waters of Lake Maitland" (110). Combining evocative mythic symbols, local geography and lore, Hurston renders a performative tale, engaging all the senses, drawing the reader into the sounds and tastes—into the space—where powerful "hands" affect movement. Also at work in that space is the ancestral time, invoking people "who have gone before to prepare the way with The Old Ones" and more who "will die in the attempt to conquer" the snake possessing the stone (110). The snake's two stones are knowledge ("embedded in her head") and a song, poetry, or language (found "in her mouth"). Knowledge and singing or tale telling are the meanings I interpret in Hurston's images. Suggesting much more than what it visually represented, the images are catalysts for stirring our perception to reach beyond the horizon of visible possibilities.

Interestingly, the snake's special knowledge "cannot be had without killing" her, while her song can only "be won by her from trickery." This supports the idea that the relationship between traditional knowledge and collective survival is ritualized through a dramatic performance in which the sacrificial agent in pivotal, as I argued at the end of Chapter Four. A collective, secular transformation defining African-American cultural identity can ensue through the actions of a pivotal individual, such as Hurston. Such a collective transformation has occurred as a result of symbolic actions represented in Hurston's work on sympathetic magic as recreated in her traditional tales.[411]

Before Uncle Monday, according to Hurston, Aunt Judy Bickerstaff was the preeminent hoodoo doctor in the area. A professional jealousy arose between them.

> Finally she [Aunt Judy Bickerstaff] began to say that she could reverse anything that he put down. She said she could not only reverse it, she could throw it back on *him*, let alone his client. Nobody talked to him about her boasts. People never talked to him except on business anyway. Perhaps Judy felt safe in boasting for this reason. (113)

As in the primary tale of Uncle Monday, the tale of Aunt Judy Bickerstaff is similar to the tale in *Dust Tracks* about the King of the 'Gators. The qualities both narratives share in common, again, have to do with the interplay between imagery and events, as well as the mythos suggested. In both stories, the female character is hurled into the lake by a power Hurston attributes to the male conjurer—an act which comes about because "it was the pride of one Hoodoo doctor to 'throw it back on the one that done it' " (a challenger). (59) The usurpation of the female conjurer's power by the male is Hurston's way of coming to terms with discrepancies between the sacred and secular worlds, and as suggested earlier, mythicizes a historical development. Her version of the conjure story, thus, becomes a vehicle for refiguring the traditional roles of men and women.

Although, as Wall has argued, there is good reason to say that women are empowered in the secular and religious tales reported in *Mules and Men*, unequal power relations are still a problem. Hurston seems to be showing that despite the prevalence of women as traditional healers, the mythic tradition perpetuates itself through male dominance. "The relative scarcity of woman-centered tales in the oral tradition must have been one of the revelations of Hurston's fieldwork," according to Wall.[112] To compensate for the absence of "tales about women told from a female point of view," Hurston had only to turn to her own recollections, not so much to her memory of tales she had heard as a child but her desire to escape the repetition of everyday life.[113] Thus she creates a tale told from a woman's perspective. At the same time, however, the tale performs a mythic function, explaining one notion of origins—in this case the process by which the male comes to dominate over the female.

Perhaps because "the most highly regarded types of performance in Afro-American culture, storytelling and sermonizing, for example, are in the main the province of men,"[114] Hurston's traditional tales, even when they are invented, must be filtered through the lens of gender to get across the overriding point she wishes to make in her work and which finally is made through the example set by her life. The established media for African-American cultural production traditionally have not made it possible for female expression to occupy a comfortable position alongside works (which is to say performances) created by men. Thus, the powerful "hands" Aunt Judy Bickerstaff used to make—all of the "hands" known in that vicinity, by Hurston's account—before Uncle Monday came, are neutralized and forgotten.

Although "within hoodoo, women were the spiritual equals of men," with "like authority to speak and to act," and although Hurston's greatest hoodoo teacher is a woman (Marie Leveau), Hurston's work and life still leave open the question of whether spiritual power is finally transferred to everyday life.[115] The only way the question can be considered resolvable is by seeing Hurston's legacy as a crucial link in a chain of transcendent symbolic actions. The symbolic actions are the African-American cultural productions created and performed throughout the historical period leading up to and following Hurston's productive period. They are transcendent in their capacity to extend beyond their immediate historical period, as Hurston's work, which influences subsequent work while also influencing the way the past is interpreted. In light of what I have already argued about the significance of an ancestral past in the mythic landscape represented in Hurston's texts, I consider the texts themselves ritual objects functioning as the means through which African-Americans collectively have been empowered to reconstitute the politics of cultural production which historically have dominated social relations, particularly with respect to gender.

10. *Scenes from* Mule Bone *with Daisy, Dave, and Jim.*

11. *A scene from* Mule Bone. *A confrontation between Rev. Singletary (played by Arthur French, far left) and Rev. Simms (played by Leonard Jackson, far right) on behalf of protagonists Dave and Jim.*

CHAPTER SIX

Staging Hurston's Life and Work

MULE BONE'S RESURRECTION

Long before the curtain arose the drama had begun. The major players were assembled: producer, literary executors, prospective directors, well-known actors, a lawyer. Meeting in the office of Gregory Mosher, a producer at Lincoln Center Theater in New York, the key players were to make a decision about whether to mount a commercial production of the 1931 play *Mule Bone, a Comedy of Negro Life*, written by Zora Hurston and Langston Hughes. Lincoln Center, being a major performing arts venue, had attracted a large gathering of black actors, playwrights, and directors to a discussion in one of the theater's rehearsal rooms, immediately preceding the meeting in Mosher's office. In both these encounters, pros and cons were being weighed in an avid debate over whether producing *Mule Bone* would be a viable pursuit in 1988.[416] Strong opinions on both sides of the question created the sort of tension associated with dramatic conflicts in plays. The dialogues that ensued can virtually stand on their own as dramatic literature. They show how ritualized action—in this instance, reading a play followed by discussions—can become a vehicle for communicating critical social differences among individuals often described as a monolithic community. The mini-drama of the *Mule Bone* debate illustrates that "the black community" is anything but monolithic. While a dispute over ownership of the play's rights had incited Hurston and Hughes to "fall out" and, thus, complicated the question of which author's aesthetic dominates the play, ownership of literary property rights has become an increasingly potent critical issue for artists as well as for scholars who question whether texts are ever governed by authors' intentions.

The conflict in *Mule Bone* is substantively different from the "real-life" conflict over how to stage the play. In both, dialogue is ordered around a central "bone of contention," and the conflict is resolved through catharsis among people directly at odds. In *Mule Bone*, on a casual afternoon in Eatonville, Florida, two young bluesmen, Jim and Dave, vie for the affection of a pretty young woman named Daisy. A subplot of *Their Eyes Were Watching God*, the conflict between Jim and Dave escalates in *Mule Bone* into a confrontation, when Jim assaults Dave with the tail bone of Matt Brazzle's dead mule.[417] Consequently, Jim is brought to trial in what proves to be as much a test of power relations between the Methodists and Baptists, as an effort to see justice prevail. A debate over whether a mule bone is in fact a weapon, based on either Christian or white law, produces a sequence combining biblical exegesis with a mockery of black self-government. The play resolves itself with both Jim and Dave rejecting Daisy when she apprises them of her dream to see her chosen mate employed in a secure job working for "white folks." I will move to a more detailed analysis of the play after enumerating the issues of proprietary rights surrounding the debate over *Mule Bone*'s 1991 production.

Both Gates, who initiated the production, and George Houston Bass, executor of Hughes's estate, had strong positions on the merits of the script, but different positions on whether anyone should have a right to tamper with the authors' work, long after their deaths. Bass was concerned with the unfinished status of the play; when Hurston and Hughes became irreconcilably embroiled in a clash because of an irrational disagreement over who had a rightful claim to the play, not only was it never produced during their lifetimes, it was never quite finished. Bass's view is supported by the evidence of numerous drafts deposited at various archives, although the one read at Lincoln Center is purported to be "the most complete draft . . . and the only one containing two scenes in Act Two."[418] The prospects for misrepresenting Hughes were too great and the stakes too high for doing so, in Bass's view. The play, as I will illustrate, because of its subject and comic style, had the potential to entertain or to alienate spectators—or both, or neither. In other words, the play reverberates on different wave lengths, depending on the spectators. More important, though, Bass saw a need to revise the script into an adaptation that would sharpen the play's structure as Hurston and Hughes might have created it had they reached the production stage.

The distinction between creative liberty and usurping an author's work in play production has perplexed traditionalists since the rise of avant-garde theater in the twentieth century, particularly since Bertolt Brecht pursued his ground-breaking work in the 1920s.[419] Brecht confronted the issue with his play *The Threepenny Opera* (1928), an adaptation of *The Beggar's Opera*, by the eighteenth century English playwright John Gay. Accused of plagiarizing a translation of Gay's play, Brecht became engaged in a dispute over property rights. Although he spoke derisively of the "bourgeois" ethics that assign material value to artistic work, he resolved the legal issue in his own favor.[420] His example set a precedent for modern theater amid changing conceptions of the role directors should have in creating performances. Avant-garde artists, following Brecht's lead, pose the questions: Are not directors equal partners in the creative process that results in a finished production? Are performers any the less creators, as well? As both a director and a playwright, Brecht innovated a dramaturgical approach to play production with the Berliner Ensemble and made collective creation seem viable, since he encouraged actors to work collaboratively on productions. Much emphasis was placed on visual documentation of productions to make stylistic choices accessible for future productions.[421] The availability of a production's history, in written form, is a critical element in staging a play such as *Mule Bone*, as with any play deemed to be of historical interest, a period piece. With *Mule Bone*, the challenges to proprietary questions were compounded by an uncertainty about Hurston's and Hughes' collaboration—what they intended versus how their relationship ended. Having never been produced, the play had no production history, so there was no original version against which the proposed 1991 production could be restored. Bass passionately broached the question of how to approach "an unfinished work." He asked, "Dare we, 57 years after two recognized geniuses of our cultural tradition, presume that we can complete their work? If we take on the responsibility to produce the play, it seems to me inherent that we must be presumptuous" (Mule Bone R 16). He was in favor of proceeding just as he would in preparing any other script for performance, with the significant difference being no authors to consult. At Brown University's Rites and Reason Theater, where he was Artistic Director, Bass instituted a research-to-performance method of production; he approached a play as if it were community property, to be made accessible to the people most likely to have strong opinions about its content. The goal was to open lines of communication between playwrights and other theater artists, scholars, and people in the community who ultimately stand to gain or to be hurt by depictions of a world in which they feel they have a stake. Questioning the logic of ignoring public taste and concern, Bass asked: "Dare we move into that troubled terrain and open ourselves up to another kind of criticism?" He argued with fervor for the artists involved with the *Mule Bone* production to adopt an open-minded attitude toward public opinion. "Unless we do that, I think what we've heard here [in the pre-production discussions] is only a glimmer of what we would hear in the public arena as people debate the merits of this text. The text has merits, there's no question about that, and the changes can be made. But the question for me is: how do we, as theater practitioners, assume the authority to finish an unfinished work?" (Mule Bone R 19)* According to Hughes's biographer Arnold Rampersad, what the text might have been had the authors completed it is an irrelevant issue; the play was never produced because Hughes and Hurston "had a falling out."[422] Although Bass thought leaving the text in its unfinished form would expose the producers to criticism for its flaws, he was convinced that Hurston and Hughes "understood the creative process of theater," meaning, they were aware that a script is not a fixed concept. "They knew that in the rehearsal process a script is changed," he argued (Mule Bone PD 7).**

The authors' knowledge about the production process aside, Bass also introduced the sensitive dilemma of Hughes's reputation. Bass voiced concern that Hughes's integrity might be jeopardized if the play were construed as stereotypical. Motivated to protect Hughes, Bass intimated, "Hughes suffered enough in his own life. He does not need to be dug up and beat up again because we misunderstand his aesthetic intention and purpose" (Mule Bone PD 8). Rampersad held the view that

*Citations designated Mule Bone R refer to the discussion immediately following the reading of one play in a rehearsal room at Lincoln Center Theater. (Unpublished transcript, New York: Lincoln Center Theater, November 28, 1988.) In addition to the people I quote, participants in the Mule Bone discussion included actors Paul Winfield, Isabell Monk, Christine Campbell, Brenda Thomas, Graham Brown, Roger Robinson, Giancarlo Esposito, Richard Gant, Ruby Dee, Joe Morton, and Minnie Gentry; playwrights Ntozake Shange, Ron Milner, and Steve Carter; director Oz Scott; and Peggy Davis, Professor of Law at New York University.
**Citations designated Mule Bone PD refer to the discussion following the rehearsal room discussion. The second discussion occurred in Producer Gregory Mosher's office. (Unpublished transcript, New York: Lincoln Center Theater, November 28, 1988.)

Hughes would have enjoyed hearing the play being read at Lincoln Center (that afternoon). Not only did "Hughes put on worse plays than this himself" (Mule Bone PD 13), according to Rampersad, the fact that Hughes is "not in a position now to be unhappy" (Mule Bone PD 14) precludes any concerns an executor or anyone else should have about the playwright's hypothetical reaction to a production of his work. Rampersad argued, "if we can put on *Love's Labors Lost*, we can put on a flawed play by Hughes and Hurston" (Mule Bone PD 7). In other words, Shakespeare's mature work doesn't get diminished by an early comedy ranked below his great work, so why should Hughes's or Hurston's.[423] Rampersad's view was corroborated by Gates: both agreed that "the play as written by Hughes and Hurston should be respected" (Mule Bone PD 6–7). Both Gates and Rampersad insisted the text stands on its own merit. "I didn't actually know Zora Neale Hurston," said Gates, "but I'm representing her here and I'm not arrogant enough to tamper with" her text (Mule Bone PD 14). According to Gates, "Zora wanted to get the play produced. She didn't have any problems with the play." (Mule Bone R 17) Although "the play is Hurston's much more than it is Langston Hughes'" (Mule Bone PD 6)—a point conceded by the participants in the reading and discussions—according to Rampersad, "Hughes had no real problems with the play," no "objections to the play itself" (Mule Bone R 16).

When a text is viewed according to a literary definition, which accords permanence to the written word not so much in contrast with spoken language as over and above the nonverbal, including the paralinguistic and kinesic dimensions of the text, the text's meaning beyond what an author intended remains a question. To what extent is it possible to know what the author had in mind or to know what choices an author would have made when confronted, for example, with the difficulties of realizing written images in performance? Or, more pertinent to the sorest point of the *Mule Bone* debate, if the social and political climate seem to dictate subtle rather than flamboyant humor, to what extent is it possible to speculate on how Hurston and Hughes would think in the current context? "It's futile to say that Zora Neale Hurston and Langston Hughes would have written a different kind of play if they were writing today" (Mule Bone R 4), argued the actor Graham Brown.

What becomes apparent from the *Mule Bone* debate is the inflammability of the line between politics and art. The crucial question of who has the authority to stage an unfinished play cannot be separated from the question of who owns a play. Since staging it is a collective enterprise and a process, do not the playwrights relinquish a certain amount of their claim to the finished product? A script, as wrought by an author, must necessarily take a different form when translated to the stage. This basic tenent of contemporary directing, so well known to Bass, is at odds with the literary notion of a text as a static, tangible, entity in its own right. Declining to produce an author's work as written, according to Gates, is censorship, and "censorship is to art as lynching is to justice" (Mule Bone R 17). (Applause followed his remark.) Leaving aside the perception that suppressing artists' work is tantamount to mob violence, it is important to note that the inclination to resist suppression of any kind is well grounded in Gates's heroic and successful mission to restore and legitimize lost work by African-American writers, as well as in a conscientious attitude toward social justice. Rampersad concurs with Gates's point about censorship. "The will to censor the black artist is still fairly strong in the community, and that's very unfortunate," Rampersad said.[124] There is a problem, however, in seeing the debate surrounding *Mule Bone* as a matter of being compelled to stage the play because not to do so would be censorship. Questions as to whether the play ought to be staged teeter on a narrow line between art and politics. If to forego presenting the play is censorship, then staging it must mean any work by a great author needs to be seen performed, even if the author, like Shakespeare with *Love's Labors Lost*, created a text less perfect than plays showing greater mastery of the craft. But who is to say that even all of Shakespeare's plays ought to be staged? "We're not talking about censorship. We're talking about craft," Bass insisted (Mule Bone R 17). When trying to decipher the merits of a play, producers can claim no triumph if to stage it is a travesty while not to stage it is an act of political repression. The idea that a play assumes a life of its own through the terms established in the script is a contested area of theater practice. The privileging of a written script has been challenged, historically, since avant-garde theater gained ascendancy beginning at the end of the nineteenth century. Both Hughes and Hurston can be positioned within the historical avant garde, even if one may resist doing so because the traditional folk styles they favored and the modernist styles associated with avant-garde work seem diametrically opposed. Such a resistance is unfounded, however, for both authors were skilled at combining aesthetics.

When attempting to evaluate a play on its own terms, what does it mean to arrive at the conclusion that the play is a "classic"? Gates asserts he "suggested this play to Greg [Mosher] because it seemed to me that it was a lost classic of the African-American experience and we have a chance to resurrect that play from the dead" (Mule Bone R 17). Committed to the idea that *Mule Bone* is a classic, Gates took the initiative to have it produced by giving the manuscript to Mosher. The viability of the play's production would rest, according to Gates, in the text's appeal to the public's familiarity with Hurston and Hughes. The assumption that the authors' reputations would attract audiences was an impetus in making the production "a literary event." Gates proposed the title "An Evening of Langston Hughes and Zora Neale Hurston" and suggested framing the play's performance "with readings from some of their other works" (Mule Bone PD 1–2). Rampersad concurred with the "classic" idea, although in different terms: "It's a very successful play," he asserted, "I think it should be presented as the world premier of a long lost comedy by Langston Hughes and Zora Neale Hurston, and that is that" (Mule Bone PD 7). He did not make his reasons for calling the play successful apparent during the debate; however, the weight of his judgment lies in his authority as a scrupulous commentator on Hughes in particular and the period, in general. "I think it's a wonderful thing to stage a play that these two great writers created and that has never been presented. It's a spectacular opportunity," Rampersad said (Mule Bone PD 7).

Ultimately, to attach "classic" status to a text is to grant it authority. "An authoritative text, by definition, is one that is maximally protected from compromising transformation," according to Richard Bauman and Charles Briggs."[425] The text, consequently, has a higher status than the people who might alter it and thus is elevated to a position fixed above and beyond the desires, preferences, and tastes brought to bear on a specific performance context.

Between the text and the circumstances surrounding its performance, a tension arises. This tension, manifested in the debate surrounding *Mule Bone*'s production, is born out of the struggle to resolve, in practice, a theoretical problem. And at the core, the problem itself consists of the ambiguous relationship between theory and practice. The dilemna centers on whether to view *Mule Bone* as a text, as a potential performance of a text, or as a performance text. Unlike Hurston's unscripted productions of the 1930s, *Mule Bone*, though drawing upon some of the same material as the other productions, could not be reconstructed based on programs, photos, or other evidence of its full meaning as a staged event. The meaning a performance acquires as an event can, according to Bauman and Briggs, be separated from its context. Indeed, they argue, a unique attribute of performance is its capacity to stand on its own—to *become* a text including all the discourses surrounding it subsumed under the umbrella of its detachable meaning. Its detachability ensures not that the context will determine what the performance is to be but that the discourses emerging as part of the context are implicit in the performance. Thus, the staged version of *Mule Bone* must necessarily contain ambivalent messages—the pros and cons of what is to be realized and how.

Once the group gathered at Lincoln Center decided to produce the play, Bass was asked to revise the text as he thought it should be, although the final decision about which text should prevail was to be reserved until his version could be reviewed by the producers. Bass agreed, and put the play through a workshop at Rites and Reason, which included a staged reading with a discussion forum, during the winter of 1989–1990. His revision was not used for the production; however, the final production script did take into account some of the pleas for the staging to include more of a context for the remote turn-of-the-century world of the play. Michael Schultz, who at the time of the 1988 reading had not yet been named as the director, was emphatic in stating his position on the need for framing: "I don't think you can do this play in today's time without having some kind of frame for it because of all the political ramifications," he said (Mule Bone PD 5). Thus, for the Broadway production a prologue was added, a monologue of Hurston (played by Joy Lee, who also plays Teets) recalling her opening lines in *Mules and Men*: "I was glad when somebody told me 'You may go out and collect Negro folklore.' " Taken almost verbatim from *Mules and Men*, this opening speech summarizes the circumstances surrounding Hurston's first field research trip to Eatonville, Florida, under the auspices of Boas. The beginning sequence is followed by an interlude with Dave, Jim, and Daisy. "Jim. Jim. Lissen to dis new hambone rhyme I made up in my sleep last night," Dave says. Through song, he enters a contest with Jim for Daisy and "wins," getting to walk her home. The Zora character returns with the entering set: "Folk-lore is not as easy to collect as it sounds," she continues. Her description of the Eatonville hometown she remembers from childhood becomes a fade-out, as the frame shifts; the scene Hurston describes comes into full focus, an on-stage "enlargement of life." The concept here was to foreground the action of the play by illustrating that the world portrayed is drawn from supposed ethnographic sources. Ultimately, this approach was akin to mounting a museum piece for exhibition. Bass's version, similarly, included a frame, projecting a vision of the play rooted in his sense that Hughes's blues aesthetic was more prominent and, therefore, should give the play its (unrealized) structure.

> The play begins and ends at the same place and nothing happens. But something does happen. It's the blues. It's an exorcising of pain, of grief, of anger, of rage. It's people at war with themselves, trapped with a historical predicament beyond their control, and there is a structure there. A specific structure that is enunciated subtly. But, because they did not have the dramaturgical skills yet to know it [note on early point in careers of Hughes and Hurston] they did not pursue the opportunity to work it out. (Mule Bone R 16)

In Bass's opening, Jim and Dave poeticize their lives as blues musicians, and the entire cast joins in a ritualized poem shedding light on the fantasy life behind their collective everyday reality. Dave begins: "When I get to be a composer/I'm gonna write me some music about/Daybreak in Alabama." To which the Actors respond: "And I'm gonna put the purtiest songs in it/ Rising out of the ground like a swamp mist/ And falling out of heaven like soft dew./ I'm gonna put some tall trees in it/ And the scent of pine needles/ And the smell of red clay after rain. . ." (4).

Both production scripts differ from the published text. When the "authorized" version of the script was turned over to Mosher, analyzed by dramaturg Anne Cattaneo, and entrusted to Schultz, the decision was to restore the original text, to add a musical score composed by blues musician Taj Mahal and based on the blues poetry of Hughes, and to stage the play on Broadway at the Ethel Barrymore Theater—all of this in addition to the prologue extracted from *Mules and Men*. It is this variation from the "authorized" text that speaks to the demands implicit in adapting a literary text for performance. There is simply no way literally to translate written words to the stage.

Bass and Rampersad considered the content of *Mule Bone* to be composed of Hurston's content in its use of stories, characters, and the setting of her folklore and of Hughes's dramatic structure; both authors were relatively new to the craft of playwriting when they collaborated on the play in 1931. Based on "The Bone of Contention," a short story of

Hurston's, purported to be a folktale she collected, *Mule Bone* has a straightforward plot revolving around a confrontation between two young men over Daisy, a confrontation that results in one being assaulted. The striking differences between the story and the play rest with the changes in the plot. Whereas "The Bone of Contention" turns upon a dispute over who has rightful claim to a turkey both young men were hunting, its central focus is an ensuing rigmarole among Baptists and Methodists—the only two churches in town, with the members of each denomination claiming allegiance to one young man. As Hurston writes: "It was evident to the simplest person in the village long before three oclock that this was to be a religious and political fight. The assault and the gobbler were unimportant." ("The Bone of Contention," *Mule Bone* 33) Although the play's plot is simplified and its focus redirected, with the turkey being replaced by a female (pun intended?), its structure is rather complexly organized around a cast of thirty-some characters, storytelling sequences, and a long trial scene in the second act. With music and dancing added, the Broadway production was envisioned as a celebration of the play's rare glimpse into an intimate social subtext. As Gates describes: "It's like overhearing a cultural ritual practiced by black people when no white people are around."[426]

Although the prevailing concept for the production was to remain close to the script in realistic detail, an attempt was made to historicize the debut of the play, by inviting the public to a series of panels and forums on topics related to the work and lives of the playwrights. These events, ostensibly held to encourage awareness of the cultural history surrounding the play, also worked as a form of audience development. Indeed, by the time the play went up, as Hurston prophesied, "the mule remained with them in song and story as simile, as a metaphor, to point a moral or adorn a tale" ("The Bone of Contention" *Mule Bone* 28). *Mule Bone* had become a sign of larger social and political trials than the play's clinching argument over whether a mule bone presented as evidence in an assault case is a weapon. In keeping with an opinion voiced by Rick Kahn, director of Crossroads Theater, the play's elaborate structure could not be faulted for confusing the authors' intentions. "The biggest problem is not so much the structure, it's something else," he said (*Mule Bone* PD 8). Kahn agreed with Schultz, who perhaps stated the issue most succinctly when he noted that despite "how good the artistry is" artists have a social responsibility because "artistry is always interpreted based on the political context" (*Mule Bone* PD 5).

Emphasizing the play's folk content became a way to diffuse political controversy anticipated in connection with the production. It can be argued, however, that *Mule Bone* is an aestheticized representation of black folk culture. The insecurities Gates and Rampersad see as black spectators' discomfort with everything unglamorous in their heritage is a side-effect rather than a cause for all the clamor surrounding *Mule Bone*'s controversial debut. Opposing views about whether the play speaks for or against black humanity are similar to the ambivalent responses provoked when ethnographic subjects are put on display. The folklorist Barbara Kirshenblatt-Gimblett has provided insight into the way that perceptions change according to how artifacts and cultural performances are framed. For example, she shows how a "museum effect" occurs when everyday objects and activities are framed and mounted. They become aesthetic artifacts, cultural performances, glimpses of the quotidien in relief: the ordinary becomes special, and the exhibited version of the ordinary becomes a model for lived experience. By analogy, in the *Mule Bone* drama, something deemed authentic black culture is given special status and in turn held up as a measure of black spectators' lifestyles. The ambiguity involved with making ordinary life into art and then using the work to set standards for behavior makes staging folk culture a difficult step toward freeing artists from either stereotypes or efforts to suppress them. As with ethnographic museum displays, particularly when live people are included and thus become "signs of themselves," in Kirshenblatt-Gimblett's terms, "repulsion and attraction, condemnation and celebration [are] typical of the reception"; the ambivalent response "reveals that the source of the critique is also the basis of the appeal."[427]

In a sense, *Mule Bone* contains no folklore—which is to say, it has no ethnographic content, as the Broadway production script suggests—in the same sense that *Their Eyes* contains none. In her unpublished essay "The Chick with One Hen," a commentary on Locke's review of *Their Eyes*, Hurston argues, "There is not a folk tale in the entire book. A folk *character*[428] *is mentioned* in one connection that does not affect the story in any way."[429] Using a strict definition of the term "folklore," Hurston tries here to be more lucid about her writing technique than she ordinarily is known to be. *Their Eyes* contains the stuff of which folklore is made, while the storytelling situations in the book are representations of folklife. The technical distinction between folklife and depictions of folklore is the difference between ritual and descriptions of ritualistic events. Hurston's fictional recreations of folklife are taken as folklore generally, because of her skillful use of ritualistic language—hieroglyphics encoded with nonverbal signs. Here the process of entextualization explains how folklore which is performative is represented in the text but in turn becomes a distinct variety of text. Rather than being composed of folklore, the text is a commentary on folklife—indeed, at times is critical of folklife, as the numerous examples of Janie's nonconformity attest.

Whether *Mule Bone* offers a commentary on folklife is not so much the question in the debates surrounding the production. There seems little doubt that everyone coming into contact with the play can readily see the humor has targets among all strata in the small-town setting, a microcosm of the segment one might take to be "the black community." Because the comedic quality of the play can be viewed as broadly pertaining to black folklife, its style is similar to broad portrayals in vaudeville, burlesque, and (more damning) the minstrel show—where characters tend to be types rather than fully developed people. Schultz as well as others directly engaged in the production were acutely aware of disadvantages broad portrayals present. They sought to counter the depersonalized style broad "typing" produces. In an effort to be more sensitive to the sense of community felt to be a distinguishing feature of the play, as Cattaneo noted, Lincoln Center Theater strove for a romantic portrait. Thus, it is no accident that the show opened on St. Valentine's Day. Although sympathetic observers, including critics, have taken the play as loving and quaint in its manner of poking fun at ordinary human foibles, and although I, too, enjoyed the nostalgia, delightful familiarity, and charm of the Broadway production, in my view, the play comes close to being a parody of black folklife. At the same time, it manages not to recede into minstrelsy. It has a jocular innocence, similar to the humor found in other Hughes plays, even though the content of the play is derived from Hurston's work. For example, the children mime hawks and chickens in a game of chick-me, chick-me, cranie crow. The hawks' preying upon the chickens mirrors the action of a checkers game that occupies a large episode of Act One. This mirroring, like the musical vying for Daisy's attention in the opening sequence, is to magnify that the central action is formally structured as a contest. Similarly, the card game Florida Flip introduces elements of cunning and chance into the fabric of the play. The humor in *Mule Bone* generally is broader than in Hurston's other plays—*The Fiery*

Chariot and *The First One*, for example. Nevertheless, Hughes's humor in plays like *Simply Heavenly* and *Little Ham* make conscious use of framing devices to alert readers (and viewers) to the tone and tenor of comedic references, providing implicitly in the structure the double-edged blues ribaldry. This is not always the case in *Mule Bone*, as became evident during the production stage.

Replete with sayings that give the work a texture uniquely identifiable with Hurston's milieu, the play does at times invoke oral tradition, while adding a modern gloss. The following tale, for example, is recounted in a similar fashion as tales are told in *Mules and Men*:

> Lige: Say, dat puts me in de mind of a Baptist brother that was crazy 'bout de preachers and de preacher was crazy 'bout feeding his face. So his son got tired of trying to beat dese stump-knockers to de grub on the table, so one day he throwed out some slams 'bout dese preachers. Dat made his old man mad, so he tole his son to git out. He boy ast him, "Where must I go, papa?" He says, "Go to hell I reckon. . . . I don't keer where you go."
>
> So de boy left and was gone seven years. He come back one cold, windy night and rapped on de door. "Who dat?" de old man ast him. "It's me, Jack." De old man opened de door, so glad to see his son agin, and tole Jack to come in. He did and looked all round de place. Seven or eight preachers was sitting round de fire eatin' and drinkin'.
>
> "Where you been all dis time, Jack?" de old man ast him.
>
> "I been to hell," Jack tole him.
>
> "Tell us how it is down there, Jack."
>
> "Well," he says, "It's just like it is here . . . you cain't git to de fire for de preachers."

Here, as in *The Fiery Chariot* and "How the Woodpecker Nearly Drowned the Whole World," Hurston uses vernacular expression—an ordinary yarn told within the context of a male bonding ritual, a "lying session"—to counter the stereotypical idea that black religion is a naive sort of faith similar to the romanticized devotion so carefully drawn by Harriet Beecher Stowe's characterization of the slave Tom in *Uncle Tom's Cabin*. Hell is more present than heaven, on the porch, and too, is a reflection of everyday life. The romanticizing, in *Mule Bone*'s Broadway production, of a scene critiquing the romanticization of black folk culture, creates ambiguous frame for the play. The critique, romanticized, gets neutralized and thus leaves the audience to speculate as to whether characters themselves are the target of parody or whether a world in which ordinary folks' lives are trivialized is the target.

"Much of Hurston's work (and life) used conventions of self-parody," according to Bass. In an attempt to come to terms with Hurston's theory of mimicry, Bass speculated about her conception of its practice in black culture and the consequent implications for the stage. "Hurston's use of self-parody is very complex in that she takes the black comic masks of popular culture and enlarges them through exaggeration," said Bass.* The workshop at Rites and Reason was conducted in an attempt to resolve performance-related difficulties discussed at the Lincoln Center reading in 1988. At Rites and Reason, the play-development process created by Bass emphasizes playwriting and directing based on historical and sociological research.

Not unlike Hurston's method of staging productions using material she collected while doing folklore research, the research-to-performance concept at Rites and Reason stems from Bass's awareness that black theater and other ethnic theaters can increase their viability when research on cultural history is integrated into the artistic process. Intrigued by the means through which cultural traditions, particularly performance traditions, are passed on, Bass, as a director, passed on to performers his understanding of traditional forms of expression as they are practiced in their social context. More important, he focused on how the forms of folk expression take on different meanings when staged. Staging Hurston's work places one in the complex situation of reenacting parodic social rituals such as the "lying sessions" on Joe Clarke's porch vividly re-created in *Mule Bone*. In trying not to create a performance in which literal and naturalistic interpretations of the text lead to realistic staging conventions, Bass sought to avoid turning a parodic play into a parody of itself.

The Broadway production of *Mule Bone* is a landmark in American theater history because for the first time mainstream theater produced a play by a nonliving major black playwright. In this case, two major black writers were involved in an intriguing personal and professional conflict which ended their friendship, all of which has been brought to public attention through the publication of *Mule Bone*, in a volume edited by Bass and Gates, including letters documenting the real-life drama. There is no better place to begin establishing Hurston's importance as a challenge to the aesthetic direction of black theater, in par-

*George Bass, "Editor/Dramaturg's Notes on *Mule Bone*." Unpublished paper (Providence, R.I.: Rites and Reason Theatre, Brown University, 1989), unnumbered pages.

ticular, and American theater, in general, than with the precedent set by *Mule Bone*. In my view the aesthetic challenges she poses were illuminated rather than resolved in the production.[430]

The main aesthetic issues, as already suggested, center around the contradictions in reproducing literally that which is meant to be parodic. The aesthetic issues took form in the rehearsal process. Casting and directing the performers, according to Schultz, depended on their "having a natural affinity with the dialect," on their feeling an emotional and psychological connection with the heritage of the characters. In New York City, locating performers with the range to handle the language of early twentieth century rural Florida and to perform comic roles without using broad portrayals common in popular, variety entertainment, presented a challenge, as well. It points to the need for specialized training, following the model of the workshop and rehearsal process practiced at Rites and Reason. Indeed, Bass's ideas about the need to codify styles of movement, gesture, facial expression, and voice intonation in black performance seem to address the training requirements for a production like *Mule Bone*, drawn from the folk culture of a remote historical period. The objective is to develop dramaturgical methods for black theater, methods that can be transferred from a community context to a major commercial venue. Because such a method has yet to be developed, adapting works for the stage from the canon of early black writers can result in a short run, as happened with *Mule Bone*.

Despite predominantly favorable critical responses, the play's early closing is symptomatic of some hazards involved in tilting the balance too far toward the text as a medium for measuring the auhenticity of an author's work. When directors and performers assume liberties and refigure a text according to the demands of a particular performance context, the results can be provocative and engage audiences on a number of levels, even over extended runs. The work of director and playwright George Wolfe stands as an example of the importance innovative approaches to texts can have on a show's running time. His adaptation of Hurston's short stories, *Spunk* is discussed later in this chapter. Interestingly, the one severe critical response to *Mule Bone*, voiced by Frank Rich in *The New York Times*, though unsympathetic to the romanticized tone of the production, praises the performances. Enthusiasm over the cast was consistent in all of the reviews and supports my idea that through performance, over and above the words from which performances emerge, Hurston's texts acquire another meaning apart from the script. The reviewers' responses show how a performance can be contextualized, to employ another term Bauman and Briggs associate with the detachability of discourses and the performances they engender. Indeed, reviewers single out some actors for special mention because their performances in *Mule Bone* can be compared with previous stage appearances. The actors, thus, "carry" the revered text and become its raison d'etre; the formidable text becomes an opportunity to treat audiences to the talents and charms of adored personalities. This consequence need not be the primary value of a performance. In the *Mule Bone* resurrection, decontextualizing the performance, divorcing the actors' accomplishments from the play and from the staged event as a whole, is another by-product of the controversy behind the production. Bauman and Briggs assert that social power is exerted through processes that involve extrapolating from texts. "To decontextualize and recontextualize a text is thus an act of control," they write.[431] Imbalances of power can be accentuated through separating, for example, commendable performances at the expense of the text's authority; reviewers then see performers as unjustly beholden to flawed directional and authorial choices. This was the view of *New York Times* critic Rich, whose tough criticism must be seen as aiding in the show's demise. *Mule Bone*, nevertheless, retains its legendary significance in black theater history.

POLK COUNTY: PERFORMANCE IN THE ARCHIVE

The popular, critical, and commercial success or failure of a production has significance for the current Hurston revival because her work and life are a focal point for the convergence of ideology and aesthetics. While seeking financial benefits as well as broad audiences, Hurston was determined not to compromise her aesthetic preferences. She was conscious of the need for growth and willingly worked on projects she considered merely a means to an end. Whether *Polk County, a Comedy of Negro Life on a Sawmill Camp*, a play she co-authored with Dorothy Waring in 1944, qualifies among her efforts to survive or to continue her commitment to the development of the type of black drama she thought would have an import on public perceptions of black culture is not clear.[432] When Dorothy Waring suggested they model the work after Gershwin's style, Hurston was mortified by Waring's lack of knowledge and perhaps also by her insensitivity. Though never produced or published, *Polk County* illustrates Hurston's aesthetic concerns. The plot centers on the courtship, engagement, and marriage between Leafy Lee, a young new arrival to the camp, and My Honey, a worker, as well as on the friendship between Big Sweet and Leafy. Leafy, in contrast with Big Sweet and the other women in the camp, has more refined manners—that is, she does not use violence to solve her problems and expects her relationship with My Honey to result in marriage, when common-law arrangements are customary. Her rival, Dicey, resorts to vicious tactics to fight for her claim to My Honey, but because Big Sweet finds Leafy to be a trustworthy friend, she uses her considerable strength to shield Leafy. These episodes mirror the situation from which Hurston escapes in *Mules and Men*. The play has the ending of a classic romantic comedy, complete with a wedding scene requiring that a rainbow carry away the surviving, happy characters. Although it reflects some crude circumstances that are part of black culture, it is written as light comedy, with each scene being an opportunity for illustrating the way expressive culture often emerges from harsh situations (as a way of fashioning an alternative view of the world).

Because *Polk County* draws heavily from *Mules and Men*, including its autobiographical episodes, Hurston's role in the collaboration seems to have been dominant. Set at the Loften Lumber Company "deep in the primeval woods of South Central Florida," *Polk County* transports the would-be spectator to a location as far from the glittering, sophisticated world of Broadway theater as could be imagined. This is not an imaginary world, but a place where an ironically sad logic causes one character, Lonnie, to question why, in addition to being poor and without power or authority, people in the camp have troubles: "We ain't got nothing but the little wages we makes," he says. "Looks like then us ought not to be bothered with trouble. That's for big, rich folks that got their many pleasures. Why we got to have troubles too?" The irony arises because the trouble to which Lonnie refers has to do with his girlfriend Big Sweet's being ordered to leave the camp after killing a man (the fourth she has murdered); otherwise, the Boss says to her, she will have to face the Judge who has said the next time she comes "up before him for a killing" he would "go hard" on her, meaning she will get ninety days in the county jail. Here it is possible to see the bitter sensibility expressed in the blues and implicit in the spells and curses of Hoodoo. Both the blues and Hoodoo are used in the play as vehicles for articulating an alternative value system. In the speech just mentioned, involving Lonnie's remarks on why Big Sweet's and his troubles seem unwarranted, harmonica playing and chanting inflect the spoken words. Similarly, the character Dicey, who seeks to resolve her problems through Hoodoo, communicates deeply rooted bitterness over being "ugly," by singing an indictment against her rivals—Big Sweet and Leafy Lee, who are lighter skinned than Dicey. Her song resembles the laments of Hurston's other two characters afflicted with self-despisement—Emmaline of *Color Struck* and Arvay in *Seraph on the Suwannee*. In *Polk County*, though, Hurston very directly demonstrates that cultural performances are the means through which rivalries and other social conflicts are resolved.

The terms "autotext" and "autoperformance" come to mind when reading *Polk County*. "Autotext" or "autoperformance" can be defined as any rendition or performance in which the author/performer is also the subject of the text. Although Zora Hurston is not the name of a character in *Polk County*, Hurston's personal experiences are part of the plot. Moreover, the autobiographical dimension does not in itself mean that the play needs to be conceived as anything other than a drama *about* events overlapping with Hurston's field research. In this sense, there is no difference between an autobiographical play and a fictional one. We expect actors to assume the characters' roles, while the playwright remains in the background. *Polk County*'s unperformed status only helps to reinforce the idea that it is an autoperformance. Hurston does not stay in the background. Once again, we are able to see the way her words provide access to a third dimension: the enlargement of her life and work becomes a ritualized transference to previous moments from her field trips, fiction and theatrical productions. Hurston was resisting a trivialized fulfillment of her theatrical desire, just as the importance of guarding against the commercialization of her work informs the *Mule Bone* episode.

RECREATING THE LEGACY

Being the Character: Holder's Hurston

According to Laurence Holder, author of *Zora Neale Hurston*, she was misunderstood by most people. Holder's affinity with that form of social and intellectual alienation made him feel capable of writing a convincing character. His play examines some of the threats to Hurston's genius and some of the reasons her being misunderstood also meant being mistreated by the art world.[433] "At age 49, I am on my way home, I'm broke and am explaining and exploring, asking and answering the question—'How did I get that way?'" This is how Van Dyke, the lead actress, describes the basic situation, the central action which gives the performance its structure.[434] In creating a play that tries to present the tragic aspects of Hurston's life, Holder has found a medium that enables a female performer such as Van Dyke to embody the spirit of the neglected genius, while reviving the powerful human forces which drove Hurston to create and to leave a legacy. Originally a one-character script, the play presented at American Place Theater in New York in 1989 included a male actor, Tim Johnson, playing various men with strong influences on Hurston's life—Herbert Sheen (her first husband), Langston Hughes, Alain Locke, and Richard Wright. The male characters seem to encircle Hurston, confining her to a mold, but no one knows exactly why the shape of the mold is drawn as it is since it never reproduces a perfect Hurston, at least not to the men who judge and condemn her.

Juxtaposed with her male peers, Hurston, although surrounded and entrapped, remains unwilling to submit to their pressures. Lack of submissiveness seems to cause her demise, according to the trajectory established in the play. In her relationships with men, a difficult arena where the stakes are high, Hurston encounters problems, from her earliest years with her father, through a short-lived marriage and her outstanding career. The play outlines her life, allowing the autobiographical details to determine the dramatic structure. Because Hurston's fascinating life, including her unbelievable disappearance from public attention, propels the drama, the production has demonstrated its power to attract audiences; it has been touring nationally in its current form since 1988.

Bursting from the mold imposed by the scrutiny of male characters, Van Dyke exudes Hurston's energy, flamboyance, and style in a radiating performance. Van Dyke's own exuberance comes across in the glow of her face and eyes, the spring of her dance steps, in the range of her voice—from low and throaty to loud and forceful, to sweet and eloquent. With a red scarf, signifying the brilliance of an era and a woman who thrived in the limelight, Van Dyke mimes clothing accessories like belts, boas, and bandannas, illustrating Hurston's elegant style and versatility.

Much of the lore about Hurston emphasizes the irrepressible quality of her character, her capacity to mesmerize, to command the center of attention, and to confound. Her life has inspired intriguing dramas also because of her entanglements with socially prominent people. "When sources said she was bold, brash, or brazen, I incorporated that because it is a clue to her character," said Van Dyke. Hurston's animated story-telling at fashionable parties and her ability to command an audience, present challenges for Van Dyke which she effectively meets by elaborating factual details about Hurston, using her autobiography and Robert Hemenway's biography, embellishing the facts with a subjunctive mood, a sense of what might have been, how Hurston might have looked based on her photos, how she might have walked, posed, gestured. When Van Dyke tells a tale from Hurston's folklore collection, "Why Women Always Take Advantage of Men," for example, placed within the context of an awards reception where Hurston decides to entertain everyone by telling a story, the audience watching the play becomes a collective character in the drama and eventually becomes the collective witness of her life's tragedy.

Because of the blurred boundaries between past and present, changes occur from one performance to the next. Although the script remains the same, "in some places people had no idea who Zora was and some adjustments were made," said Van Dyke. At a performance at the Billie Holiday Theater in Brooklyn, New York, Van Dyke coaxed her audience by breaking further through the fourth wall than already occurs in the production; she directly addressed people in the audience when reenacting certain scenes such as Hurston's trip to Harlem as an anthropology student of Franz Boas, to measure head sizes. Van Dyke pointed and called out to specific people: "Hey, you, there, how would you like to be part of an experiment?" In contrast, at a performance presented by the Paul Robeson Performing Arts Company in Syracuse, New York, Van Dyke was able to build toward the high moments in part through the energy supplied by an audience that laughed at all the jokes and remained hypnotically still during sad moments. The play's flexibility from one context to another exemplifies the kind of bridge-building Hurston envisioned for her own theatrical work.

Van Dyke's attunement with audiences has meant not only ensuring a long life for the production but broadening public awareness of Hurston. The performance generates energy, says Van Dyke, because it is insightful. The relationship between the performer and the audience creates a space for Hurston and for a reevaluation of her life and work, on the one hand, and the dialogue contemporary black artists are having with Hurston's personal history, on the other. The current productions connect Hurston to an ongoing black theater tradition, while making it possible to reassess her value as a woman artist and to bring that assessment to the public for a final gloss.

Ruby Dee's Video Hurston

A line of continuity stretches from an individual's culture and gender to her work; defining what that work should be, maintaining control of the work, and having it reach the desired audience are a small part of what Hurston, as an African American woman, had to manage as she pursued her theatrical career. A difficult childhood, harsh economic circumstances, and complicated personal relationships caused tensions along her journey toward self-fulfillment and recognition. Whereas Holder's play confronts "the lies of enemies and the envious hostility of friends" that clouded Hurston's brilliance during her lifetime.

Actor Ruby Dee's production *Zora Is My Name*, also autobiographical, presents another perspective.[435] Here, Hurston's genius is explored through a kind of imagery and narrative structure that test the boundaries of realism, therefore proposing an alternative to the literal interpretations of Hurston's life and work. Whereas the Hurston of Holder's play reflects upon events that threatened Hurston's independence, Dee's Hurston takes charge of the image being constructed on stage. Holder's Hurston confronts the spectator, implying that her image was a product of others' perceptions of her and suggesting that the audience as witness is somehow an accomplice, in isolating her from the center of attention she needed to thrive, if not survive; Dee's Hurston, in contrast, never alludes to any tragedy related to her career but only to the devastating effect her mother's death had on her sense of security.

The mother, and other characters depicting women as influences in Hurston's early life and her refiguring of their images in her folklore and fiction, constitutes a central motif in Dee's production. "I have memories within me that came out of the material that went to make me" is Dee's opening line. Remembering, collecting, and documenting are actions performed by Hurston as narrator, played by Dee. The Hurston who acts, who listens as a child to storytellers, who experiences the trauma of her mother's death, who leaves home, is a separate character, the Hurston of history, played by Lynn Whitfield, related through memory to the writer she becomes (Dee). This device of having two women play Hurston, allows actions in the present to refer mimetically to the past and future, because both characters simultaneously appear in some instances. Hurston as an adult ethnographer returning to her hometown to collect folklore enters the world she inhabited as a child. The young Hurston plays games and enacts other scenes as they are narrated by her Double—Hurston as an adult. At two crucial moments the two Zoras embrace and thereby suggest that narrative chronology is an illusion—past, present, and future coexisting—made concrete through the simultaneous presence of a woman who reminisces and her Double, a woman who experiences, and both, of course, are the self-same person, each the Double of the other. Conflating the past and the future by having the young and old Hurston appear together in the present concretely represents the ethnographic present used by the narrator; it also demonstrates that the retelling of Hurston's life story, particularly through a dramatic performance, signifies her relationship to herself and to others.

The adaptation's fidelity to Hurston's autobiography and to her folklore collection *Mules and Men* is realistic. The Eatonville of Hurston's youth and of her fiction and folklore comes to life from tableaux, as if to illustrate Hurston's concept of the way African-Americans interpret the English language in pictorial terms, what she calls hieroglyphics. By this she means that objects, thoughts, and actions are represented in language through visual metaphors. When Dee's Hurston narrates, the scenes pictured in her words are enacted through actors' miming the characters. The spectator sees Hurston controlling her role, her relationship to her past, her reality as represented in her written works.

Hurston's motivation to write and the act of writing are the substance of Dee's adaptation. In contrast with Holder's play, which also examines Hurston's literary career, *Zora Is My Name* celebrates the world view rendered in her folklore texts and her commitment to her community. It attempts to explain why Hurston worked, "so every one would know they had a history and a culture to be proud of"—an objective which has taken on new meaning with the renewed interest in her work. It is an interpretation on Dee's part, in keeping with her role as an actress, which she sees in part as being a tradition-bearer and educator, particularly for young black Americans. Whether attributing this objective to Hurston as an overriding motivation can be borne out through all of her actions remains a subject of conjecture.

Bell Hooks has suggested that although Hurston was interested in preserving black folk culture, "she never directly states for whom she wished to preserve the culture, whether for black folks, that we may be ever mindful of the rich imaginative folkways that are our tradition and legacy, or for white folks, that they may laugh at the quaint dialect and amusing stories as they voyeuristically peep into the private inner world of poor Southern black people."[436] In my view, avoiding direct statements that would allow her motives or her work itself to be strictly classified was exactly Hurston's point: she opposed the paradigms that rigidly constrain our interpretations of culture to either/or categories, even as she paid respect to the value of the forms she worked against, by appearing to work within the formal conventions of novel writing, ethnography, and drama. Although she realized the patronage that went along with cultivating a white audience, she did not pursue the attention because she condoned the derision that often came with it. Her work, rather, grew from a long view of history, what can be seen as Hurston's vision, indeed her genius, which has inspired the current movement toward restoring her work and her ideas.

A Tea with Zora and Marjorie

The playwright Barbara Speisman's drama *A Tea with Zora and Marjorie*, is structured in a way that enables a spectator or reader to perceive the parallels in the lives of Hurston and the novelist Marjorie Keenan Rawlings and to hear the echoes reverberating when specific incidents in one charater's life are mirrored in the other's experience. The "plot" consists of monologues delivered alternately and two dialogues between Hurston and Rawlings. The dialogues occur when they meet for tea— once in 1941 and again ten years later. Rawlings, a northerner, establishes her residence in Florida because she found it to be the most nurturing environment in which to feed her passion for writing. Like Hurston, Rawlings was taken with the rural setting and made ample use of it in her books. The sequestered setting of her home in Cross Creek, Florida, where she maintained an orange grove the Florida's "folk" became the source of her novels *Cross Creek* and *The Yearling*. Because Rawlings recreated the way of life she observed among her rural neighbors and Hurston also made her community the subject of her novels, Speisman brought the two authors together as characters in a play, to give a sense of what the two remarkable women might have been like in each other's presence when they meet for tea at Rawlings' invitation. Rawlings has to bypass segregation codes that forbid Hurston to come in through the lobby entrance of the hotel where Rawlings is staying in St. Augustine, the designated rendezvous place. On the other hand, Hurston slips in through the servants' entrance and shows her acclimation to the code of the Jim-Crow South; we see her humility when faced with the prospect of meeting a writer she admired. The play's concept is not unlike the idea behind all the stagings of Hurston's life and work—all of which hint at the enormous dramatic potential implicit in her enigmatic persona.

A Tea with Zora and Marjorie does justice to Hurston's complex, often contradictory motivations—for example, to sail to Honduras on her houseboat in search of a lost civilization, or freeing herself of relationships with men even though she discovers, as she advises Rawlings, that "finishing a book don't make your heart sing. Loving people does that."[437] A fine element in the play includes language that brings out subtle differences in the voices of the two women. These distinctions, all the more pronounced in performance, involve tone as well as illocution. Whereas Rawlings speaks with long full phrases drawn out to accentuate an upper-class precision, Hurston mixes dialect into her informal monologues that burst alternately with raucousness and pathos. Both characters exude carefree energy and duel with their wits.

George Wolfe's Adaptation: Spunk

Of the productions discussed in this essay, the one that perhaps best captures the complexity of Hurston's vision is *Spunk*, the director George Wolfe's adaptation of Hurston's stories "Sweat," "Story in Harlem Slang," and "The Gilded Six Bits." *Spunk* combines several non-realistic staging techniques with storytelling, masking, and the blues.[438] Under Wolfe's Obie-Award-winning direction, the performance strikes a balance between loyalty to Hurston's texts and innovative blends of movement, gestures, facial expressions, music, and visual imagery—including tableaux with characters frozen in expressionistic postures. Wolfe sees himself as translating some principles of Japanese Noh Drama into the context of southern black culture, as when masked figures serving as a chorus, float in and out of scenes.[439] The visual language of the production "moves from a heightened reality into some ritual, abstract world."[440] The language of the stories, part prose narrative and part dialogue, deconstructs the action (in an effort to show underlying contradictions of everyday-life behavior) as characters speak the narrative, sometimes referring to themselves in the third person, sometimes sharing the same narrative with one or more characters in a polyvocal chain linking one moment to the next. While Wolfe rigorously adheres to Hurston's text, short riffs of blues music and lyrics bridge scenes and set the mood.

Hurston's stories provide rich material for Wolfe's Brechtian technique of focusing on the core meanings produced by words, on their sense and the external displays that illustrate a character's feelings. In poetical language Hurston captures specific emotional landscapes, each of which "excludes the psychological, the subconscious, the metaphysical unless they can be conveyed in concrete terms."[441] Wolfe's decision to stage the stories is ambitious, considering that his understanding was that they were not meant to be performed.

There are obvious biblical references from the Old and New Testaments in the opening vignette, based on Hurston's story "Sweat." The transparent reference to Genesis and the Fall is inverted: whereas Eve was responsible for the fate that would cause man to have to work for his bread, here the main female character, Delia, is condemned to "sweat, sweat, sweat! Work and sweat, cry and sweat, pray and sweat!" (75) Moreover, she supports her husband Sykes. Sykes introduces the snake into the scene. Foreshadowed in the form of a bull whip, the snake invokes a slave driver's tool of oppression. Additional references to "driving" in the story, as when Delia "drives" through town on her pony, magnify the forced-labor imagery. Not only is the landscape accented with this antebellum frame, but the suggestion that Sykes had assumed the role of a slave driver also gives the effect of a polemic against injustice, brutality, oppression; however, the story never recedes into anything overtly polemical, as is the case with Hurston's work as a whole. Stark as the brutality may be, there is none of the hopelessness evident in stories of social oppression such as appear in Wright's *Uncle Tom's Children* published the decade after "Sweat" had appeared. Whatever cringing and feelings of utter despair Sykes's stereotypical shiftless black male role causes fade in light of the story's poetry and economy.

Structured in three parts, "Sweat," the story, can be read as a three-act play. In parts I and II, the central actions between the two main characters occur. Delia, in part I, is transformed into a defensive pillar when her unfaithful husband Sykes torments her with a bull whip. A territorial conflict ensues, as Sykes is determined to drive Delia from the house, so that he can have his mistress move in, while Delia is equally determined to hold onto the house, for she, being the primary wage earner, is likewise the owner. Thus, the whip and in part III a snake Sykes brings home upset the balance of power. The story sings, or one might say hisses, with the alliterative sound of the letter "S" in nearly every paragraph. A remarkable transformation in iconography can be seen in the prevalence of S, with its resemblance to the snake symbolizing Damballah Wedo, the serpent deity of Voodoo. Initially appearing in the story as a menacing presence, a disruption of Delia's routine and a threat to her self-possession, the snake, by the end of the story, becomes her ally. Indeed, from the point of view of Sykes, who writhes on the floor in the snake's grasp and looks to Delia for help only to find her returning his gaze, it must seem as if Delia has been possessed by Damballah. Delia is not only possessor of the house but is also possessed. In contrast, the New Testament allusion when Delia crawls "over the earth in Gethsemane and up the rocks of Calvary," hints at the prospect of a resolution, a redemption. The syncretic blend of Voodoo and Christian imagery contributes to the intense heat of the story, prevents it from being simply a stereotypical folksy tale—indeed imbues the tale with a deep structure stretching from the recesses of a hellish interior to the free-flowing display of exaggerated emotions in an outback region where community gossip creates a tragi-comic interlude.

The men on Joe Clarke's porch provide, in part II, a backdrop to the action, as they chew cane stalks while chatting about the past, present, and future of Delia and Sykes's marriage. The men devote considerable talk to Sykes's infidelity in a scene that plays upon the ritualistic significance of community talk. Talking becomes a ritual of its own, an enactment of words that initiate anyone within their range into the codes of small-town survival. On the store porch, the context for the central characters' actions can be seen through the men's gossip. Their judgments about Delia's and Sykes's life together give the picture of what it means in this rural outpost to be tried and condemned for going against the community's norms. Creating the effect of a jury—and thereby invoking another ritualistic process—the store porch gossip scene reminds us that Delia and Sykes are bound by the heavy-laden air of a village mentality. The setting is thus established as a place where one's private actions are adjudicated in the public domain—albeit a microcosmic domain. For each action is examined in such microscopic detail that the picture is unrecognizable, blown up to such proportions that the invisible does not merely become visible but (as in "Black Death") becomes a reversed image and projection of the central characters' mental state. Everything the men are saying reinforces the terrible sense of violation that has brought about a breach in the couple's marriage. By part III, "It was plain that the breaches must remain agape."

The technique of splitting the narrative and the dialogue between two or more characters effectively represents in dramatic form a quality used in the novel *Their Eyes Were Watching God*—what Gates identifies as "free-indirect discourse." Gates credits this style of narrating with having the power to make a written text show its potential responsiveness to the surrounding oral and performative contexts. Building upon Mikhail Bahktin's idea of dialogical exchange, Gates explicates the interrelated oral and written discourses presented, respectively, by Janie and a narrator who speaks as if in Janie's voice but from an omniscient perspective, similar to Hurston's, a narrator who also, in contrast, writes in Hurstonesque language from a position bound by Janie's rural world. Although Hurston uses an omniscient point of view in "Sweat," in his adaption, Wolfe takes the liberty of putting the words of a would-be omniscient narrator into the characters' mouths, while they mime the actions they describe. Allowing characters to speak of themselves in the third person, as when Delia and Sykes narrate their final encounter, Wolfe optimizes his use of the distancing technique he learned from studying Brecht's work—the Alienation (or "A")—Effect Brecht accomplished, particularly through the use of placards or printed titles to establish the situation in episodically structured scenes.

> Sykes: Closer, right underfoot this time. He leaped—onto the bed.
> *In isolated light, the actor playing Sykes becomes both Sykes and the snake.*
> Delia: Outside Delia heard a cry.
> *Sykes cries out in pain.*

Rather than placards, Wolfe has the characters step aside from their roles. Indeed, a spectator must question whether the character is temporarily displaced by the actor. In other words, it appears that the actor slips into the role of the narrator at one moment and the character the next. The advantage of this technique lies in its automatic undermining of the realism implied when characters are given only dialog to speak.

For the narrator and the character, as played by the actor, are simultaneously the same and different. The narrated words spoken about a character from the lips of the same actor playing the character are the verbal equivalent of holding up a mirror, enabling spectators to see that a performance amounts to much more than a character's emotional and material struggles.

Also innovative is the use of the title "Spunk," which is the title of a short story by Hurston not included in Wolfe's production. True to her high regard for irony, Hurston named the story after its main character, although Spunk's arrogance becomes the first step toward unraveling a dark tale of betrayal and death. Spunk, in a sense, is unmasked and undone by his name. What is more, Hurston in 1931 had plans for a play of the same title.

"I shall do something good with 'Spunk,'" she wrote to her patron Charlotte Osgood Mason. "I am working on that also [in addition to *Fast and Furious* and *Jungle Scandals*, the revues mentioned previously] and it looks like a very good play can be made from it. Anyway, I like the idea of going from the light and trivial to something better, rather than coming down from a 'Spunk' to 'Fast and Furious.' The public will see growth rather than decline, you see."[442] As the public has seen, perhaps much later than Hurston had hoped, the theater practice she envisioned has a greater resonance now than the French composer George Antheil might have predicted when he told Hurston in 1931 she "would be the most stolen-from Negro in the world for the next ten years at least. He said that this sort of thievery is unavoidable. Unpleasant of course but at the bottom a tribute to one's originality."[443]

As an afterword to her paraphrase of Antheil's comment about her position within the performance traditions I have discussed, Hurston's remarks on imitation, mimicry, and parody in black culture reinforce the continuing power of her ideas as dramatic theory: "If you look at a man and mistrust your eyes, do something and see if he will imitate you right away," she wrote, "If he does, that's My People" (*Dust Tracks* 220). Thus, as she apparently exalts mimicry, she draws attention to the peculiar contradiction involved in classifying the "essential" quality of a culture and its forms of expression.[444] In her refusal to be categorized, she is a progenitor, indeed an archetype, for theater artists who recognize that her life and work have empowered a new generation to be, above all, unrelenting.

CONCLUSION

I began my work on Hurston to develop a methodology for performance studies, particularly an interdisciplinary approach to the study of African-American cultural performances. I have attempted to define the area of African-American cultural performance according to the example set by Hurston's interdisciplinary work. The methodology emerging from the study of Hurston's work is defined as a dramaturgical practice; it involves ethnographic and historical research, analysis of iconology, the codifying of performance styles, training, directing, and writing critical texts (academic or artistic) based on a histrionic conception of African-American cultures. Beyond my initial expectations, this effort to find a method specific to African-American performance studies has produced a study more broadly applicable to performance studies. Situating Hurston's work within the field of performance studies, I have found that the techniques she used in composing her texts supply abundant examples to illustrate the complex ways that written texts need not merely be *related* to performance texts but can *be* performances.

One important aspect of this method has been to analyze the intertextuality of performances, to assess distinctive features of performances as they are written, performed, or not performed, as it were. The study of sympathetic magic is crucial to the performance-centered approach Hurston's work exemplifies. Included under a broad rubric called sympathetic magic, healing, conjuring, and other varieties of traditional medicine and religion (or nontraditional, depending on one's perspective), bring to light the relationship between the metaphorical content of Hurston's texts and the social scientific field research she used to her advantage as a fiction writer. Although one may question why it is desirable to venture into an area so far removed from conventional literary studies, not to mention mainstream scientific approaches, the answer lies in a serious consideration of anthropology and its history as a discipline. My aim in writing this conclusion is not to detail the history of anthropology; the subject has received significant attention in work by James Clifford, George Stocking, Michael Taussig, and other scholars cited in the preceding chapters. The point is to reiterate that there is a sensory dimension to performance-centered approaches, and the ethnographic field research context provides models for interactive writing. This is not to say that all anthropology looks to magic for the answers to scientific questions or that literary texts can be reduced to magical formulas. It is, rather, to stress that alongside of cultural and intellectual history, the history of anthropology reveals that ritualistic practices are an important source of cultural knowledge and that this knowledge permeates language in all its forms.

The idea of creating an interactive type of critical text initially caused me to experiment with interviews and other structured discussions with artists directly involved in the productions I was studying. This method, though primarily pertinent to my final chapter, "Staging Hurston's Life and Work," also has ramifications for the type of dramaturgical practice that Hurston's work inspires. Once it is possible to see that field research provides the substance of performances "not seen," it is possible to see the dialogues a researcher has in the field as part of a drama— the script to which remains to be written. I am not suggesting that it is necessary to produce a studious *script* in place of a scholarly book. I am, however, arguing that it is crucial to incorporate the dialogues in which one is engaged while producing a text (academic or artistic) into the text—to claim all the voices belonging to the work—in an effort to maintain vigilant watch over one's own agenda.

Both values stemming from field research—the historical and ritual significance of traditional religion and healing, as well as the exchanges from which one obtains cultural knowledge—can be seen as sources for imagery in Hurston's work. Following W.T.J. Mitchell, I have considered imagery, or typology, in Hurston's work as theoretically based. The theoretical is important because it represents a way of conceptualizing the world with reference to visual metaphors, and as Mitchell has shown, visual languages ultimately expose powerful, even controlling attitudes. Indeed, Mitchell as well as Taussig have gone farther, to show that the prominence of visual references in language reflects a pervasive concern for a controlling point of view and, conversely, for resisting it. Building upon Mitchell's and Taussig's work, and that of others who consider the significance of visual and other sensory languages, I began my work on Hurston to examine her use of vivid word-pictures—what she calls hieroglyphics. Here, it seemed to me, was the kernel of her own performance theory. Why a performance theory?

The value of a performance theory can be measured only through its practical application. Thus, I have sought to discover ways Hurston's example could be the basis for communicating knowledge of specific performances from one generation to the next. This is one of the major challenges theater artists face, since unlike literary texts, performances (or performance texts) are momentary. The fact that particular performances do not endure beyond the time required to stage them does not, however, mean they must be forgotten or never repeated. In that her theatrical career is virtually a lost segment of Hurston's work, the goal to create codes using her work as examples is difficult. To begin, reconstructing Hurston's own staged productions, though it can be done, requires an intimate knowledge of the performances which can only be acquired through the minimal evidence available. As far as I have been able to determine, there were no scripts for *The Great Day, From Sun to Sun,* and *All De Live Long Day.* "The Fiery Chariot" appears to be the only extant script from the three productions, and it is only one episode in *From Sun to Sun.* Nevertheless, the program notes, if read alongside *Mules and Men, Jonah's Gourd Vine,* and Hurston's entire body of written work, provide the complete content of the rich events. The only exception to completeness lies in segments identified only by the name of a performer. An example of this occurs in *The Great Day,* where the name Leigh Whipper appears. Recordings of the songs performed in each scene, available to researchers at the American Folklife Center, give an idea of the musical style of the performances. All of the available information from the program notes for *From Sun to Sun* made it possible for organizers of the annual Zora Neale Hurston Festival in Eatonville, Florida, to stage an adaptation in 1991. There remains no way to pursue extended analysis of the script or the performance of their production, because neither the text of the adaptation nor the videotape of the production is available for release.

Having available documentation of staged productions is essential not only to be able to write a thorough historical account but to reproduce the play, in writing or on stage. One of the perpetual dilemmas of contemporary experimental theater, as Richard Schechner points out in his essay "Decline and Fall of the (American) Avant-Garde," with reference to the American avant-garde or experimental theater is how to pass on a performance text to subsequent audiences if no one has ever bothered to keep a record of everything that went into the text.[445] Codifying performances by using elaborate notation system as composers document musical scores offers an option; however the idea of codification in drama is usually associated with ancient performance traditions and archaic master texts. Although historical longevity is not a necessary cause for codification, the precedent set by, for example Asian performance traditions such as Indian Kathakali or Japanese Noh drama, suggests the possibility that codification offers certain benefits in training as well as in systematic elaboration of performance knowledge and perhaps cultural knowledge, more broadly. Codifying African-American expressive forms, it would seem, involves modifying particular styles of performance into practical, collaborative dramaturgy and directing. George Houston Bass, whom I have mentioned in conjunction with the *Mule Bone* discussion, practiced an experimental research-to-performance based theater, with an emphasis on ritual; his work was moving toward codifying black performance styles.

There are, however, within African-American performance contexts, resistances to codification, many of which stem from pressures related to production. The *Mule Bone* production, according to Bass, offered prospects for examining a variety of archetypal characters and developing a sense of the ritualistic behavior associated with their presentational styles. The major loss of Bass and the reverberations from the *Mule Bone* production hint at yet another set of circumstances amounting to a "social drama" requiring exactly the sort of formal, ritualistic performances (along with necessary training and, more far-reaching, codification) that Bass's work at Rites and Reason had come to symbolize. Aside from these highly particular concerns, there is the more general question of whether or not formalized codes are desirable, particularly if they lead to reification and idealization of types.

Despite some problems, there seems to be (perhaps because of *Mule Bone*) sound justification for continuing the work Bass conceived. As with Rites and Reason, an experimental method promises the possibility for development, over time, of a concept of performance and cultural production embracing social, historical, and humanistic objectives intended to bring about changes in the way cultural communities define themselves and interact with one another. Some attributes of the method include historical, sociological, and anthropological research; an approach to directing that emphasizes dramaturgical research and attention to details of the dramatic text in relation to the performance text; ritual rather than realistic structure; documentions of rehearsals and performances; discussions surrounding productions; use of recorded documentation (aural and visual), as well as diagrams, as a basis for formalizing performance knowledge and structuring performance training; whenever possible, the building of repertory and other cultural institutions oriented toward research, as well as educational and artistic training.

Not only is field research part of the work needed to create performances (or other cultural productions) that are viable to communities, but the productions, likewise, are part of the field, part of the culture being examined. This is to say that history must be seen as something the performance helps to produce. In an attempt to come to terms with social, historical, performative, and textual practices, I have ultimately taken a turn toward closer consideration of myth and myth-making. The extent to which individuals engaged in creating performances are aware of their role in making history can, possibly, influence the broader social context surrounding the immediate and extended communities attached to the production. Thus, training and directing based on field research requires having knowledge of production history as well as cultural history. Although the method is useful in adapting performances from texts authored in remote historical or cultural contexts, it also can apply to creating contemporary performances which should be acknowledged for their potential to construct or deconstruct history and myth. Field research and the knowledge it represents must take into account the influence that cultural productions have had in constituting the "real world." This work can be explored in experimental workshops.

My final objective has been to contribute to a concept of critical writing about performances as another form of cultural production. Effective criticism, in my view, must expose underlying structures of production and performance, laying bare controversies for scrutiny and reconsideration. Hurston's work illustrates a method of combining textual practices. I have tried to show how combining different forms of narrative produces a unique discourse in which text and metatext are represented as one language, a mythic recreation of worlds, and a commentary on structural conventions of narrative, genre, and other aspects of text production—above all, performances and the illusions of surface images. In that her productions and performances constitute a type of mythography, the texts provide ample evidence of a critical approach to cultural representation. Distinctions between genres determined by disciplines are erased. Thus, Hurston's work, and the work involved in making this book, establish a foundation for continued efforts at examining the possibilities for interdisciplinary exchange and intertextual analysis. Toward this end, finally, I have not escaped transgressing certain generic, disciplinary, and methodological boundaries.

NOTES

PREFACE

1. First published in *Negro,* edited by Nancy Cunard (1934); reprinted in *The Sanctified Church: The Folklore Writings of Zora Neale Hurston* (Berkeley: Turtle Island, 1981). See the Appendix at the back of this book, pp. 243–258.

INTRODUCTION

2. The main biographical sources I consulted are Robert Hemenway, *Zora Neale Hurston, a Literary Biography* (Urbana, IL: University of Illinois Press, 1977); Zora Neale Hurston, *Dust Tracks on a Road* (1942); *Hurston, Folklore, Memoirs, and Other Writings,* edited by Cheryl Wall (New York: Library of America, 1995). Until recently, Hurston's birthplace was thought to have been Eatonville, Florida, and her birthdate 1901, as reported in Hemenway's biography. After publication of the biography, Wall's research showed Hurston was born ten years earlier and not in Florida. The inconsistency is in part a consequence of Hurston's elusiveness concerning her age and other personal details. My conversations with Barbara Speisman were helpful to me in sorting out the conflicting reports surrounding Hurston's birthdate. Speisman is the author of the play "A Tea With Zora and Marjorie: A Series of Vignettes Based on the Unique Friendship of Zora Neale Hurston and Marjorie Kinnan Rawlings," *Rawlings Journal* (1988), 67–100, as well as two other plays on Hurston and Rawlings. Speisman's current research on Hurston's early life in Alabama and Florida is part of her work in progress. Zora Hurston's niece Lucy Ann Hurston used her father's records to corroborate Wall's and Speisman's accounts.

3. See Cyrena N. Pondrom, "The Role of Myth in *Their Eyes Were Watching God,*" *American Literature* 58, 2 (May 1986): 183–84, for a discussion of this episode in *Dust Tracks,* with reference to Hurston's exposure to classical myth.

4. The idea of transcendental homelessness, invoked in Walter Benjamin's essay "The Storyteller," supplies a point of connection between the oral storyteller's and novelist's roles. Whereas the epic has given rise to tragic drama, the latter has expanded into a modern form of tragedy, displacement. Georg Lukacs calls this displaced sensibility "transcendental homelessness," which finds expression in the novel. Lukacs, *The Theory of the Novel (1914–15),* (Cambridge, Mass.: MIT Press, 1971; 1990).

5. See George Houston Bass and Henry Louis Gates, Jr., editors, *Mule Bone, a Comedy of Negro Life* (New York: HarperCollins Publishers, 1991).

6. Kathy Perkins offers a concise summary of Hurston's theater career in *Black Female Playwrights: An Anthology of Plays before 1950* (Bloomington: Indiana University Press, 1989), 77–79.

Notes

7. Ibid., p. 77.

8. Pondrom makes the connection between mythic references and modernism, in "The Role of Myth in *Their Eyes Were Watching God*," 201–02. Michael North discusses Hurston's performative style as an alternative to the limits modernism imposed in 1934. Given a choice between radical left politics, on the one hand, and romanticized or stereotypical representations of African-American culture, on the other, Hurston preempts the dichotomy by making her language reflect ambiguities of genre and tone and by avoiding a distinction between presentation and representation, according to North. North covers some of the same topics I explore in Chapters One and Two, including an analysis of "Characteristics of Negro Expression," See North," 'Characteristics of Negro Expression', Zora Neale Hurston and the *Negro* Anthology," *The Dialect of Modernism* (New York: Oxford University Press, 1994), pp. 175–95.

9. Sister M. Francesca Thompson, O.S.F., "The Lafayette Players, 1917–1932," in *The Theatre of Black Americans*, edited by Errol Hill (New York: Applause Theater Books, 1980), 223.

10. Fanin Belcher, Jr., details critical views on blacks in the theater in *The Place of the Negro in the Evolution of the American Theatre, 1767–1940*. Ph.D. Dissertation. Yale University, 1945 (Ann Arbor, MI: UMI Research, 1969) Belcher does not critique the dominant perspectives; his analysis, rather, reinforces them. I am grateful to Ron Argelander at New York University, Tisch School of the Arts, Department of Undergraduate Drama for introducing me to Belcher.

11. Jessie Fauset, "Negro Laughter," in *The New Negro* (1925), edited by Alain Locke (New York: Atheneum, 1968), 164.

12. Richard Poirier examines masking techniques writers use in *The Performing Self: Compositions and Decompositions in the Language of Contemporary Life* (New York: Oxford University Press, 1971). My colleagues Carolyn Karcher and Daniel O'Hara drew my attention to Poirier's contribution to performance theory.

13. J.L. Austin is credited with introducing the notion of performative language into theories of rhetoric and meaning. He explains how certain utterances are the equivalent of performing actions particularly in legally binding situations. See *How To Do Things with Words*, edited by J.O. Urmson (New York: Oxford University Press, 1962).

14. John MacAloon, "Introduction: Cultural Performances, Culture Theory," in *Rite, Drama, Festival, Spectacle: Rehearsals Toward a Theory of Cultural Performance*, edited by John J. MacAloon (Philadelphia: Institute for the Study of Human Issues, 1984), 8, 10.

15. In *The Souls of Black Folk*, African-American music, particularly the spiritual, becomes the vehicle for profound cultural meaning which Baker designates as cultural performance. Here, in *Modernism and the Harlem Renaissance* (Chicago: University of Chicago Press, 1987), Baker revises his previous position on Du Bois and culture presented in *Long Black Song* (Charlottesville: University of Virginia Press, 1972).

16. Baker, *Modernism and the Harlem Renaissance*, 64.

17. Schechner explains his term "twice-behaved behavior" in "Restoration of Behavior," *Between Theatre and Anthropology* (Philadelphia: University of Pennsylvania Press, 1985), 35–116.

18. The historian Eric Hobsbawm distinguishes custom, which changes, from tradition, which even if invented is static and repetitive. See Hobsbawm "Introduction: Invented Traditions," in *The Invention of Tradition*, edited by Hobsbawm and Terrence Ranger (Cambridge: Cambridge University Press, 1983), 1–14.

19. See Roy Wagner, *The Invention of Culture* (Chicago: University of Chicago Press, 1975; 1981).

20. See Turner, *From Ritual to Theatre: The Human Seriousness of Play* (New York:

Performing Arts Journal Publications, 1982), 74. Watergate, one of Turner's examples from recent history, illustrates how such a process unfolds. When the public was apprised that "dirty tricks," including burglary, were part of campaign politics in the early 1970s, the knowledge was startling, unprecedented; it represented a "breach" in what might be called a democratic social contract. Although a full-scale crisis, in Turner's sense, did not ensue, redressive action was pursued through Senate hearings, aired for months on national television, through an intensely charged atmosphere which climaxed with Nixon's resignation. Watergate illustrates Turner's idea that the meaning of cultural events shaping a community's history as well as its future cannot be fully grasped through observation only.

21. Turner, *From Ritual to Theatre*, 94.

22. Dell Hymes, "Breakthrough into Performance," in *Folklore: Performance and Communication*, edited by Dan Ben-Amos, Kenneth S. Goldstein (The Hague: Mouton, 1975), 11–74. The essay establishes a critical bridge across disciplines in approaches to verbal arts.

23. Ibid., p. 18.

24. In "The Arts of Impression Management," *The Presentation of Self in Everyday Life* (New York: Doubleday, 1959), 208–237, Goffman talks about impression management as a culminating example of what can happen when people become conscious of themselves as having public and private behavior.

25. Goffman shows how behavior is organized into discrete segments, in *Frame Analysis: An Essay on the Organizing of Experience* (Boston: Northeastern University Press, 1986).

26. Goffman and psychologists such as Paul Eckman and Ray Birdwhistell have pursued nonverbal studies in an effort to demonstrate the semiotics of facial expressions, bodily movements and other coded patterns. See Eckman, ed. *Emotion in the Human Face* (Cambridge: Cambridge University Press, 1972; 1982); Birdwhistell, *Kinesics and Context* (Philadelphia: University of Pennsylvania Press, 1970). Another comprehensive look at nonverbal communication, though focused on therapeutic encounters, can be found in Albert Scheflen's book *How Behavior Means: Exploring the Context of Speech and Meaning: Kinesics, Posture, Interaction, Setting and Culture* (New York: Doubleday, 1974).

27. See Schechner, "Drama, Script, Theater and Performance," *Performance Theory* (New York: Routledge, 1977), 68–105.

28. Ruth Benedict's book *Patterns of Culture* (Boston: Houghton Mifflin, 1934; 1959) illustrates prominent concepts central to the theory Boas had concerning behavior among specific groups identified by linguistic and other features classifiable as cultural.

29. Boas to Hurston, May 3, 1927.

30. The use of the term "primitive" here reflects the dominant thinking of the time toward non-Western cultures. I explore the term's significance in relation to Hurston's work in Chapter Five.

31. Hurston to Boas, April 21, 1929.

32. Ibid.

33. Boas to Hurston April 24, 1929.

34. Hurston, "The Florida Expedition," 1.

35. Gates presents his argument in *The Signifying Monkey: A Theory of African-American Literary Criticism* (New York: Oxford University Press, 1988). Other studies that offer vernacular and performative models directly addressing African-American oral traditions are among Roger Abrahams' work, particularly *Deep Down in the Jungle: Negro Narrative Folklore from the Streets of Philadelphia* (Chicago: Aldine Press, 1970). Folklorist John Roberts critiques what he calls the tendency to interpret black vernacular culture as pathological, particularly with reference to male identity. See Roberts, "African-American Diversity and

the Study of Folklore," *Western Folklore* 52, no. 2 (April 1993): 164–65. Richard Bauman's work establishes a basis for looking at oral traditions and vernacular expression using formal characteristics that reach across cultures. See *Verbal Art as Performance* (Prospect Heights, IL: Waveland Press, 1977), as well as Bauman's collaborative articles: Bauman and Charles Briggs, "Poetics and Performance: Critical Perspectives on Language and Social Life," *Annual Review of Anthropology* 19 (1990): 59–88; and Briggs and Bauman, "Genre, Intertextuality and Social Power," *Journal of Linguistic Anthropology* 2, no. 2 (1992): 13–72. More recently, the literary critic John Lowe has produced an in-depth study of Hurston's humor and brings a generous range of vernacular theories to bear on Hurston's texts. Lowe, *Jump at the Sun: Zora Neale Hurston's Cosmic Comedy* (Urbana, Ill.: University of Illinois Press, 1994).

CHAPTER ONE: THE DRAMA OF EVERYDAY LIFE

36. William Pickens, "Aftermath of a Lynching," *Negro* (New York: Negro Universities Press, 1934): 38.

37. Her position can be viewed in light of contemporary intellectuals' work such as Gayatri Spivak, Edward Said, and Henry Louis Gates, Jr.

38. Said's book *Orientalism* (New York: Vintage Books, 1979) is a critical marker for contemporary debates over the problems essentialist thinking presents for cultural studies.

39. Gayatri Spivak's essay "Can the Subaltern Speak?" explains the problem intellectuals presuming to speak on behalf of disenfranchised groups face when cultural identities are classified according to broad labels. She proffers a class analysis that is helpful in sorting out the complex situations Hurston faced. Spivak's essay appears in *Marxism and the Interpretation of Culture*, edited by Cary Nelson and Lawrence Grossberg, (Urbana: University of Illinois Press, 1988), 271–313. See Homi Bhaba's critique of Said, in "The Other Question: Stereotype Discrimination and the Discourse of Colonialism," *The Location of Culture* (London: Routledge, 1994), 66–84.

40. A key source championing another look at relativism is Charles Taylor's *The Ethics of Authenticity* (Cambridge, MA: Harvard University Press, 1991). Taylor challenges the principles behind relativistic thinking. Paul Gilroy, in *The Black Atlantic: Modernity and Double Consciousness* (Cambridge, MA: Harvard University Press, 1993), offers a historicized critique of essentialist ideas about black American, Caribbean, and British cultures. Folklorists John Roberts and Amy Shuman have approached the topic of essentialism from the angle of gender; see Roberts, "African-American Diversity and the Study of Folklore," and Shuman, "Dismantling Local Culture," *Western Folklore* 52, 2 (April 1993): 345–364. See also Deborah Kapchan, "Hybridization and the Marketplace: Emerging Paradigms of Folkloristics," *Western Folklore 52, 2* (April 1993): 303–326.

41. Werner Sollors defines "race as one aspect of ethnicity," in *Beyond Ethnicity: Consent and Descent in American Culture* (New York: Oxford University Press, 1986), 39. Although I agree it is not helpful to insist on separate categories, Sollors broadens the discourse on race by viewing it in the larger frame of American identity and by pointing out the contradictions involved in placing individuals and groups into categories based on such a nebulous variable.

42. Gates, *The Signifying Monkey*, 118.

43. Ibid. Gates discusses the practice of imitation in African-American oral and literary texts and its implications for criticism, 117 et passim.

44. Allan Chase, in *The Legacy of Malthus: The Social Costs of the New Scientific Racism* (New York: Alfred A. Knopf, Inc., 1975) goes into intricate detail documenting the eugenics movement and its consequences; Audrey Smedley, *Race in North America: Origin and*

Evolution of a Worldview (Boulder: Westview Press, 1993), offers a concise history of major developments in the intellectual history surrounding racialist discourse.

45. See Audrey Smedley, "Dismantling the Cultural Construction of Race: Twentieth Century Transformations in Science," *Race in North America: Origin and Evolution of a Worldview* (Boulder: Westview Press, 1993), 273–93.

46. See also Stoddard, *The Revolt Against Civilization: The Menace of the Under Man* (New York: Charles Scribner's Sons, 1922). The review by Boas of *The Rising Tide of Color* appears in *The Nation*, 111 (December 8, 1920): 656. Locke's review is cited in my text.

47. Melville Herskovits, *Franz Boas: The Science of Man in the Making* (New York: Charles Scribner's Sons, 1953), 117.

48. Alain Locke, Letter to the Editor of *The Forum*, December 1927, LXXVIII: 542–43. The citation is from a reprint of the letter in "The High Cost of Prejudice," in *A Documentary History*, vol. 3, edited by Herbert Aptheker (New York: Carol Publishing Group, 1973, 1990), 563.

49. "Aryans and Non-Aryans," *The American Mercury*, Vol. XXXII, No. 125 (May 1934): 221. Melville Herskovits, *Franz Boas* (New York: Charles Scribner's Sons, 1953): 118.

50. Boas, "Aryans and Non-Aryans," 222–23.

51. Boas, "The Instability of Human Types," in *Papers on Inter-Racial Problems Communicated to the First Universal Race Congress Held at the University of London, July 26–29, 1911*, edited by G. Spiller (London: P.S. King & Son, 1911), 103.

52. Boas, "The Aims of Anthropological Research," Address of the President of the American Association for the Advancement of Science, *Science* N.S., vol. 76 (1932); reprinted in *Race, Language and Culture* (New York: Macmillan, 1940): 250. For a review of literature on the topic, published during the same period, see Otto Klineberg, "Physique and Mentality," *Race Differences* (New York: Harper & Brothers, 1935), 73–92.

53. Ibid., 251.

54. Ibid.

55. "She completed a year and a half of college course work during her intermittent study at Howard between 1919 and 1924," and having been encouraged in her literary pursuits, "she was admitted to membership in the campus literary club, the Stylus," under the direction of Locke; her first short story 'John Redding Goes to Sea,' was published in *Stylus*, May 1921. "She came to New York in 1925 as a writer and left Barnard two years later as a serious social scientist, the result of her study of anthropology under Franz Boas." She graduated in 1928. See Robert Hemenway, *Zora Neale Hurston*, 18, 19, 21.

56. Jeffrey Stewart, editor, *Race Contacts and Interracial Relations: Lectures on the Theory and Practice of Race* (Washington, D.C.: Howard University Press, 1992), xxv.

57. Boas, "The History of Anthropology," Address at the International Congress of Arts and Sciences, 1904, *Congress of Arts and Sciences*, edited by H.J. Rogers (Boston: Houghton Mifflin, 1906); *Science* 20 (1904); reprinted in *The Shaping of American Anthropology 1883–1911*, edited by George Stocking, Jr. (New York: Basic Books, 1974), 31.

58. George Edmund Haynes, "The Trend of the Races" (1922) in *Documentary History of the Negro People in the United States*, vol. 3, edited by Herbert Aptheker (New York: Carol Publishing Group, 1973; 1990), 360n.

59. George E. Marcus and Michael M.J. Fischer, "A Crisis of Representation in the Human Sciences," *Anthropology as Cultural Critique: An Experimental Moment in the Human Sciences* (Chicago: University of Chicago Press, 1986), 13.

60. Ibid.

61. Alice Kaplan and Kristin Ross, "Introduction," *Everyday Life*, Yale French Studies, no. 73: 4.

62. "Verbal expression," as one of the two means by which actions are performed (the other being song-composition), means "the composition of the verses as a whole, i.e., the clothing of them in suitable language," *Aristotle Poetics*, trans. Gerald Else (Ann Arbor: The University of Michigan Press, 1990), 26 n56.

63. The quote is from Kaplan and Ross, "Introduction," 4.

64. Hurston's commentary on class distinctions is discussed in Chapter Two.

65. Walter J. Ong, "From Mimesis to Irony: The Distancing of Voice," in *The Horizon of Literature*, edited by Paul Hernadi (Lincoln: University of Nebraska Press, 1982), 27.

66. Jeffrey Stewart, *Race Contacts*, xxxii.

67. Ibid.

68. A professor of philosophy at Howard University, Locke had been the first African-American Rhodes Scholar at Oxford (1907–1909) and held a B.A. from Harvard College (1907) and a Ph.D. from Harvard University (1918).

69. Alain Locke Papers, Manuscript Division, Moorland-Spingarn Research Center, Howard University.

70. Stewart, *Race Contacts*, xlvi.

71. For example, while pursuing field research that she later used as the basis for her theories in "Characteristics," Hurston experienced a conflict of interest because Mason's contract with Hurston restricted her from any other commitments; however, she was discussing the prospect of engaging in research on Creole culture in New Orleans with the anthropologist Otto Klineberg, under Boas's direction. Klineberg, writing to Boas in November of 1929, said that Hurston had explained she was not sure whether she would be able to work on the project and told Klineberg, after first saying he should keep it a secret, to tell Boas, as well, that she was being paid a salary by rich patrons in New York and would have to be released from them. It seems she worked out an arrangement to pursue independent research and in that way participated in the research with Klineberg. Klineberg to Boas, November 18, 1929, Franz Boas Papers, The American Philosophical Society.

72. Walter E. Stephens, "Mimesis, Mediation and Counterfeit," in *Mimesis in Contemporary Theory: An Interdisciplinary Approach*, edited by, Mihai Spariosu (Philadelphia: John Benjamins Publishing Company, 1984), 238.

73. Ibid.

74. See Herbert Lindenberger, "The Mimetic Bias in Modern Anglo-American Criticism," in *Mimesis in Contemporary Theory*, 1–26.

75. Edward Said, "On Originality," *The World, the Text, and the Critic* (Cambridge, Mass.: Harvard University Press, 1983), 129.

76. Ibid., 131, 129. The analogy with Scheflen refers to his book entitled *How Behavior Means: Exploring the Contexts of Speech and Meaning: Kinesics, Posture, Interaction, Setting, and Culture* (New York: Doubleday, 1974).

77. Ibid.

78. Ibid.

79. See Jerrold Hirsch, "Modernity, Nostalgia, and Southern Folklore Studies: The Case of John Lomax," *Journal of American Folklore*, vol. 105, no. 416 (Spring 1992): 183–207. During the mid-1930s, Hurston traveled with John Lomax and Mary Elizabeth Barnicle on an expedition to collect folk songs for the Music Division of the Library of Congress. It is also worth noting that much of the work published in the *Negro* anthology presupposes attitudes similar to Hurston's.

80. Said, "On Originality," 134.

81. Ibid.

82. Michel Foucault, *The Archaeology of Knowledge and the Discourse on Language* (New York: Pantheon, 1972), 141.

Notes

83. Stephens, "Mimesis, Mediation and Counterfeit," 238.

84. *Negro*, 63. The reference to Shakespeare in Hurston and Buttitta indicates what Lawrence Levine characterizes as a shift from Shakespearean plays' having broad popular appeal in nineteenth century American theater to their developing an elitist appeal and "high art" status during the first half of the twentieth century. See Levine, "William Shakespeare and the American People: A Study in Cultural Transformation," in *Rethinking Popular Culture: Contemporary Perspectives in Cultural Studies*, edited by Chandra Mukerji and Michael Schudson (Berkeley: University of California Press, 1991), 157–97; reprinted from *American Historical Review* 89, No. 1 (February 1984): 34–66.

85. Hirsch, "Modernity, Nostalgia, and Southern Folklore Studies," 191.

86. Ibid.

87. Franz Boas Papers, The American Philosophical Society.

88. Buttitta, "Negro Folklore in North Carolina," *Negro*, 62. Like the term 'Negro,' the reference to 'poor white trash' was standard in folklore writing of the period and into the Federal Folklore Project of the late 1930s.

89. Baker's idea of the "mastery of form" and the "deformation of mastery" can be seen in this light, in *Modernism and the Harlem Renaissance*; see Gates, *Figures in Black: Words, Signs, and the "Racial" Self* (New York: Oxford University Press, 1989) and *The Signifying Monkey*.

90. The quote is from Gates, *The Signifying Monkey*, 181.

91. See Gregory Bateson, *Steps to an Ecology of Mind* (New York: Ballantine, 1972), 184.

92. Said, "On Originality," 135.

93. See David Levering Lewis, *When Harlem Was in Vogue*, 304.

94. See Monty Noam Penkower, *The Federal Writers' Project: A Study in Government Patronage of the Arts* (Urbana: University of Illinois Press, 1977), on the impact research developments during the 1930s had for advancements in African-American studies 147, and for folklore research 147 et passim. I discuss Hurston's involvement in the Federal Writers' Project in Chapter Three.

95. Locke's commentary on Brown's folklore appears in the *Negro* anthology 111–15. The phrase is a reference to William Stott's book *Documentary Expression and Thirties American* (Chicago: The University of Chicago Press, 1986).

CHAPTER TWO: HURSTON'S THEORY OF IMITATION

96. The problem of performing oneself as an exhibition will be explored subsequently.

97. North designates Hurston's early work "The Eatonville Anthology" 192 as her first example of ethnography. In my view, the collection is correctly placed under "Fiction" in *I Love Myself When I Am Laughing*. It was composed before Hurston's field research expeditions (first published in 1926), and the stories bear no apparent relation to the information documented in her field research notes. North accounts for the resemblance to fiction by concluding that "The Eatonville Anthology" blends the genre of folklore, autobiography, and fiction.

98. Hurston to Thomas E. Jones, October 12, 1934; James Weldon Johnson Collection, Beinecke Library. Jones was president of Fisk University at the time.

99. Hurston, "Dance Songs and Tales from the Bahamas," *Journal of American Folklore* vol. 43, no. 169 (July–Oct. 1930): 294.

100. See Hazel Carby, "The Politics of Fiction, Anthropology, and the Folk: Zora Neale Hurston," in *New Essays on Their Eyes Were Watching God*, edited by Michael Awkward (New York: Cambridge University Press, 1990), 71–93.

Notes

101. June Jordan passionately espouses this view in her article, "On Richard Wright and Zora Neale Hurston: Notes Toward a Balancing of Love and Hatred," *Black World* (August 1974), 4–8.

102. According to Allen Woll, "the world of the New Negro and the world of the Broadway musical tended to remain separate," *Black Musical Theatre from Coontown to Dreamgirls* (Baton Rouge: Louisiana State University Press, 1989), 111.

103. These productions are discussed in more detail in subsequent chapters. Concerning *Fast and Furious* and *Jungle Scandals*, Hurston wrote to Mason: "I do not consider either of the revues as great work, but they are making the public know me and come to me, and that is important." (July 23, 1931; ALP, MSRC)

104. Lloyd Lewis, "Worried 'De Lawd,' " review clipping, Rollins College Archive.

105. Ibid. This comment has resonance in the debate over whether to produce *Mule Bone* at Lincoln Center Theater, which is discussed in Chapter Six.

106. She apparently collaborated with a radio personality, Andrew Dobson, as well.

107. Clippings file, Rollins College Archive.

108. See Sollors, *Beyond Ethnicity*, 250.

109. James Clifford, *The Predicament of Culture: Twentieth-Century Ethnography, Literature, and Art* (Cambridge, Mass.: Harvard University Press, 1988), 129.

110. Clifford does not use the term "metonym" in this context.

111. Clifford, *The Predicament of Culture*, 135.

112. This topic is explored in more detail in Chapters Four and Six.

113. Letter from Boas to Andrew Carnegie, November 30, 1906. Reprinted in *The Shaping of American Anthropology*, edited by Stocking, 317.

114. Ibid.

115. Stocking, "The Basic Assumptions of Boasian Anthropology," in *The Shaping of American Anthropology*, 1.

116. Key works by the three colleagues of Boas include: Benedict, *Race: Science and Politics* (New York: Modern Age Books, 1940); rev. ed. with *Races of Mankind* (New York: Viking, 1945). Herskovits (see bibliography), between 1923 and 1973, published numerous articles and books on black culture; see the bibliography in George Eaton Simpson, *Melville J. Herskovits* (New York: Columbia University Press, 1973), 189–94. Klineberg, *Negro Intelligence and Selective Migration* (New York: Columbia University Press, 1935); *Race Differences* (New York: Harper & Brother Publishers, 1935).

117. In Margaret Mead, *An Anthropologist at Work: Writings of Ruth Benedict* (Boston: Houghton Mifflin, 1959), 139.

118. Ibid.

119. The idea of cultural pluralism predates the 1930s and is identified with Horace M. Kallen, whose article "Democracy versus the Melting Pot: A Study of American Nationality" appeared in *The Nation*, February 1915. In 1924 "Kallen introduced the term 'cultural pluralism' to designate his radically anti-assimilationist viewpoint," arguing for a "federation of nationalities"; see Philip Gleason, "American Identity and Americanization," *Harvard Encyclopedia of American Ethnic Groups*, edited by Stephen Thernstrom (Cambridge, Mass.: Harvard University Press, 1980), 43. Also see, in the same volume, Harold J. Abramson, "Assimilation and Pluralism," 150–60; Michael Novak, "Pluralism: A Humanistic Perspective" 772–81; and Michael Walzer, "Pluralism: A Political Perspective," 781–87.

120. See Abrahams, "The American Folklore Society: One Hundred Years of Folklore Study and Presentation," *1988 Festival of American Folklife* (Washington, D.C.: Smithsonian Institution, 1988), 46–47. See also Deborah Gordon, "The Politics of Ethnographic Authority: Race and Writing in the Ethnography of Margaret Mead and Zora Neale

Hurston," in *Modernist Anthropology: From Fieldwork to Text,* edited by Marc Manganaro (Princeton, N.J.: Princeton University Press, 1990), 146–62, for a discussion firmly positioning Hurston's field research historically and in relation to Boas's orientation on the one hand, and Mason's on the other.

121. Jerrold Hirsch, "Cultural Pluralism," 51.

122. Herskovits, "Acculturation and the American Negro," *The Southwestern Political and Social Science Quarterly* Vol. VIII, No. 3 (December 1927): 215, 217.

123. Herskovits, "The Significance of the Study of Acculturation for Anthropology," *American Anthropologist* Vol. 39 (1937): 263.

124. See Hirsch, "Cultural Pluralism," 51.

125. Hirsch, "Cultural Pluralism," 52.

126. Hirsch, "Cultural Pluralism," 54.

127. Hirsch, "Modernity, Nostalgia, and Southern Folklore Studies: The Case of John Lomax," *Journal of American Folklore,* Vol. 105, No. 416 (Spring 1992): 193; see also in the same article the section on John Lomax, the FWP, and Literal and Radical Variation on Romantic Nationalism, 198–203.

128. According to Hirsch, this still remains elusive for contemporary folklorists: "The FWP was unable to face the issue of whether the revitalized American culture they hoped for could be created without changes in social and economic arrangements. The question this raises for public sector folklorists today is whether the values that underlie their efforts must be presented in the form of myths that can never address key problems and how to weigh what is lost as well as gained in such circumstances," in "Cultural Pluralism," 52.

129. "The Failure of Folklore in Richard Wright's *Black Boy*," *Journal of American Folklore,* Vol. 104, No. 413 (Summer 1991): 292.

130. See Cunard, "A Reactionary Negro Organisation: A Short Review of Dr. DuBois, *The Crisis,* and the N.A.A.C.P. in 1932," in *Negro,* 142–47; and Du Bois, "Black America," *Negro,* 148–52. Ironically, Cunard does not apply the same criticism to her own involvement in promoting black reliance on the Communist Party. Part of the Party's strategy in the Scottsboro Case involved "discrediting the NAACP, thus portraying the CPUSA as the only organization sincerely committed to the defense of black Americans," according to Fraser M. Ottanelli, in *The Communist Party of the United States from the Depression to World War II* (New Brunswick, N.J.: Rutgers University Press, 1991).

131. "Wandering: Zora Neale Hurston's Search for Self and Method," *Specifying: Black Women Writing the American Experience* (Madison: The University of Wisconsin Press, 1987), 28.

132. See Susan Stewart, *Nonsense: Aspects of Intertextuality in Folklore and Literature* (Baltimore: Johns Hopkins University Press, 1989), 93. According to Stewart, "When the text draws attention to its own boundaries it is questioning the limits put upon the range of its possible interpretations and asserting its own possibilities for multiple meanings."

133. Ibid., 91.

134. Martin Laba, in his essay "Popular Culture and Folklore: The Social Dimension," explains how expressive behavior in folk culture can interpret popular culture forms found in technologically or mechanically oriented material culture. Significantly, "in the recurrent and ritual exchanges in the small group audience context, the item of popular culture may take on a meaning and function apart from the intention of the original producers of the item" 14; also, "the social practice of folkloric communication is structured by the symbolic forms in popular culture and serves as a means by which individuals and groups ritualize, organize and make sense of those forms of their day-to-day experience" 17. In *Media Sense: The Folklore-Popular Culture Continuum,* edited by Peter Navarez and Martin Laba (Bowling Green, Ohio: Bowling Green State University Popular Press, 1986).

135. A broad range of topics and styles are represented in the *Negro* anthology.

136. Douglass Kahn, in his book *John Heartfield: Art and Mass Media*, refers to mimicry as "a model for opposition" and as "a vantage point to observe recent cultural actions" (New York: Tanam Press, 1985), 105.

137. Goffman, *Frame Analysis*, 538.

138. It is significant that while Hurston was conducting her research, Boas wrote to Hurston, noting that material she had recently sent to him duplicated much of what had already been collected by others. He reminded her that he had asked her "to pay attention, not so much to the content, but rather to the form of diction, movements, and so on"; material he considered "essentially new" included "methods of dancing, habitual movements in telling tales, or in ordinary conversation," adding that "in transmission from Africa to America most of the contents of the culture have been adopted from the surrounding peoples while the mannerisms have, to a great extent, been retained." Boas to Hurston, May 3, 1927. Franz Boas Papers, American Philosophical Society. This is to say that her emphasis on formal aspects of expression, including mimesis, is another example of Boas's influence. Regarding Boas's similar influence on Benedict, see the section on mastering pattern, in Richard Handler, "Ruth Benedict and the Modernist Sensibility," in *Modernist Anthropology*, edited by Manganaro, 169–77.

139. According to Tzvetan Todorov, utterances and enunciations combine to form a symbolic meaning, such that a "speaking subject does not assume his utterance." Thus, Hurston "is rather imitating some other utterance," to use Todorov's lexicon. See Todorov, *Symbolism and Interpretation*, trans. Catherine Porter (Ithaca, N.Y.: Cornell University Press, 1982), 62–3.

140. Barthes, *S/Z*, trans. Richard Miller (New York: Hill and Wang; The Noonday Press, 1974), 45.

141. Ibid., 44–45.

142. See Andre Bazin, *What Is Cinema?*, Vol I, trans. Hugh Gray (Berkeley, Calif.: University of California Press, 1967), 74.

143. Later in this chapter, I discuss the idea of masking with reference to Ralph Ellison's essay "Change the Joke and Slip the Yoke," in *Shadow and Act* (New York: New American Library; Signet, 1966), 61–73.

144. Bhaba, "Sly Civility," *The Location of Culture*, 93–101.

145. Hemenway, *Zora Neale Hurston*, 126.

146. Ibid. See the letter to Hughes. Hemenway's claim concerning the emphasis on "accuracy" in transcription, then versus now, is highly debatable; part of what accounts for the recent interest in Hurston's folklore research is that she shares some experimental techniques in common with some contemporary field researchers; the interest in experimentation also was a major tenet of folklore collecting under the Federal Writers' Project. I explore the topic in Chapter Three.

147. Ibid., 167–68.

148. Ibid., 213.

149. Ibid.

150. Again, see Gordon, particularly her discussion of Hurston in relation to Boas, Mason, and Locke, "Politics of Ethnographic Authority," 159–62.

151. Gunter Lenz, "Southern Exposures: The Urban Experience and the Re-Construction of Black Folk Culture and Community in the Works of Richard Wright and Zora Neale Hurston, *New York Folklore* Vol. 7 (Summer 1981): 30.

152. See Susan Stewart, "Notes on Distressed Genres," *Journal of American Folklore*, Vol 104, No. 411 (Winter 1991): 5–31, on how the nostalgia over lost elements of the past accounts for the appropriating of folklore genres in literary texts, the idealization of liter-

ary tradition and, consequently, the "separation of speech and writing . . . anchored in a mimetic theory of representation" which "always posits speech as a form of nature"; what Stewart calls the severance of the individual from the folk context is interpreted as "a preference for individuals severed from context and 'collected' from the lower classes by an aristocracy eager to promote them," 8. Stewart's sense of the "distress" across genres has significant bearing on the boundary crossing and the interplay between folklore, fiction, and drama in Hurston's work.

153. Roger D. Abrahams and Susan Kalcik, "Folklore and Cultural Pluralism," in *Folklore in the Modern World*, edited by Richard M. Dorson (The Hague: Mouton Publishers, 1978), 229.

154. See Allen Woll, *Black Musical Performance: From Coontown to Dreamgirls* (Baton Rouge: Louisiana State University Press, 1989), 116.

155. Abrahams and Kalcik, "Folklore and Cultural Pluralism," 229.

156. Hobsbawm, "Introduction: Inventing Traditions," in *The Invention of Tradition*, edited by Hobsbawm and Terence Ranger (Cambridge: Cambridge University Press, 1983), 10.

157. E.H. Gombrich, "Meditations on a Hobby Horse or the Roots of Artistic Form," *Meditations on a Hobby Horse and other Essays on the Theory of Art* (London: Phaidon, 1963), 10.

158. Else, 20.

159. Ibid.

160. See Hurston, *Dust Tracks on a Road*, Chapter I, "My Birthplace," 1–6.

161. At the same time she was planning to begin graduate study at Columbia University under the Julius Rosenwald Fund Fellowship, Hurston was debating whether to study with Herskovits at Northwestern. Writing to Boas, she said: "I realize that Dr. Herskovits has been to Haiti and otherwise working with Negroes and that he could be a great deal of help to me." Hurston to Boas, January 4, 1935. Franz Boas Papers, American Philosophical Society.

162. Melville Herskovits, "The Negro's Americanism," in *The New Negro* (1925), edited by Alain Locke (New York: Atheneum, 1968), 353–360; *The Myth of the Negro Past* (1941) (Boston: Beacon Press, 1990). In 1936, Herskovits published some early speculations on continuities between West Africans and American Negroes in "The Significance of West Africa for Negro Research," reprinted in Simpson, *Melville J. Herskovits*, 127–39. Herskovits writes: "The traditions of African origin peculiar to New World Negroes persist in those portions of the United States even where the strongest acculturation to European patterns of behavior has taken place," 138.

163. In a postscript to Boas, Hurston adds: "Perhaps Dr. Herskovits can with my feeble contribution work out something that would help others who wish to study the American Negro as well as me." Hurston to Boas, January 4, 1935. Franz Boas Papers, American Philosophical Society.

164. "Change the Joke and Slip the Yoke," *Shadow and Act*, 69.

165. Ellison points out that white and black Americans are subjected to the same criticism in the second portion of the passage just quoted: "just as he himself [the white man] has been so charged by European and American critics with a nostalgia for the stability once typical of European cultures," in "Change the Joke," 69; and elsewhere in the essay he suggests the same idea.

166. Ellison, "Change the Joke," 68.

167. Ellison, 69–70.

168. Ellison, 70.

169. As she wrote to Boas: "You see, the negro is not living his lore to the extent of

the Indian. He is not on a reservation being kept pure. His negroness is being rubbed off by close contact with white culture." Hurston to Boas, March 29, 1927. Franz Boas Papers, American Philosophical Society.

170. Pierre Bourdieu's analysis of the relationship between aesthetic values and social status usefully explains some assumptions pertaining to distinctions between high and low art. I have found his sociological approach an aid in interpreting Hurston's remarks on high, low, folk and popular arts. See Bourdieu, *Distinction, a Social Critique of the Judgement of Taste*, trans. Richard Nice (Cambridge, MA: Harvard University Press, 1984).

171. The school was then called North Carolina College for Negroes.

172. See Robert Hemenway, *Zora Neale Hurston*, 253–56. It is interesting to note that Buttitta criticized Paul Green for perpetuating images of African-Americans "complacently pictured in the patronising, master-slave relationship," in "Negro Folklore in North Carolina," 62.

173. Frederick Koch, "Making a Native Folk Drama," *Southern Folklore Quarterly*, Vol. 1, No. 3 (September 1977): 29.

174. David Driskell, "The Evolution of a Black Aesthetic 1920–1950," in *Two Centuries of Black American Art* (New York: Los Angeles County Museum of Art/Alfred A. Knopf, 1976), 59–79.

175. Koch, "Making a Native Folk Drama," 30.

176. Hemenway's quotation in *Zora Neale Hurston* 102 and his quotation of Hurston, 255 illustrate two different situations in Hurston's life when she confronted her preference for performing arts as a form of communication. In a sense, she proposes an alternative to analytic discourse or language which she saw as a necessary by-product of field research. Although she respects scientific methods, in writing, she humanizes and personalizes her scientific subject—the people she researches and discusses, particularly in *Mules and Men* (1935) and *Tell My Horse* (1938). The idea of Enlightenment thinking or dominant approaches to cultural production and representation arises here in connection with a discussion of Hegel's view that "there is a strong link between modern science and Protestantism, viewed as a religion of the heart, of feeling, of hearing after an absent God," in Merold Westphal, *History and Truth in Hegel's Phenomenology* (Atlantic Highlands, NJ: Humanities Press, 1978), 50. The humanizing of people objectified by scientific method can be seen as yearning for a kind of Hegelian "common sense" in the face of exalted reason as characterized by the Enlightenment. Westphal continues, "He [Hegel] is equally concerned about what we would call positivism, the view which makes the natural sciences the paradigm of knowing and tends to discredit all knowledge claims which cannot be assimilated to that model. . . . The results of the exact sciences are so impressive in their certainty, and their usefulness, that they are easily taken to be the highest use of reason. When this happens a reality that is finite and a knowing that is empirical tend to be absolutized," 50–51. This struggle, Hegel exemplified as rationality (or Reason) on the one hand versus "the ethical life of a nation" (or Spirit), on the other—with both concepts having a universal as well as particular (individual) significance.

177. This topic is explored in further detail in Chapter Four.

CHAPTER THREE: NEGOTIATING THE FIELD

178. I follow the spelling used in each text being discussed.

179. See his comments in *Dust Tracks*, 288.

180. Hurston to Boas, March 29, 1927. Franz Boas Papers, American Philosophical Society.

181. A footnote to "T'appin (Terrapin)," *New Negro*, edited by Alain Locke, 245–49, points out that Fauset collected the tale along with "Brer Buzzard" in August 1925. The subtitle states that the tales were "Told by Cugo Lewis, Plateau, Alabama. Brought to American from West Coast Africa, 1859," 245. See also Hemenway, *Zora Neale Hurston*, 96–98.

182. "Cudjo's Own Story of the Last African Slaver," in *The Journal of Negro History*, Vol. XII, No. 4 (October 1927): 648–63. In a footnote, Hurston comments on the context for her research, as "an investigator of the Association for the Study of Negro Life and History" and acknowledges her use of sources of the Mobile Historical Society. Referring to *The Mobile Register* (11/9/58), in the article Hurston summarizes events surrounding passage of the ship *Clotilde* with its "cargo of slaves" from West Africa to the United States.

183. In Hemenway, *Zora Neale Hurston*, the linguist William Stewart is credited with discovering the plagiarism in the article, in 1972. Hemenway's "is the first public discussion of Stewart's discovery," 97.

184. Robert Hemenway, *Zora Neale Hurston, a Literary Biography*, 98. Hemenway's discussion of the plagiarism relies on the discovery having been pointed out to him by John Szwed, note 23, p. 103.

185. Ibid., 99.

186. Ibid.

187. The manuscript totals 117 pages, including an appendix of tales and games.

188. According to Hemenway's analysis of the previously mentioned investigation, she copied portions of the article's historical content from *Historic Sketches of the Old South*, by Emma Langdon Roche, a book available at the Historical Society in Mobile, Alabama. Hemenway, *Zora Neale Hurston*, 96–7.

189. Herskovits, "The Negro's Americanism," 354.

190. Ibid.

191. "Hurston's career needs no absurd apologetics," according to Hemenway, "she never plagiarized again," *Zora Neale Hurston*, 98.

192. Hemenway, *Zora Neale Hurston*, 100–1.

193. Ibid., 101.

194. Hemenway, ibid.; Hurston, "Barracoon," 2.

195. Hemenway, *Zora Neale Hurston*, 101.

196. According to J.L. Dillard, Cudjo's language as represented in Hurston's text is an excellent rendition. Dillard, *Black English: Its History and Usage in the United States* (New York: Random House, 1972; Vintage, 1973), 96.

197. B.A. Botkin is a primary example of an ethnographer also using fictional techniques contemporaneously with Hurston; see Hirsch, "Cultural Pluralism." For discussions on Hurston's ethnography as an alternative method, see John Dorst, "Rereading *Mules and Men*: Toward the Death of the Ethnographer," *Cultural Anthropology*, Vol. 2, No. 3, August 1987, 305–18; Gordon, "The Politics of Ethnographic Authority," 146–62. See also Hazel Carby, "The Politics of Fiction, Anthropology, and the Folk: Zora Neale Hurston," in *New Essays on Their Eyes Were Watching God*, edited by Michael Awkward (Cambridge: Cambridge University Press, 1990), 71–93; Christopher D. Felker, "Adaptation of the Source: Ethnocentricity and 'The Florida Negro,' " in *Zora in Florida*, edited by Steve Glassman and Kathryn Lee Seidel (Orlando: University of Central Florida Press, 1991), 146–58. Broader discussions of recent critical developments relevant to the ideas presented in this chapter can be found in James Clifford, *The Predicament of Culture: Twentieth-Century Ethnography, Literature, and Art* (Cambridge,

Mass.: Harvard University Press, 1988); James Clifford and George Marcus, editors, *Writing Culture: The Poetics and Politics of Ethnography* (Berkeley: University of California Press, 1986); Clifford Geertz, "Blurred Genres: The Refiguration of Social Thought," *Local Knowledge* (New York: Basic Books, 1983), 19–35; Manganaro, editor, *Modernist Anthropology*; Edward Said, "Representing the Colonized: Anthropology's Interlocutors," *Critical Inquiry*, 15 (Winter 1989): 205–25.

198. *American Mercury*, vol. 58 (March 1944): 358.

199. Andrews, "A Poetics of Afro-American Autobiography," in *Afro-American Literary Study in the 1990s*, edited by Houston A. Baker, Jr., and Patricia Redmond (Chicago: The University of Chicago Press, 1989), 81.

200. The quotation is from Andrews, "Reunion in the Postbellum Slave Narrative: Frederick Douglass and Elizabeth Keckley," *Black American Literature Forum*, vol. 23, no. 1 (spring 1989): 9. Andrews notes that critics have neglected postbellum narratives because they contradict notions of selfhood compatible with the prevailing trends in African-American literary study, in "A Poetics of Afro-American Autobiography."

201. Ibid., 82.

202. See Botkin, editor, *Lay My Burden Down: A Folk History of Slavery* (Athens, GA: The University of Georgia Press, 1945; Brown Thrasher Books, 1989), Tom E. Terrill and Jerrold Hirsch, editors, *Such as Us: Southern Voices of the Thirties* (Chapel Hill: The University of North Carolina Press, 1978). John Edgar Wideman, "Charles Chesnutt and the WPA Narratives: The Oral and Literate Roots of Afro-American Literature," in Charles T. Davis and Henry Louis Gates, Jr., editors, *The Slave Narrative* (New York: Oxford University Press, 1985), 59–78.

203. Andrews, "Afro-American Autobiography," 85.

204. Ibid.

205. "You has don more for then any one elce in this world since I ben in this cuntry no one has thought enough of me to look out for my well fair as you has [*sic*]," Kossula wrote to Mason, September 4, 1930. Alain Locke Papers, Manuscript Division, Moorland-Spingarn Research Center, Howard University.

206. The frequently cited male critics of Hurston's, writing during the Harlem Renaissance, are salient. Ralph D. Story suggests that Hurston's male colleagues accuse her of the same type of behavior they, too, displayed. Story "Gender Ambition: Zora Neale Hurston in the Harlem Renaissance," *The Black Scholar* (Summer/fall 1989): 25–30.

207. Allen D. Grimshaw, "Some Problematic Aspects of Communication in Cross-Racial Research in the United States" (1970); in *Language as Social Resource*, edited by Anwar S. Dil (Stanford: Stanford University Press, 1981), 65.

208. Hemenway, *Zora Neale Hurston*, 337, 341–2

209. See, in particular, Hemenway, "The Personal Dimension in *Their Eyes Were Watching God*," in *New Essays on Their Eyes Were Watching God*, edited by Michael Awkward (New York: Cambridge University Press, 1990), 34–36.

210. Mason mentions to Hurston's "mission" in her February 13, 1938 letter, and the allusion arises throughout their correspondence. Alain Locke Papers, Manuscript Division, Moorland-Spingarn Research Center, Howard University.

211. See Arnold Rampersad's comments on Hughes's story "The Blues I'm Playing" in *The Life of Langston Hughes*, Vol I (New York: Oxford 1986), 282.

212. Kossula wrote to Mason, "in reply to what you said about I letting the white folks read my history." Cudjo Lewis to Mason, September 4, 1930. Alain Locke Papers, Manuscript Division, Moorland-Spingarn Research Center, Howard University.

213. He writes: "You may have seen in the papers about my history but this has been over three years since I has let any one take it off to copy. I only did that so they would

help me but there is no one did for me as you did." Lewis to Mason, September 4, 1930. Alain Locke Papers, Manuscript Division, Moorland-Spingarn Research Center, Howard University.

214. Mason to Hurston, February 13, 1938; James Weldon Johnson Collection, Beinecke Library, Yale University Library. Paul Radin is well known for his work on the Winnebago trickster figures.

215. Cudjo Lewis to Mason, September 4, 1930; Hurston to Mason, May 26, 1932. Alain Locke Papers, Manuscript Division, Moorland-Spingarn Research Center, Howard University.

216. John Dollard, *Caste and Class in a Southern Town* (Madison: The University of Wisconsin Press, 1988; 1937): 306.

217. Hurston, "Black Death," Alain Locke Papers, Manuscript Division, Moorland-Spingarn Research Center, Howard University.

218. Dollard, *Caste and Class*, 310.

219. See Hemenway's discussion of "Black Death," *Zora Neale Hurston*, 74–79.

220. My discussion of "Black Death" continues in more detail in Chapter Five.

221. Neal, "A Profile: Zora Neale Hurston," *Southern Exposure*, 1 (Winter, 1974): 166.

222. Ibid.

223. Ibid.

224. Hemenway, *Zora Neale Hurston*, 78.

225. See Cheryl A. Wall, "*Mules and Men* and Women: Zora Neale Hurston's Strategies of Narration and Visions of Female Empowerment," *Black American Literature Forum*, Vol. 23, No. 4 (Winter 1989): 661–80.

226. This is a contract letter from Mason to Hurston, January 20, 1932, Alain Locke Papers, Manuscript Division, Moorland-Spingarn Research Center, Howard University. It is signed by Mason and Hurston and witnessed and signed by Mason's legal representative.

227. Harold Peerce, "The Negro Folk Cult," *The Crisis* 43 (1936): 374.

228. Ibid.

229. Ibid.

230. Ibid.

231. Neal, "A Profile," 166, 167.

232. Felker, "Adaptation of the Source: Ethnocentricity and 'the Florida Negro,' " *Zora in Florida*, edited by Steve Glassman and Kathryn Lee Seidel (Orlando: University of Central Florida Press, 1991), 153.

233. Stetson Kennedy, "Florida Folklife and the WPA, an Introduction," *A Reference Guide to Florida Folklore from the Federal WPA*, compiled by Jill I. Linzee and edited by Deborah S. Fant and Ormond H. Loomis (White Springs, FL: Bureau of Florida Folklife Programs, Florida Department of State, 1990), xix.

234. Kennedy, *Guide to WPA Collection of Florida Folklore*, xxvi.

235. Felker, "Ethnocentricity," 148.

236. Neal, "A Profile," 166.

237. Felker, "Ethnocentricity," 153.

238. Monty Noam Penkower in *The Federal Writers' Project: A Study in Government Patronage of the Arts* (Urbana: University Of Illinois Press, 1977), discusses the problems of how to define who should be included in the "writer" category when hiring, the vast differences in levels of training, experience, and production level.

239. Felker, "Ethnocentricity," 149.

240. Her field research notes on tales she collected from Joe Wiley, who appears in *Mules and Men*, support her statement about fragmentations. Alain Locke Papers, Moorland-Spingarn Research Center, Howard University—1928 sent to Mason.

241. See Paul Oliver, *Blues Fell This Morning: Meaning in the Blues* (Cambridge: Cambridge University Press, 1960; 1990), 278.

242. I am grateful to Elaine Charnow of the Margaret Mead Film Festival, Museum of Natural History in New York, and the Anthropology Department of New York University, for screening of a videotape she transcribed, based on Hurston's films.

243. Felker discusses the relationship between Hurston's essentialist, or what he calls ethnocentric, view of black culture as being aesthetic—seeing expressive forms as the efforts of people "to lead lives that are things of beauty." Felker, "Ethnocentricity," 151.

244. Felker, "Ethnocentricity," 150–51.

245. Kennedy, *A Reference Guide*, xxvi, note.

246. Hirsch, "Foreword," *Lay My Burden Down*, xx.

247. Hirsch, "Foreword," xxi.

248. Hurston, "Turpentine Camp—Cross City," August 1939, 15. WPA Federal Writers' Project, Florida Folklife Archives, Bureau of Florida Folklife Programs, Florida Department of State.

249. Hurston, "Turpentine Camp," 15.

250. Hurston, "Turpentine Camp," 7.

251. Kennedy, "Introduction," *A Reference Guide*, xxxiii.

252. Hurston, "Turpentine Camp," 3.

253. Herskovits to Boas, January 25, 1928, Franz Boas Papers, American Philosophical Society. Panels a the Institute on Race Relations included the following. (1) Race and Culture; Dealing with the Biological Issues of Race and Race Differences; The Theory and Significance of Race; The Scientific Problem of the Negro; The Force of Tradition in determining human behavior. (2) World Race Problems: Historical, Political, and Psychological Factors in Race Contact Generally; Contemporary Problems; South America (Particularly Brazil), the West Indies, South Africa; Racial and Cultural Factors in Conflict Situations in India, China, and Japan; Race and the World's Religions; Comparisons with Patterns of Race Contact and Accommodation in the United States. (3) Cultural and Historical Factors in the American Negro-White Race Problems (such as African background, culture and acculturation, slavery). (4) Social Philosophies, Techniques and Methods: Aspects of the General Social Philosophy Bearing upon the American Race Problem; Programs of Organizations and Methods of Approach to Race Problems Presented and Appraised; Minority Groups under Political Organization; Fascism, Communism, Democracy. (Margaret Mead Papers, Manuscript Division, Library of Congress.) An example of an effort to institute a change in black performance history, a Committee for the Establishment of a Permanent Negro Repertory Theater was established in 1931 by Alain Locke, Paul Green, and others. (Alain Locke Papers, Manuscript Division, Moorland-Spingarn Research Center, Howard University.)

254. Jane Belo and Zora Neale Hurston, "Bishop R.A.R. Johnson of the Holy Church of the Living God, the Pillar and the Ground of the Truth, House of Prayer for all People, Inc." Included with Notes on Sanctified Church in Beaufort, S.C., April 29, 1940, 3–5. Margaret Mead Papers, Manuscript Division, Library of Congress.

255. Belo and Hurston, "Bishop R.A.R. Johnson," 5.

256. Belo and Hurston, "Bishop R.A.R. Johnson," 5.

257. Mead wrote to Hurston with specific instructions on what to observe. See Mead to Hurston, May 20, 1940, Margaret Mead Papers, Manuscript Division, Library of Congress.

258. See Belo to Hurston, April 29, 1940, Margaret Mead Papers, Manuscript Division, Library of Congress.

259. Belo indicates her perception and expectation of Hurston as being "to handle to the personal end." Belo to Hurston, April 29, 1940, Margaret Mead Papers, Manuscript Division, Library of Congress.

260. Hurston to Green, May 3, 1940, Paul Green Papers, in the Southern Historical Collection of the Manuscripts Department, University of North Carolina, Chapel Hill.

261. Ronald Patrick Ross, "Black Drama in the Federal Theater, 1935–39," (Ph.D. Dissertation, University of Southern California, 1972), 25.

262. John Houseman, *Run-Through, a Memoir* (New York: Simon and Schuster, 1972): 182.

263. Houseman, 205; Perkins, in *Black Female Playwrights* 78, reiterates Houseman's account.

264. Ronald Patrick Ross, "Black Drama in the Federal Theater 1935–39," (Ph.D. Dissertation, University of Southern California, 1972), 182–83.

265. Hurston to Knott, January 26, 1938; James Weldon Johnson Collection, Beinecke Library, Yale University Library.

266. Knott to Johnson, January 29, 1938.

267. Johnson to Knott, February 4, 1938.

268. Barbara Kirshenblatt-Gimblett, in "Objects of Ethnography," in *Exhibiting Cultures: The Poetics and Politics of Museum Display*, edited by Ivan Karp and Steven D. Lavine (Washington, D.C.: Smithsonian, 1990), 386–443, examines the topic in fine detail with reference to performance related concerns I cover in the Introduction. I explore the topic of cultural display further in Chapter Six.

269. Johnson to Knott, May 1, 1934; James Weldon Johnson Collection, Beinecke Library, Yale University Library.

CHAPTER FOUR: THE AUTHENTICITY DEBATE

270. In Perkins, *Black Female Playwrights Before 1950*, 81.

271. Ibid., 84.

272. Ibid., 84.

273. Ibid., 88.

274. Lawrence Levine, *Black Culture and Black Consciousness: Afro-American Folk Thought from Slavery to Freedom* (New York: Oxford, 1968), 84.

275. See Hazel V. Carby, "The Politics of Fiction, Anthropology, and the Folk: Zora Neale Hurston," in *New Essays on "Their Eyes Were Watching God,"* edited by Michael Awkward (New York: Cambridge University Press, 1990), 71–93.

276. All citations are from Crevecouer in *Letters from an American Farmer and Sketches of Eighteenth Century America* (New York: Penguin Books, 1981; 1986), 69.

277. Gates, "Editor's Introduction: Writing 'Race' and the Difference it Makes," *"Race," Writing and Difference*, edited by Gates. (Chicago: The University of Chicago Press, 1986): 9.

278. Gates, "Writing 'Race,' " 8.

279. Gates, "Writing 'Race,' " 5.

280. Charles Taylor, *The Ethics of Authenticity* (Cambridge, Mass.: Harvard University Press, 1991), 63.

281. Taylor, 63.

282. See Werner Sollors' discussion of Zangwill's play and of Horace Kallen.

283. Sollors, "Ethnicity and Literary Form," 249.

284. Woll, *Black Musical Theatre*, 78.

285. Woll, *Black Musical Theatre*, 78.

286. Hatch, "The White Folks Guide to 200 Years of Black & White Drama," *The Drama Review* vol. 16, no. 4 (December 1972): 18.

287. Baker, *Modernism and the Harlem Renaissance* (Chicago: University of Chicago Press, 1987) 33.

288. Hurston to Mason, October 15, 1931, Alain Locke Papers, Manuscript Division, Moorland-Spingarn Research Center, Howard University.

289. Ibid.

290. Ibid.

291. Ibid.

292. See Spivak, "Can the Subaltern Speak?"

293. Ibid.

294. Kennedy, "Introduction," *Guide to the WPA Collection of Florida Folklore*, xxii.

295. Gwaltney, *Drylongso: A Self-Portrait of Black America* (New York: The New Press, 1993; Random House, 1980), xv.

296. In Perkins, 93.

297. Johnson, "Preface to the First Edition," *The Book of American Negro Poetry*, (1922). (New York: Harcourt, Brace, Jovanovich, 1969), 10–11.

298. Boas, *Anthropology and Modern Life* (New York: W.W. Norton and Co., 1928; Dover, 1986), 79.

299. Tausig, *Mimesis and Alterity: A Particular History of the Senses* (New York: Routledge, 1993), 141.

300. Hurston to Mason, October 15, 1931. Alain Locke Papers, Manuscript Division, Moorland-Spingarn Research Center, Howard University.

301. Hurston to Mason, September 25, 1931.

302. Mitchell, *Black Drama: The Story of the American Negro in the Theater* (New York: Hawthorn Books, 1967), 24–25.

303. Alain Locke Papers, Manuscript Division, Moorland-Spingarn Research Center, Howard University.

304. Ibid.

305. Alain Locke Papers, Manuscript Division, Moorland-Spingarn Research Center, Howard University.

306. See Miles Orvell, *The Real Thing: Imitation and Authenticity in American Culture, 1880–1940* (Chapel Hill, NC: University of North Carolina Press, 1989).

307. Ibid., 121.

308. Ibid., 122.

309. Ibid., 104.

310. Ibid., 125.

311. See James Hatch and Ted Shine, editors, *Black Theater U.S.A.*, for the text of Brown's play and historical commentary. Hill's article discusses, along with other plays, the first documented play written and produced by a black person, William Henry Brown, in the United States, *King Shotaway* (c. 1820s). Brown, who had started his own theater in New York, staged the play about a slave rebellion in St. Vincent, thus introducing the protagonist King Shotaway as the first black nationalist hero known in American theater. See Hill, "The Revolutionary Tradition in Black Drama," *Theater Journal*, Vol. 38, No. 4 (December 1986): 408–26.

312. James, "The Art of Fiction," in *The Future of the Novel: Essays on the Art of Fiction*, edited by Leon Edel (New York: Vintage, 1956), 13.

313. Harold Cruse, *The Crisis of the Negro Intellectual* (New York: William Morrow & Co., 1967), 38.

314. Huggins, *Harlem Renaissance* (New York: Oxford University Press, 1971), 118.

315. Huggins, *Harlem Renaissance*, 118.

316. Lewis, *When Harlem Was in Vogue*, 99.

317. Cruse, *The Crisis of the Negro Intellectual*, 38.

318. Gates, "Writing 'Race,' " 5.

319. See Larry Neal, Proposal for Harlem Urban Renewal, Unpublished Manuscript. Larry Neal Papers, New York Public Library: Schomburg Center for Research in Black Culture, Archive, Box 2.

320. Huggins, *Harlem Renaissance*, 118.

321. Gwaltney, xvii.

322. Hurston had, according to Hemenway, worked as a domestic between the ages of 14 and 20. Since Cheryl Wall's research has shown Hurston's birth to have been ten years earlier than Hemenway reports (1891 rather than 1901), rereading *Dust Tracks* and Hemenway's passages on those years of Hurston's life, leaves open the possibility that she spent considerably more time in the workforce.

323. Arthur Huff Fauset, "Intelligentsia," *Fire!!*, Vol. 1, no. 1, 1926. Reprinted by The Fire Press, Metuchen, N.J. 1982, p. 45.

324. Gates, "Why the 'Mule Bone' Debate Goes On," *The New York Times*, February 10, 1991.

325. Ibid.

326. Ibid.

327. Ibid.

328. See Mance Williams, *Black Theater of the 60s and 70s: A Historical-Critical Analysis of the Movement* (Westport, Conn.: Greenwood Press, 1983), 17.

329. Detailed expense reports which Mason required from Hurston are in the Alain Locke Papers, Manuscript Division, Moorland-Spingarn Research Center, Howard University.

330. Euba, *Archetypes, Imprecators, and Victims of Fate: Origins and Developments of Satire in Black Drama* (New York: Greenwood Press, 1989), 132.

CHAPTER FIVE: HURSTON'S HIEROGLYPHICS: THE WORD MAGIC OF RITUAL ACTION

331. Susan Buck-Morss, *The Dialectics of Seeing: Walter Benjamin and the Arcades Project* (Cambridge, Mass.: The MIT Press), 172.

332. The source being used here is H. Frankfort, *Ancient Egyptian Religion* (New York: Harper & Row, 1961; Columbia University Press, 1948), 135–6.

333. Buck-Morss, ibid.

334. Hughes, Bambara.

335. Fernandez, "Some Reflections on Looking in Mirrors," 31.

336. Ibid., 33–34.

337. Ibid., 34.

338. Taussig, *Mimesis and Alterity*, 224.

339. Ibid., 250.

340. Hemenway, *Zora Neale Hurston*, 78.

341. Stephen Tyler, "Ethnography, Intertextuality and the End of Description," *American Journal of Semiotics*, Vol. 3, No. 4 (1985): 88.

342. The other stories I am referring to are "Father Abraham," "Mother Catherine," and "Uncle Monday." See *The Sanctified Church*, 15–40. "Mother Catherine" and "Uncle Monday" also appear in *Negro*, 54–61. "Mother Catherine" and "Uncle Monday" also appear in Zora Neale Hurston, *The Complete Stories* (New York: HarperCollins, 1995), 99–116.

343. The reader is invited to compare my discussion of tales in this chapter with Cyrena N. Pondrom's informative discussion of Hurston's best known novel, in "The Role of Myth in Hurston's *Their Eyes Were Watching God*," *American Literature* vol. 58, No. 2 (May 1986): 181–202.

344. Thompson, "Myths and Folktales," *Journal of American Folklore*, Vol. 68, No. 270 (October-December 1955): 484.

345. Ibid.

346. I examined a version of the story deposited in the Alain Locke Papers at the Moorland-Spingarn Research Center; other versions include the manuscript submitted to *Opportunity*, in the Charles Johnson Collection at Fisk University Library, which is the version published in *The Complete Stories* (HarperCollins 1995). As mentioned, another variation appears in the *Journal of American Folklore* article "Hoodoo in America." All citations in my discussion relate to the story as published in *The Complete Stories*.

347. Here, I extrapolate from Stanley Jeyaraja Tambiah's formulations based on his analysis of Trobriand thought, in "The Magical Power of Words," *Culture, Thought, and Social Action: An Anthropological Perspective* (Cambridge, Mass.: Harvard University Press, 1985), 28–30.

348. Mulira, "The Case of Voodoo in New Orleans," 58.

349. Ibid., 56. Spellings of Marie Leveau's name vary. The quoted passage has remained as published.

350. Ibid.

351. Joan Dayan, "Vodoun, or the Voice of the Gods," *Raritan: A Quarterly Review*, 10, 3 (winter 1991): 32.

352. Baker, *Modernism and the Harlem Renaissance*, 15.

353. Hurston to Boas, December 27, 1928; Franz Boas Papers, American Philosophical Society.

354. Bambara, "Some Forward Remarks," *The Sanctified Church*, 11.

355. Mulira, 49–63.

356. See Michael Riffaterre, "Truth in Diegesis," in *Fictional Truth* (Baltimore: The Johns Hopkins Press, 1990), 1–28.

357. Tambiah, "The Magical Power of Words," 22.

358. Bambara, 11.

359. Dayan, 32.

360. Metraux, *Voodoo in Haiti* (New York: Schocken Books, 1972), 85.

361. Dayan, 36–37.

362. I am referring to Stith Thompson's critique of the idea that ritual gives rise to myth, in "Myths and Folktales," *Journal of American Folklore*, Vol. 68, No. 270 (October-December 1955): 482–488; see also, in the same *Journal of American Folklore* issue on myth, Lord Raglan, "Myth and Ritual," 454–461, and Stanley Edgar Hyman, "The Ritual View of Myth and the Mythic," 462–472.

363. Thompson sees no reason for associating myth with ritual since for him the subject matter, which is not to say the meaning, of myths is more important than their alleged purposes or functions.

364. Tambiah, "Form and Meaning of Magical Acts: A Point of View," *Culture, Thought, and Social Action*, 83.

365. Boas to Hurston, May 3, 1937, Franz Boas Papers, American Philosophical Society.

366. Wall, "*Mules and Men* and Women: Zora Neale Hurston's Strategies of Narration and Visions of Female Empowerment," *Black American Literature Forum*, Vol. 23, No. 4 (winter 1989): 673.

367. Soyinka discusses Obatala, Shango, and Ogun; I am drawing an analogy with his

idea of the Yoruba gods as archetypes and the underlying worldview presented in Hurston's conjure narratives. The quote is from *Myth, Literature and the African World,* 4.

368. See Dayan, 49.

369. Not accidentally, the title and substance of Jamaica Kincaid's book *At the Bottom of the River* echo this idea. See Metraux, 258. The same idea is repeated in "Uncle Monday," which I discuss subsequently, in this chapter.

370. Metraux, 258.

371. Fernandez, 30–31.

372. Dutton, "The Problem of Invisibility: Voodoo and Zora Neale Hurston," *Frontiers,* Vol. 23, No. 2 (1992): 140.

373. Karen McCarthy Brown is one recent scholar who has attempted to reconcile the two in her work *Mama Lola, a Vodoun Priestess in Brooklyn* (Berkeley: University of California Press, 1991).

374. Dutton, 145.

375. Taussig, *Mimesis and Alterity,* 16.

376. Hurston to Mason, October 10, 1931, Alain Locke Papers, Manuscript Division, Moorland-Spingarn Research Center, Howard University.

377. Hurston to Belo, May 2, 1940, Margaret Mead Papers, Manuscript Division, Library of Congress.

378. See critical overviews in Nathan Irvin Huggins, *Harlem Renaissance* (New York: Oxford University Press, 1971), 295–98 et passim; David Levering Lewis, *When Harlem Was in Vogue,* 206–7 et passim.

379. William Rubin, "Modernist Primitivism: An Introduction," in *"Primitivism" in 20th Century Art* (New York: The Museum of Modern Art), 1.

380. Rubin, "Modernist Primitivism: An Introduction," 5.

381. Hal Foster, "The 'Primitive' Unconscious," *Recordings: Art, Spectacle, Cultural Politics* (Seattle: Bay Press, 1985), 199. Similarly, James Clifford shows discrepancies in the exhibit's fascination with "primitivist" aesthetics and lack of concern with cultural context. See Clifford, *The Predicament of Culture,* 189–214.

382. Torgovnick *Gone Primitive: Savage Intellects, Modern Lives* (Chicago: University of Chicago Press), 71.

383. See Jiri Veltrucky, "Dramatic Text as a Component of Theater," in *Semiotics of Art,* edited by Ladislav Matejka and Irwin Titunik (Cambridge, Mass.: MIT, 1976; 1984), 103–05.

384. Both models of Erving Goffman's make it possible to analyze everyday-life behavior as performance. The world-as-stage model used in *The Presentation of Self in Everyday Life* (New York: Doubleday, 1959) shows how people manage the impressions they make on others. *Frame Analysis* shows how context structures behavior. Whereas the first places more emphasis on persona and the individual's role-playing techniques in various contexts, the latter stresses the ways that organizational structures influence the meaning of behavior.

385. Hurston, *The Sanctified Church,* 30.

386. Baker, "Workings of the Spirit," 87.

387. Hurston, *Dust Tracks on a Road,* 30.

388. Baker, "Workings of the Spirit," 92. Also, for the moment I am putting aside Umberto Eco's argument that the idea of the iconic is incoherent, preferring instead to proceed from W.J.T. Mitchell's claim that the icon is the most difficult sign-type to assimilate into semiotics. *Iconology: Image, Text, Ideology* (Chicago: University of Chicago Press, 1986), 56.

389. See Dillard, *Black English,* 151; and Eugene D. Genovese, *Roll, Jordan, Roll: The World the Slaves Made* (New York: Random House, 1972; Vintage, 1976): 448–50.

390. Tambiah, "The Magical Power of Words," 27.

391. Eliade, *The Sacred and the Profane*, (New York: Harcourt, Brave, and World; Harvest, 1959), 95.

392. My sources are William Bascom, *The Yoruba of Southwestern Nigeria* (New York: Holt, Rinehart and Winston, 1969): 88; Robert Farris Thompson, *Flash of the Spirit: African & Afro-American Art & Philosophy*, (New York: Vintage Books, 1984), 72–79.

393. John Roberts, *From Trickster to Badman: The Black Folk Hero in Slavery and Freedom* (Philadelphia: University of Pennsylvania Press, 1989), 93.

394. Ibid.

395. Soyinka, 8.

396. Euba's chapter on "The Drama of Epidemic" is especially informative on this subject, in *Archetypes, Imprecators, and Victims of Fate*, 121–64.

397. This argument takes into account speculations presented by Paul Carter Harrison, *The Drama of Nommo* (New York: Grove Press, 1972) and *Totem Voices: Plays from the Black World Repertory* (New York: Grove Press, 1989), with an introduction by Harrison. (My review of *Totem Voices* appears in *Black American Literature Forum*, Vol. 25, no. 1 [Spring 1991].) See also, Jahnheinz Jahn, *Muntu: The New African Culture* (New York: Grove Press, 1961).

398. Willis D. Weatherford and Charles S. Johnson, *Race Relations: Adjustment of Whites and Negroes in the United States* (D.C. Heath and Company, 1934), 96.

399. E. Franklin Frazier, *The Negro in the United States* (New York: Macmillan; revised edition, 1957), 21.

400. Ibid.

401. See Frazier, 20–21.

402. Boas to Hurston, May 3, 1927. Franz Boas Papers, American Philosophical Society.

403. Ibid.

404. Frazier, *The Negro in the United States*, 689.

405. R.F. Thompson, 90.

406. Armstrong, *The Affecting Presence: an Essay in Humanistic Anthropology* (Urbana: University of Illinois, 1971), 120.

407. Ibid.

408. Mitchell, *Iconology*, 198.

409. Wall, "*Mules and Men* and Women," 664.

410. Bascom, *The Yoruba*, 88.

411. By extension, I am also including her fiction and drama based on the traditional tales and her ethnographic research.

412. Wall, "*Mules and Men* and Women," 665.

413. Ibid.

414. Wall, 664.

415. See Wall, 672.

CHAPTER SIX: STAGING HURSTON'S LIFE AND WORK

416. The discussions were held on November 28, 1988; portions were later published upon the show's production in 1991 in a special supplement of *The New Theater Review*, a Lincoln Center Theater Publication. My citations are drawn from the discussion in the rehearsal room at Lincoln Center (designated as "Mule Bone R") and the discussions in the producer's office (designated as "Mule Bone PD").

417. Matt Brazzle is the same character as Matt Bonner in *Their Eyes Were Watching God*.

418. See Bass and Gates, editors, *Mule Bone*, 43.

419. This is not to diminish the importance of other influential innovators of the early twentieth century. The Russian director Vsevelod Meyerhold, according to theater historian Michael Kirby, is Brecht's precursor in agit prop theater. The French dramatist Antonin Artaud also rearticulated the relationship between text and performance. Kirby emphasized the point concerning Brecht and Meyerhold in lectures at the Performance Studies Department, New York University.

420. See John Fuegi, *Bertolt Brecht: Chaos According to Plan* (Cambridge: Cambridge University Press, 1987), 59–60.

421. The *Modellbuch* and the *Theaterarbeit*, both documenting the Berliner Ensemble's work, are the two main examples I have in mind. See John Willett, *The Theater of Bertolt Brecht: A Study from Eight Aspects* (New York: New Directions, 1959), 21.

422. Transcript, 16.

423. My colleague Evelyn Tribble, a Renaissance specialist, was helpful to me in providing support for the view that *Love's Labors Lost* is among Shakespeare's weaker plays.

424. Interview, "Black Theater's What-Might-Have-Been," *New York Newsday* (January 31, 1991): 112.

425. Bauman and Briggs, "Poetics and Performance as Critical Perspectives on Language and Social Life," *Annual Review of Anthropology* 19 (1990): 77.

426. Don Nelsen, "Digging Up Prized 'Bone': Why a Collaboration Between Zora Neale Hurston & Langston Hughes Took 61 Years to Reach Broadway." *The New York Daily News* (February 3, 1991), 9.

427. Barbara Kirshenblatt-Gimblett, "Objects of Ethnography," 412.

428. This is a reference to Big John or Ole John.

429. Hurston, "The Chick with One Hen," unpublished manuscript, James Weldon Johnson Collection, Beineicke Library, Yale University Library. Locke's review appeared in *Opportunity*, January 1938.

430. Information regarding *Mule Bone*'s production has been compiled through my discussions with Lincoln Center Dramaturg Anne Cattaneo, Director Michael Schultz, and George Houston Bass. An unpublished transcript of the discussion among producers, literary and estate executors of Hurston and Hughes, and prospective directors, following the initial reading of the play at Lincoln Center Theater in New York, November 28, 1988, supplied some of the background for the discussion of the dramaturgical, directorial, and political issues. See Langston Hughes and Zora Neale Hurston, *Mule Bone: A Comedy of Negro Life*, edited by Bass and Gates (New York: Harper Collins, 1991).

431. Bauman and Briggs, "Poetics and Performance," 76.

432. So far as I have been able to discern very little is known about how the collaboration between Hurston and Waring came about. See also Hemenway, *Zora Neale Hurston*, and Warren J. Carson, "Hurston as Dramatist: The Florida Connection," in *Zora in Florida*, edited by Glassmann and Seidel, 122–3.

433. Interview with Laurence Holder, August 8, 1991. A version of the play, entitled "Zora," appears in *New Plays from the Black Theatre*, edited by Woodie King, Jr. (Chicago: Third World Press, 1989), 137–52.

434. A series of dialogues I had with Elizabeth Van Dyke are the basis for her comments and quoted statements.

435. The quote is from Alice Walker, "Anything We Love Can Be Saved: The Resurrection of Zora Neale Hurston and Her Work," *Zora! Zora Neale Hurston, a Woman and Her Community*, edited by N.Y. Nathiri (Orlando, Fla.: Orlando Sentinel, Sentinel Communications Co., 1991): 82. *Zora Is My Name* is a 1990 American Playhouse production which aired on the Public Broadcast System.

436. Bell Hooks, "Saving Black Folk Culture: Zora Neale Hurston as Anthropologist and Writer," *Yearning: Race, Gender, and Cultural Politics* (Boston, Mass.: South End Press, 1990): 136.

437. Speisman, *A Tea With Zora and Marjorie, The Rawlings Journal*, I (1988), 95.

438. The production was initiated at the Mark Taper Forum in Los Angeles in May 1989; premiered at Crossroads Theater in New Brunswick, New Jersey, on November 1, 1989; and was produced in 1990 at the Public Theater's New York Shakespeare Festival.

439. See Rosemary Bray, "An Unpredictable Playwright Reverses Himself," *The New York Times* (April 15, 1990): 7.

440. Program Notes, *Spunk* (New Brunswick, N.J.: Crossroads Theater Company, Nov. 2–Dec. 10, 1989).

441. John Willett, *The Theater of Bertolt Brecht, a Study from Eight Aspects* (Norfolk, CT: James Laughlin; New Directions, 1959): 175.

442. Hurston to Mason, July 23, 1931, Alain Locke Papers, Manuscript Division, Moorland-Spingarn Research Center, Howard University.

443. Hurston to Mason, October 15, 1931, Alain Locke Papers, Manuscript Division, Moorland-Spingarn Research Center, Howard University.

444. For a discussion of Hurston's nonessentialist self-concept, see Barbara Johnson, "Thresholds of Difference: Structures of Address in Zora Neale Hurston," in *"Race," Writing, and Difference,* edited by Gates 317–38; see also Michelle Wallace, "Who Owns Zora Neale Hurston? Critics Carve Up the Legend," *Invisibility Blues: From Pop to Theory* (London: Verso, 1990): 172–86.

CONCLUSION

445. Schechner, *The End of Humanism: Writings on Performance* (New York: Performing Arts Journal Publications, 1982), 11–76; see, in particular, pages 30–44.

BIBLIOGRAPHY

Abbott, Dorothy. "Recovering Zora Neale Hurston's Work," *Frontiers* 12, no. 1 (1991): 175–213.

Abrahams, Roger. "The American Folklore Society: One Hundred Years of Folklore Study and Presentation." *1988 Festival of American Folklife.* Washington, D.C.: Smithsonian Institution, 1988, 46–47.

———. "Folklore and History in the Study of Afro-America." In *Folklore Today: A Festschrift for Richard M. Dorson*, edited by Linda Degh, Henry Glassie, and Felix J. Oinas, 1–9. Bloomington: Indiana University Press, 1976.

———. "Phantoms of Romantic Nationalism in Folkloristics," *Journal of American Folklore* 106, 419 (1933): 3–37.

———. "Toward an Enactment-Centered Theory of Folklore." In *Frontiers of Folklore*, edited by William Bascom. Boulder: Westview Press, 1977.

Abrahams, Roger, and Susan Kalcik. "Folklore and Cultural Pluralism." In *Folklore in the Modern World*, edited by Richard M. Dorson, 223–36. The Hague: Mouton Publishers, 1978.

Abramson, Harold J. "Assimilation and Pluralism," In *Harvard Encyclopedia of American Ethnic Groups*, edited by Stephan Thernstrom, 150–60. Cambridge, Mass.: Harvard University Press, 1980.

Andrews, William L. "A Poetics of Afro-American Autobiography." In *Afro-American Literary Study in the 1990s*, edited by Houston A. Baker, Jr., and Patricia Redmond, 78–90. Chicago: University of Chicago Press, 1989.

Anozie, Sunday O. *Structural Models and African Poetics: Towards a Pragmatic Theory of Literature.* London: Routledge & Kegan Paul, 1981.

Aptheker, Herbert, ed. *Documentary History of the Negro People in the United States*, Vols. 3 and 4, New York: Carol Publishing Group, 1973; 1990.

Armstrong, Robert Plant. *The Affecting Presence: An Essay in Humanistic Anthropology.* Urbana: University of Illinois Press, 1971.

Aschenbrenner, Joyce. *Katherine Dunham: Reflections on the Social and Political Contexts of Afro-American Dance.* New York: Congress on Research in Dance, 1981.

Austin, Gayle. *Feminist Theories for Dramatic Criticism.* Ann Arbor: University of Michigan Press, 1990.

Austin, J. L. *How To Do Things With Words.* Edited by J.O. Urmson. New York: Oxford University Press, 1962.

Awkward, Michael, ed. *New Essays on "Their Eyes Were Watching God."* Cambridge: Cambridge University Press, 1990.

Baker, Houston A., Jr. *Modernism and the Harlem Renaissance.* Chicago: University of Chicago, 1987.

————. "Workings of the Spirit: Conjure and the Space of Black Women's Creativity." In *Workings of the Spirit: The Poetics of Afro-American Women's Writing*, 69–101. Chicago: University of Chicago Press, 1991.

Bakhtin, Mikhail. *The Dialogic Imagination.* Edited by Michael Holquist. Translated by Caryl Emerson and Michael Holquist. Austin: University of Texas Press, 1981.

————. *Rabelais and His World.* Translated by Helene Iswolsky. Bloomington: Indiana University Press, 1984.

Barthes, Roland. *Image—Music—Text.* Translated by Stephen Heath. New York: Farrar, Straus and Giroux; the Noonday Press, 1977.

————. *S/Z.* Translated by Richard Miller. New York: Hill and Wang; Noonday Press, 1974.

Bascom, William. *The Yoruba of Southwestern Nigeria.* New York: Holt, Rinehart and Winston, 1969.

Bass, George Houston. "Editor/Dramaturg's Notes on *Mulebone*." Unpublished Paper. Providence, R.I.: Rites and Reason Theatre, Brown University, 1989.

————. "A Playwright's Note on the Art of Re-Creation." *Theater Three* (Fall 1987): 61–67.

Bateson, Gregory. "A Theory of Play and Fantasy." In *Steps to an Ecology of Mind*, 177–93. New York: Ballantine, 1972.

Battersby, Christine. *Gender and Genius: Towards a Feminist Aesthetics.* Bloomington: Indiana University Press, 1989.

Baudrillard, Jean. *For a Critique of the Political Economy of the Sign.* Translated by Charles Levin. Telos Press, 1981.

Bauman, Richard. "American Folklore Studies and Social Transformation: A Performance-Centered Perspective," *Text and Performance Quarterly* 9, no. 3 (July 1989): 175–84.

————. *Verbal Art as Performance.* Prospect Heights, Ill.: Waveland Press, 1977.

Bauman, Richard, and Charles Briggs. "Poetics and Performance: Critical Perspectives on Language and Social Life." *Annual Review of Anthropology* 19 (1990): 59–88.

Benedict, Ruth. *Race: Science and Politics.* New York: Modern Age Books, 1940.

Benjamin, Walter. *Illuminations: Essays and Reflections.* Edited by Hannah Arendt. New York: Schocken Books, 1968.

————. *Reflections: Essays, Aphorisms, Autobiographical Writings.* Edited by Peter Demetz. New York: Schocken Books, 1978.

Bethel, Lorraine. " 'This Infinity of Conscious Pain': Zora Neale Hurston and the Black Female Literary Tradition." In *All the Women Are White, all the Blacks Are Men, but Some of Us Are Brave: Black Women's Studies*, 176–188. New York: The Feminist Press, 1982.

Bhabha, Homi K. *The Location of Culture.* London: Routledge, 1994.

Bhabha, Homi. "Representation and the Colonial Text: a Critical Exploration of Some Forms of Mimeticism." In *The Theory of Reading*, edited by Frank Gloversmith, 93–122. Totowa, N. J.: Harvester; Barnes & Noble, 1984.

Biddiss, Michael D., ed. *Gobineau Selected Political Writings.* New York: Harper & Row, 1970.

Bloom, Harold, ed. *Zora Neale Hurston's Their Eyes Were Watching God.* New York: Chelsea House Publishers, 1987.

Boas, Franz. *Anthropology and Modern Life.* New York: W. W. Norton, 1928; Dover, 1986.

————. "Aryans and Non-Aryans," *The American Mercury* 22, no. 125 (May 1934): 219–23.

————. "The Instability of Human Types." In *Papers on Inter-Racial Problems Communicated to the First Universal Race Congress Held at the University of London, July 26–29, 1911*, edited by G. Spiller, 99–103. London: P. S. King & Son, 1911.

————. *Primitive Art* (1927). New York: Dover, 1955.

————. *Race, Language and Culture.* New York: Macmillan, 1946.

Bibliography

Bobb, June D. "Taking a Stand on High Ground: The Recreated Self in *Their Eyes Were Watching God.*" *The Zora Neale Hurston Forum* 2, no. 1 (Fall 1987): 10–17.

Bontemps, Arna, ed. *The Harlem Renaissance Remembered.* New York: Dodd, Mead, 1972.

Botkin, B. A. *Lay My Burden Down, a Folk History of Slavery.* Athens, Ga.: The University of Georgia Press, 1989.

———. "WPA and Folklore Research: 'Bread and Song.'" *Southern Folklore Quarterly* 3, no. 1 (March 1939): 1–14.

Bourdieu, Pierre. *Distinction, a Critique of the Judgement of Taste.* Translated by Richard Nice. Cambridge, Mass.: Harvard University Press, 1984.

Braxton, Joanne M. *Black Women Writing Autobiography: A Tradition Within a Tradition.* Philadelphia: Temple University Press, 1989.

Briggs, Charles. "Metadiscursive Practices and Scholarly Authority in Folkloristics," *Journal of American Folklore* 106, no. 422 (Fall 1993): 387–434.

Briggs, Charles, and Richard Bauman. "Genre, Intertextuality and Social Power," *Journal of Linguistic Anthropology* 2, no. 2 (1992): 131–72.

Brown, Karen McCarthy. *Mama Lola, a Vodon Priestess in Brooklyn.* Berkeley: University of California Press, 1991.

Brown-Guillory, Elizabeth. *Their Place on the Stage: Black Women Playwrights in America.* New York: Greenwood Press, 1988.

Buck-Morss, Susan. *The Dialectics of Seeing: Walter Benjamin and the Arcades Project.* Cambridge, Mass.: MIT Press, 1990.

Buttitta, Anthony J. "Negro Folklore in North Carolina." In *Negro,* edited by Nancy Cunard, 62–66. New York: Negro Universities Press, 1934.

Carson, Warren J. "Hurston as Dramatist: The Florida Connection." In *Zora in Florida,* edited by Steve Glassman and Kathryn Lee Seidel, 121–129. Orlando: University of Central Florida Press, 1991.

Cassirer, Ernst. "The Place of Language and Myth in the Pattern of Human Culture," in *Language and Myth* (1946), 1–16. New York: Dover Publications, 1966.

———. "Word Magic." *Language and Myth,* 44–61.

Chase, Allan. *The Legacy of Malthus: The Social Costs of the New Scientific Racism.* New York: Alfred A. Knopf, 1977.

Clifford, James. *The Predicament of Culture: Twentieth-Century Ethnography, Literature, and Art.* Cambridge, Mass.: Harvard University Press, 1988.

Clifford, James, and Marcus, George, eds. *Writing Culture: the Poetics and Politics of Ethnography.* Berkeley: University of California Press, 1986.

Cole, John Y. "Amassing American 'Stuff': The Library of Congress and the Federal Arts Project of the 1930s," *The Quarterly Journal of the Library of Congress* 40(4): 356–89.

Craig, E. Quita. *Black Drama of the Federal Theater Era: Beyond the Formal Horizons.* Amherst: University of Massachusetts Press, 1980.

Cruse, Harold. *The Crisis of the Negro Intellectual.* New York: William Morrow, 1967.

Cunard, Nancy, ed. *Negro.* New York: Negro Universities Press, 1934.

———. "A Short Review of Dr. Du Bois, *The Crisis,* and the N. A. A. C. P. in 1932." In *Negro,* edited by Nancy Cunard, 142–47. New York: Negro Universities Press, 1934.

Dalgarno, Emily. "'Words Walking Without Masters': Ethnography and Creative Process in *Their Eyes Were Watching God,*" *American Literature* 64, no. 3 (September 1992): 519–41.

Dance, Darryl C. "Zora Neale Hurston."

Dayan, Joan. "Vodoun, or the Voice of the Gods," *Raritan: A Quarterly Review* 10, 3 (Winter 1991): 32–57.

Deck, Alice A. "Autoethnography: Zora Neale Hurston, Noni Jabavu, and Cross-

Disciplinary Discourse," *Black American Literature Forum* 24, no. 2 (Summer 1990): 237–56.

Derrida, Jacques. "The Pit and the Pyramid: Introduction to Hegel's Semiology." In *Margins of Philosophy*. Translated by Alan Bass, 69–108. Chicago: University of Chicago Press, 1982.

Devereux, George. "Art and Mythology: A General Theory." In *Art and Aesthetics in Primitive Societies: a Critical Anthology*, edited by Carol F. Jopling, 193–224. New York: Dutton, 1971. Reprinted from *Studying Personality Cross-Culturally*, 361–403. Evanston, Ill.: Row Peterson, 1961.

Diamond, Elin. "Mimesis, Mimicry, and the 'True-Real," *Modern Drama* 32, no. 1 (May 1984): 58–72.

Dillard, J. L. *Black English: Its History and Usage in the United States.* New York: Random House, 1972.

DiRocco, Lisa. "Aesthetics and Culture: A View by Larry Neal." *Drum* 9, no. 2 (Spring 1978). Larry Neal Papers. New York Public Library: Schomburg Archive.

Dollard, John. *Caste and Class in a Southern Town* (1937). Madison: The University of Wisconsin Press, 1988.

Dorson, Richard M. *American Folklore.* Chicago: University of Chicago Press, 1977.

———. *Folklore and Fakelore: Essays Toward a Discipline of Folk Studies.* Cambridge, Mass.: Harvard University Press, 1976.

———. *Folklore: Selected Essays.* Bloomington: Indiana University Press, 1972.

Dorst, John. "Rereading *Mules and Men*: Toward the Death of the Ethnographer," *Cultural Anthropology* 2, no. 3 (August 1987): 305–318.

Drewal, Margaret. "The State of Research on Performance in Africa." Paper prepared for the Joint Committee on African Studies of the American Council of Learned Societies and the Social Science Research Council, 1990.

Driskell, David C. "The Evolution of a Black Aesthetic, 1920–1950." In *Two Centuries of Black American Art*, 59–79. New York: Los Angeles County Museum of Art/Alfred A. Knopf, 1976.

Du Bois, W.E.B. "Black America." In *Negro*, edited by Nancy Cunard, 148–52. New York: Negro Universities Press, 1934.

Dutton, Wendy. "The Problem of Invisibility: Voodoo and Zora Neale Hurston," *Frontiers* 23, no. 2 (1992): 131–52.

Ecker, Gisela, ed. *Feminist Aesthetics.* Translated by Harriet Anderson. Boston: Beacon Press, 1985.

Eco, Umberto. "Theory of Sign Production." In *A Theory of Semiotics*, 151–313. Bloomington: Indiana University Press; Midland Book Edition, 1979.

Elam, Keir. *The Semiology of Theatre and Drama.* London: Methuen, 1980.

Eliade, Mircea. *The Sacred and the Profane* (1957). Translated by Willard R. Trask. New York: Harcourt, Brace & World; Harvest, 1959.

Ellis, Trey. "The New Black Aesthetic," *Callaloo* 12, no. 1 (Winter 1989): 233–43.

Ellison, Ralph. "Change the Joke and Slip the Yoke," *Shadow and Act*, 61–73. New York: New American Library; Signet, 1966.

Else, Gerald, trans. *Aristotle Poetics.* Ann Arbor: University of Michigan Press, 1990.

Euba, Femi. *Archetypes, Imprecators, and Victims of Fate: Origins and Developments of Satire in Black Drama.* New York: Greenwood Press, 1989.

Fanon, Franz. *Black Skins, White Masks* (1952). Translated by Charles Lam Markmann. New York: Grove Weidenfeld, 1967.

Fauset, Arthur Huff. "T'appin (Terrapin)." In *The New Negro.* Edited by Alain Locke, 245–49. New York: Atheneum, 1968.

Fauset, Jessie. "The Gift of Laughter." In *The New Negro*. Edited by Alain Locke, 161–67. New York: Atheneum, 1968.

Feintuch, Burt, ed. *The Conservation of Culture: Folklorists and the Public Sector*. Lexington: The University Press of Kentucky, 1988.

Felker, Christopher D. "Adaptation of the Source: Ethnocentricity and 'the Florida Negro.' " In *Zora in Florida*. Edited by Steve Glassman and Kathryn Lee Seidel, 146–58. Orlando: University of Central Florida Press, 1991.

Ferguson, Sally Ann. "Folkloric Men and Female Growth in *Their Eyes Were Watching God*," *Black American Literature Forum*, 21, nos. 1–2 (Spring–Summer, 1987): 185–198.

Fernandez, James. "Reflections on Looking in Mirrors," *Semiotica* 30, nos. 1/2 (1980): 27–39.

———. "Tolerance in a Repugnant World and Other Dilemmas in the Cultural Relativism of Melville J. Herskovits," *Ethos* 18, no. 2 (June 1990): 140–64.

Fletcher, Angus. "Iconographies of Thought," *Representations* 28 (1989): 99–112.

Foster, Hal. *Recodings: Art, Spectacle, Cultural Politics*. Seattle: Bay Press, 1985.

Foucault, Michel. *The Archaeology of Knowledge and the Discourse on Language*. New York: Pantheon, 1972.

Fox-Genovese, Elizabeth. "Myth and History: Discourse of Origins in Zora Neale Hurston and Maya Angelou," *Black American Literature Forum*, 24, no. 2 (Summer 1990): 221–36.

Frazier, E. Franklin. *The Negro in the United States* (1949). New York: Macmillan, 1957.

Galton, Francis. *Hereditary Genius, an Inquiry into its Laws and Consequences* (1869). London: Julian Friedmann Publishers, 1978.

Gates, Henry Louis, Jr. *Figures in Black: Words, Signs, and the "Racial" Self*. New York: Oxford University Press. 1987.

———. *"Race," Writing and Difference*. Chicago: University of Chicago Press, 1985.

———. *The Signifying Monkey: A Theory of African-American Literary Criticism*. New York: Oxford University Press, 1988.

Geertz, Clifford. "Blurred Genres: the Refiguration of Social Thought," in *Local Knowledge*, 19–35. New York: Basic Books, 1983.

Genovese, Eugene D. "Origins of the Folk Religion," in *Roll, Jordan, Roll: The World the Slaves Made*, 206–32. New York: Random House; Vintage, 1976.

Gilroy, Paul. *The Black Atlantic: Modernity and Double Consciousness*. Cambridge, Mass.: Harvard University Press, 1993.

Glassman, Steve, and Kathryn Lee, eds. *Zora in Florida*. Orlando, Fla.: University of Central Florida Press, 1991.

Gleason, Philip. "American Identity and Americanization." *Harvard Encyclopedia of American Ethnic Groups*, edited by Stephan Thernstrom. Cambridge, Mass.: Harvard University Press, 1980.

Goffman, Erving. *Frame Analysis: An Essay on the Organizing of Experience*. Boston: Northeastern University Press, 1986.

———. *The Presentation of Self in Everyday Life*. New York: Doubleday, 1959.

Goldenberg, Myrna. "The Barnard Connection: Zora Neale Hurston and Annie Nathan Meyer," in *All About Zora*. Winter Park, Fla.: Four-G Publishers, 1991.

Goldwater, Robert. *Primitivism in Modern Art* (1966). Cambridge, Mass.: Harvard University Press; The Belknap Press, 1986.

Gombrich, E. H. *Meditations on a Hobby Horse and Other Essays on the Theory of Art*. London: Phaidon, 1963.

Gordon, Deborah. "The Politics of Ethnographic Authority: Race and Writing in the Ethnography of Margaret Mead and Zora Neale Hurston," in *Modernist Anthropology:*

from Fieldwork to Text, edited by Marc Manganaro, 146–62. Princeton, N. J.: Princeton University Press, 1990.

Green, Paul. "The Folk Arts," 1–6; "Symphonic Drama," 14–26, in *Dramatic Heritage*. New York: Samuel French, 1953.

Grimshaw, Allen D. "Some Problematic Aspects of Communication in Cross-Racial Research in the United States," in *Language as Social Resource*, edited by Anwar S. Dil, 57–76. Stanford: Stanford University Press, 1981.

Hall, Stuart, and Paddy Whannel. *The Popular Arts*. London: Hutchinson Educational, 1964.

Harris, Leonard, ed. *The Philosophy of Alain Locke: Harlem Renaissance and Beyond*. Philadelphia: Temple University Press, 1989.

Harrison, Paul Carter. *The Drama of Nommo*. New York: Grove Press, 1972.

———. *Totem Voices: Plays from the Black World Repertory*. New York: Grove Press, 1989.

Hegel, G.W.F. "Psychology." *Philosophy of Mind*, 179–240. Translated by William Wallace. Oxford: Clarendon Press, 1971.

Hemenway, Robert. "Biography, Captive of the Written Record," *Artist and Influence*, 8 (1986): 10–18.

———. "Introduction." *Dust Tracks on a Road*, xi–xxxix. Urbana, Ill.: University of Illinois Press, 1984.

———. "Introduction: That Which the Soul Lives By." *Mules and Men*, xi–xxviii. Bloomington, In.: Indiana University Press, 1978.

———. "Zora Neale Hurston and the Eatonville Anthology." In *The Harlem Renaissance Remembered*, edited by Arna Bontemps, 190–214. New York: Dodd, Mead, 1972.

———. *Zora Neale Hurston, a Literary Biography*. Urbana, Ill.: University of Illinois Press, 1977.

Herskovits, Melville. "Acculturation and the American Negro," *The Southwestern Political and Social Science Quarterly* 7, no. 3 (December 1927): 211–24.

———. *Acculturation: The Study of Culture Contact* (1938). Gloucester, Mass.: Peter Smith, 1958.

———. "Memorandum for the Study of Acculturation," *American Anthropologist* 28 (1936): 149–52.

———. "The Significance of the Study of Acculturation for Anthropology," *American Anthropologist* 39 (1937): 259–64.

———. *Franz Boas: The Science of Man in the Making*. New York: Charles Scribner's Sons, 1953.

———. *The Myth of the Negro Past* (1941). Boston: Beacon Press, 1990.

Hill, Errol. "The Revolutionary Tradition in Black Drama," *Theater Journal* 38, no. 4 (December 1986): 408–26.

Hill, Lynda. "Staging Hurston's Life and Work." In *Acting Out: Feminist Performances*, edited by Lynda Hart and Peggy Phelan, 295–313. Ann Arbor: University of Michigan Press, 1993.

Hirsch, Jerrold. "Cultural Pluralism and Applied Folklore: The New Deal Precedent." In *The Conservation of Culture: Folklorists and the Public Sector*, edited by Burt Feintuch, 46–70.

———. "Modernity, Nostalgia, and Southern Folklore Studies: The Case of John Lomax," *Journal of American Folklore* 105, no. 416 (Spring 1992): 183–207.

Hobsbawm, Eric and Ranger, Terence, eds. *The Invention of Tradition*. Cambridge: Cambridge University Press, 1983.

Hooks, Bell. *Yearning: Race, gender, and cultural politics*. Boston: South End Press, 1990.

Hornby, Richard. *Script into Performance: A Structuralist Approach*. New York: Paragon House Publishers, 1987.

Bibliography

Hughes, Langston, and Zora Neale Hurston. *Mule Bone: A Comedy of Negro Life*. Edited by George Houston Bass and Henry Louis Gates, Jr. New York: Harper Collins, Harper Perennial, 1991.

Huggins, Nathan Irvin. *Harlem Renaissance*. New York: Oxford University Press, 1971.

Hurston, Zora Neale. "Art and Such." In *Reading Black, Reading Feminist: A Critical Anthology*, edited by Henry Louis Gates, Jr., 21–26. New York: Penguin Books, Meridian, 1990.

———. "Barracoon: The Story of the Last 'Black Cargo.' " Typescript. Manuscript Division, Moorland-Spingarn Research Center, Howard University, 1931.

———. "Black Death." In *The Complete Stories*, 202–208. New York: HarperCollins, 1995.

———. "The Bone of Contention." In *Mule Bone* 27–39; in *The Complete Stories* 209–220.

———. "The Chick with One Hen." Typescript. The Beinecke Rare Book and Manuscript Library, Yale University Library.

———. "Color Struck." In *Black Female Playwrights: An Anthology of Plays Before 1950*. Edited by Kathy Perkins, 89–102. Bloomington, Ind.: Indiana University Press, 1989.

———. *The Complete Stories*. New York: HarperCollins, 1995.

———. "Cudjo's Own Story of the Last African Slaver," *The Journal of Negro History* 12, no. 4 (October 1927): 648–69.

———. "Dance Songs and Tales from the Bahamas," *Journal of American Folklore* 43, no. 169 (July–October 1930): 294–312.

———. "Drenched in Light," *The Complete Stories*, 17–25. New York: HarperCollins, 1995.

———. *Dust Tracks on a Road: an Autobiography* (1942). New York: HarperCollins.

———. "The Fiery Chariot." Typescript. University of Florida Libraries. Special Collections, n.d.

———. "The First One." In *Black Female Playwrights: An Anthology of Plays Before 1950*. Edited by Kathy Perkins, 80–88. Bloomington, Ind.: Indiana University Press, 1989.

———. "The Florida Expedition." Typescript. Franz Boas Papers, American Philosophical Society, n.d.

———. "Florida Folklore." Typescript. Manuscript Division, Library of Congress, n.d.

———. "Folklore." First Version. Typescript. Works Progress Administration, Florida Folklife Archives, Florida Bureau of Folklife Programs, n.d.

———. *Folklore, Memoirs and Other Writings*. Edited by Cheryl Wall. New York: Library of America, 1995.

———. "Go Gator, and Muddy the Water," Typescript. Florida Bureau of Folklife Programs.

———. "Hoodoo in America," *The Journal of American Folklore* 44, no. 174 (October–December 1931): 318–405.

———. *I Love Myself When I Am Laughing . . . and Then Again When I Am Looking Mean and Impressive: a Zora Neale Hurston Reader*. Edited by Alice Walker. New York: The Feminist Press, 1979.

———. "John Redding Goes to Sea," *The Complete Stories*, 1–16. New York: HarperCollins, 1995.

———. *Jonah's Gourd Vine* (1934). New York: Harper & Row, Perennial Library, 1990.

———. "The Last Slave Ship." *The American Mercury* 58 (March 1944): 351–58.

———. *Moses, Man of the Mountain* (1939). Urbana, Ill.: University of Chicago Press, Illini Books, 1984.

———. *Mules and Men* (1935). Bloomington: Indiana University Press, 1978.

———. "Negro Legends." Typescript. Works Progress Administration, Florida Folklife Archives, Bureau of Florida Folklife Programs, n.d.

———. "Ritualistic Expression from the Lips of the Communicants of the Seventh Day

Church of God; Beaufort, South Carolina." Typescript. Manuscript Division, Library of Congress (1940).

———. *The Sanctified Church.* Berkeley, Calif.: Turtle Island, 1981.

———. "Sanctified Church in Beaufort, S.C." Field Notes. Typescript Manuscript Division, Library of Congress (1940).

———. *Seraph on the Suwanee* (1948). New York: HarperCollins, Harper Perennial, 1991.

———. *Spunk.* Berkeley, Calif.: Turtle Island, 1985.

———. *Tell My Horse* (1938). New York: HarperCollins, Harper Perennial, 1990.

———. *Their Eyes Were Watching God* (1937). Urbana, Ill.: University of Illinois Press, 1978.

———. "Turpentining." Typescript. Works Progress Administration, Florida Folklife Archives, Bureau of Florida Folklife Programs, n.d.

———. "Uncle Monday." Typescript. Works Progress Administration; Florida Folklife Archives, Bureau of Florida Folklife Programs, n.d.

Hurston, Zora Neale and Dorothy Waring. *Polk County: A Comedy of Negro Life on a Sawmill Camp with Authentic Negro Music in Three Acts.* (1944) Typescript. The Beinecke Rare Book and Manuscript Library, Yale University Library; The Library of Congress; New York Public Library: The Billy Rose Theatre Collection.

Hyatt, Marshall. *Franz Boas Social Activist: The Dynamics of Ethnicity.* New York: Greenwood Press, 1990.

Hyman, Stanley Edgar. "The Ritual View of Myth and the Mythic," *Journal of American Folklore* 68, no. 270 (October–December 1955): 462–72.

Hymes, Dell. "Breakthrough into Performance." In *Folklore: Performance and Communications.* Edited by Dan Ben-Amos and Kenneth Goldstein, 11–74. The Hague; Paris: Mouton, 1975.

Jahn, Janheinz. *Muntu: The New African Culture.* New York: Grove Press, 1961.

Jakobson, Roman. *Verbal Art, Verbal Sign, Verbal Time.* Edited by Krystyna Pomorska and Stephen Rudy. London: Basil Blackwell, 1985.

Johnson, Barbara. "Metaphor, Metonymy and Voice in *Their Eyes Were Watching God.*" In *Black Literature & Literary Theory*, edited by Henry Louis Gates, Jr., 205–20. New York: Methuen, 1984.

———. "Thresholds of Difference: Structures of Address in Zora Neale Hurston." In *"Race," Writing and Difference,* edited by Henry Louis Gates, Jr., 317–28. Chicago: University of Chicago Press, 1985.

Johnson, James Weldon. *Along This Way* (1933). New York: Penguin Books, 1990.

———. *Black Manhattan* (1930). New York: Atheneum, 1969.

Jopling, Carol F., ed. *Art and Aesthetics in Primitive Societies.* New York: Dutton, 1971.

Jordan, June. "On Richard Wright and Zora Neale Hurston: Notes Toward a Balancing of Love and Hatred," *Black World* (August 1974): 4–8.

Kahn, Douglas. *John Heartfield: Art and Mass Media.* New York: Tanam Press, 1985.

Kalb, J.D. "The Anthropological Narrator of Hurston's *Their Eyes Were Watching God,*" *Studies in American Fiction* 16, no. 2 (Autumn 1988): 169–180.

Kapchan, Deborah. "Hybridization and the Marketplace: Emerging Paradigms of Folkloristics," *Western Folklore* 52 (April 1993): 303–26.

Kaplan Alice and Ross, Kristin. "Introduction," *Everyday Life,* Yale French Studies, no. 73 (1987): 1–4.

Kennedy, Stetson. "Florida Folklife and the WPA, an Introduction." In *A Reference Guide to Florida Folklore from the Federal WPA.* Bureau of Florida Folklore, Florida Folklife Archives, Florida Department of State, 1990.

Kirshenblatt-Gimblett, Barbara. "Mistaken Dichotomies." *Journal of American Folklore* 101 (1988): 140–55.

Bibliography

———. "Objects of Ethnography." In *Exhibiting Cultures: The Poetics and Politics of Museum Display*, edited by Ivan Karp and Steven D. Lavine, 386–443. Washington, D.C.: Smithsonian Institution Press, 1991.

Klineberg, Otto. *Negro Intelligence and Selective Migration*. New York: Columbia University Press, 1935.

———. *Race Differences*. New York: Harper & Brothers, 1935.

Koch, Frederick. "Making a Native Folk Drama," *Southern Folklore Quarterly* 1, no. 3 (September 1977): 29–33.

Krasner, James. "The Life of Women: Zora Neale Hurston and Female Autobiography," *Black American Literature Forum* 23, no. 1 (Spring 1989): 113–26.

Laba, Martin. "Popular Culture and Folklore: The Social Dimension." In *Media Sense: The Folklore-Popular Culture Continuum*, edited by Peter Navarez and Martin Laba, 9–18. Bowling Green, Ohio: Bowling Green State University Popular Press, 1986.

Lenz, Gunter. "Southern Exposures: The Urban Experience and the Re-Construction of Black Folk Culture and Community in the Works of Richard Wright and Zora Neale Hurston," *New York Folklore* 7. (Summer 1981): 3–39.

Levin, Gail. "American Art." In *"Primitivism" in 20th Century Art: Affinity of the Tribal and the Modern*. 453–74. New York: The Museum of Modern Art, 1984.

Levine, Lawrence W. *Black Culture and Black Consciousness: Afro-American Folk Thought from Slavery to Freedom*. New York: Oxford University Press, 1977.

———. "William Shakespeare and the American People: A Study in Cultural Transformation." In *Rethinking Popular Culture: Contemporary Perspectives in Cultural Studies*, edited by Chandra Mukerji and Michael Schudson, 157–97. Berkeley: University of California Press, 1991. Reprinted from *American Historical Review* 89, no. 1 (February 1984): 34–66.

Levi-Strauss, Claude. "The Science of the Concrete." In *The Savage Mind*, 1–33. Chicago: University of Chicago Press, 1962.

Lewis, David Levering. *When Harlem Was in Vogue*. New York: Oxford University Press, 1981.

Lindenberger, Herbert. "The Mimetic Bias in Modern Anglo-American Criticism." In *Mimesis Contemporary Theory: an Interdisciplinary Appproach*, edited by Mihai Spariosu, 1–26. Philadelphia: John Benjamins, 1984.

Lionnet, Francoise. "Autoethnography: an Anarchic Style of *Dust Tracks on a Road*." In *Autobiographical Voices: Race, Gender, Self-Portraiture*, 97–129. Ithaca, N.Y.: Cornell University Press, 1989.

Locke, Alain, ed. *The New Negro* (1925). Edited by Robert Hayden. New York: Atheneum, 1968.

Lowe, John. *Jump at the Sun: Zora Neale Hurston's Cosmic Comedy*. Urbana, Ill.: University of Illinois Press, 1994.

Manganaro, Marc, ed. *Modernist Anthropology: From Fieldwork to Text*. Princeton, N.J.: Princeton University Press, 1990.

Marcus, George E., and Michael M.J. Fischer. *Anthropology as Cultural Critique: An Experimental Moment in the Human Science*. Chicago: University of Chicago Press, 1986.

Matejka, Ladislav, and Irwin R. Titunik, eds. *Semiotics of Art: Prague School Contributions*. Cambridge, Mass.: MIT Press, 1976.

McKay, Nellie. "The Autobiographies of Zora Neale Hurston and Gwendolyn Brooks: Alternate Versions of the Black Female Self." In *Wild Women in the Whirlwind: Afra-American Culture and the Contemporary Literary Renaissance*. Edited by Joanne Braxton and Andree McLaughlin, 264–81. New Brunswick, N.J.: Rutgers University Press, 1990.

Bibliography

Mead, Margaret. *An Anthropologist at Work: Writings of Ruth Benedict.* Boston: Houghton Mifflin Company, 1959.

————. *Blackberry Winter: My Earlier Years.* New York: Washington Square Press, 1972.

Mechling, Jay. "The Failure of Folklore in Richard Wright's *Black Boy*," *Journal of American Folklore* 104, no. 413 (Summer 1991): 275–94.

Metraux, Alfred. *Voodoo in Haiti* (1959). New York: Schocken Books, 1972.

Mitchell, W. J. T. *Iconology: Image, Text, Ideology.* Chicago: University of Chicago Press, 1986.

Mulira, Jessie Gaston. "The Case of Voodoo in New Orleans." In *Africanisms in American Culture,* edited by Joseph E. Holloway, 34–68. Bloomington: Indiana University Press, 1990.

Munn, Nancy D. "Visual Categories: An Approach to the Study of Representational Systems." In *Art and Aesthetics in Primitive Societies,* edited by Carol F. Jopling, 335–55. New York: Dutton, 1971.

Murphy, Joseph M. *Santeria, an African Religion in America.* Boston: Beacon Press, 1988.

Nathiri, N.Y., ed. *Zora! Zora Neale Hurston: A Woman and Her Community.* Orlando, Fla.: Orlando Sentinel, 1991.

Navarez, Peter, and Martin Laba, eds. introduction to *Media Sense: The Folklore-Popular Culture Continuum,* 1–8. Bowling Green, Ohio: Bowling Green State University Popular Press, 1986.

Neal, Larry. "Cultural Nationalism and Black Theatre." Unpublished Manuscript. Larry Neal Papers. New York Public Library: Schomburg Archive, n.d.

————. "A Profile: Zora Neale Hurston," *Southern Exposure* 1 (Winter 1974): 160–68.

Ngugi wa Thiongo. *Writers in Politics.* London: Heinemann, 1981.

North, Michael. *The Dialect of Modernism: Race, Language and Twentieth-Century Literature.* New York: Oxford University Press, 1994.

Novak, Michael. "Pluralism: A Humanistic Perspective." In *Harvard Encyclopedia of American Ethnic Groups,* edited by Stephan Thernstrom, 772–81. Cambridge, Mass.: Harvard University Press.

Ong, Walter J. "From Mimesis to Irony: The Distancing of Voice." In *The Horizon of Literature,* edited by Paul Hernadi, 11–42. Lincoln: University of Nebraska Press, 1982.

Ottanelli, Fraser M. *The Communist Party of the United States from the Depression to World War II.* New Brunswick, N.J.: Rutgers University Press, 1991.

Pavis, Patrice. *Languages of the Stage.* New York: Performing Arts Journal Publications, 1980.

Peerce, Harold. "The Negro Folk Cult," *The Crisis* 43 (1936): 364, 374.

Penkower, Monty Noam. *The Federal Writers' Project: A Study in Government Patronage of the Arts.* Urbana: University of Illinois Press, 1977.

Perkins, Kathy. *Black Female Playwrights: An Anthology of Plays Before 1950.* Bloomington: Indiana University Press, 1989.

Pondrom, Cyrena N. "The Role of Myth in Hurston's *Their Eyes Were Watching God*," *American Literature* 58, no. 2 (May 1986): 181–202.

Pryse, Marjorie. "Zora Neale Hurston, Alice Walker, and the 'Ancient Power' of Black Women." In *Conjuring: Black Women, Fiction, and Literary Tradition.* Edited by Marjorie Pryse and Hortense J. Spillers, 1–24. Bloomington, Ind.: Indiana University Press, 1985.

Raglan, Lord. "Myth and Ritual," *Journal of American Folklore* 68, no. 270 (October–December 1955): 454–61.

Rampersad, Arnold. *The Life of Langstorm Hughes Vol. I: 1902–1941 I, Too, Sing America.* New York: Oxford University Press, 1986.

Riffaterre, Michael. *Fictional Truth.* Baltimore: Johns Hopkins, 1990.

———. *Text Production*. Translated by Terese Lyons. New York: Columbia University Press, 1983.

Roberts, John. "African American Diversity and the Study of Folklore," *Western Folklore* 52 (April 1993): 157–71.

———. *From Trickster to Bad Man: The Black Folk Hero in Slavery and Freedom*. Philadelphia: University of Pennsylvania Press, 1989.

Rubin, William. "Modernist Primitivism: An Introduction." In *Primitivism in 20th Century Art: Affinity of the Tribal and the Modern*, 1–79. New York: Museum of Modern Art, 1984.

Said, Edward. "Representing the Colonized: Anthropology's Interlocutors," *Critical Inquiry* 15 (Winter 1989): 205–25.

———. "On Originality." *The World, the Text, and the Critic*, 126–39. Cambridge, Mass.: Harvard University Press, 1983.

Schechner, Richard. *Between Theater and Anthropology*. Philadelphia: University of Pennsylvania Press, 1985.

———. *The End of Humanism*.

———. *Performance Theory*. New York: Routledge, 1988.

Scheflen, Albert. *How Behavior Means: Exploring the Contexts of Speech and Meaning: Kinesics, Posture, Interaction, Setting, and Culture*. New York: Doubleday, 1974.

Seward, Adrienne Lanier. "The Legacy of Early Afro-American Folklore Scholarship." In *Handbook of American Folklore*, edited by Richard Dorson, 48–56. Bloomington: Indiana University Press, 1983.

Sheffey, Ruthe T. "Zora Hurston and Langston Hughes's 'Mule Bone': An Authentic Folk Comedy and the Compromised Tradition." *The Zora Neale Hurston Forum* 2, no. 1 (Fall 1987): 49–60.

Shuman, Amy. "Dismantling Local Culture," *Western Folklore* 52 (April 1993): 345–64.

Simons, Sarah E. "Social Assimilation," Part I, *The American Journal of Sociology* 6 (July 1900–May 1901): 790–822.

Simpson, George Eaton. *Melville J. Herskovits*. New York: Columbia University Press, 1973.

Sollors, Werner. "Beyond Ethnicity" 20–39; "Introduction" 3–19; "Ethnicity and Literary Form" 237–58; "Melting Pots" 66–101. In *Beyond Ethnicity: Consent and Descent in American Culture*. New York: Oxford University Press, 1986.

Soyinka, Wole. *Myth, Literature and the African World*. Cambridge: Cambridge University Press, 1976.

Spariosu, Mihai, ed. *Mimesis in Contemporary Theory: An Interdisciplinary Approach*. Philadelphia: John Benjamins, 1984.

Speisman, Barbara. "A Tea with Zora and Marjorie: A Series of Vignettes Based on the Unique Friendship of Zora Neale Hurston and Marjorie Kinnan Rawlings." *Rawlings Journal* (1988): 67–100.

Spiller, G. *Papers on Inter-Racial Problems*. London: P.S. King & Son, 1911.

Stephens, Walter E. "Mimesis, Mediation and Counterfeit." In *Mimesis and Contemporary Theory: and Interdisciplinary Approach*, edited by Mihai Spariosu. Philadelphia: John Benjamins, 1984.

Stewart, Jeffrey, ed. *Race Contacts and Interracial Relations: Lectures on the Theory and Practice of Race*. Washington, D.C.: Howard University Press, 1992.

Stewart, Susan. *Nonsense: Aspects of Intertextuality in Folklore and Literature*. Baltimore: Johns Hopkins University Press, 1989.

———. "Notes on Distressed Genres." *Journal of American Folklore* 104, no. 411 (Winter 1991): 5–31.

Bibliography

Stocking, George, Jr., ed. *The Shaping of American Anthropology 1883–1911*. New York: Basic Books, 1974.

Stoddard, Lothrop. *The Revolt Against Civilization: The Menace of the Under Man*. New York: Charles Scribner's Sons, 1922.

———. *The Rising Tide of Color Against White World-Supremacy*. New York: Charles Scribner's Sons, 1921.

Story, Ralph D. "Gender Ambition: Zora Neale Hurston in the Harlem Renaissance," *The Black Scholar* (Summer/Fall, 1989): 25–31.

Stott, William. *Documentary Expression and Thirties America*. Chicago: University of Chicago Press, 1986.

Tambiah, Stanley Jeyaraja. "Form and Meaning of Magical Acts." In *Culture, Thought, and Social Action: An Anthropological Perspective*, 60–86. Cambridge, Mass.: Harvard University Press, 1985.

———. "The Magical Power of Words," *Culture, Thought, and Social Action* 17–59.

Taussig, Michael. *The Devil and Commodity Fetishism in South America*. Chapel Hill, N.C.: University of North Carolina Press, 1980.

———. "Homesickness & Dada." *The Nervous System*, 149–81. New York: Routledge, 1992.

———. *Mimesis and Alterity: A Particular History of the Senses*. New York: Routledge, 1993.

Taylor, Charles. *The Ethics of Authenticity*. Cambridge, Mass.: Harvard University Press, 1991.

Terrill, Tom E., and Jerrold Hirsch, *Such as Us: Southern Voices of the Thirties*. Chapel Hill, N.C.: University of North Carolina Press, 1978.

Thompson, E.P. "Folklore, Anthropology, and Social History," *Indian Historical Review* 3, no. 2 (1977): 247–66.

Thompson, Robert Farris. *Flash of the Spirit: African & Afro-American Art & Philosophy*. New York: Random House, Vintage, 1984.

Thompson, Stith. "Myths and Folktales," *Journal of American Folklore* 68, no. 27 (October–December 1955): 482–88.

Todorov, Tzvetan. *Symbolism and Interpretation*. Translated by Catherine Porter. Ithaca, NY: Cornell University Press, 1982.

Torgovnick, Marianna. *Gone Primitive: Savage Intellects, Modern Lives*. Chicago: University of Chicago Press, 1990.

Tracy, Steven C. *Langston Hughes & the Blues*. Urbana, Ill.: University of Illinois Press, 1988.

Turner, Victor. *From Ritual to Theatre: The Human Seriousness of Play*. New York: PAJ Publications, 1982.

Turner, Victor. *The Ritual Process: Structure and Anti-Structure*. Ithaca, N.Y.: Cornell University Press, 1969.

Tyler, Stephen A. "Ethnography, Intertextuality and the End of Description," *American Journal of Semiotics* 3, no. 4 (1985): 83–98.

Van Gennep, Arnold. *The Rites of Passage* (1908). Chicago: University of Chicago Press, 1960.

Varnedoe, Kirk. "Gaugin." In *"Primitivism" in 20th Century Art: Affinity of the Tribal and the Modern*, 179–210. New York: Museum of Modern Art, 1984.

Walker, Alice. "Anything We Love Can Be Saved: The Resurrection of Zora Neale Hurston and Her Work." In *Zora! Zora Neale Hurston, a Woman and Her Community*, edited by N.Y. Nathiri, 79–84. Orlando, Fla.: Sentinel Communications Company, 1991.

———. "Saving the Life That Is Your Own: The Importance of Models in the Artist's Life" (1976). *In Search of our Mothers' Garden's*, 3–14. New York: Harcourt Brace Jovanovich, 1983.

Wall, Cheryl. "*Mules and Men* and Women: Zora Neale Hurston's Strategies of Narration and Visions of Female Empowerment," *Black American Literature Forum* 23, no. 4 (Winter 1989): 661–80.

Wallace, Michelle. "Who Owns Zora Neale Hurston? Critics Carve Up the Legend." In *Invisibility Blues: From Pop to Theory,* 172–86. London: Verso, 1990.

Walzer, Michael. "Pluralism: A Political Perspective." In *Harvard Encyclopedia of American Ethnic Groups,* edited Stephan Thernstrom, 781–87. Cambridge, Mass.: Harvard University Press, 1980.

Weatherford, Willis D., and Charles S. Johnson. *Race Relations: Adjustment of Whites and Negroes in the United States.* Boston: D.C. Heath, 1934.

White, Hayden. *Tropics of Discourse: Essays in Cultural Criticism.* Baltimore: Johns Hopkins University Press, 1978.

Wideman, John E. "Charles Chesnutt and the WPA Narratives: The Oral and Literate Roots of Afro-American Literature." In *The Slave Narrative,* edited by Charles T. Davis and Henry Louis Gates, Jr., 59–78. New York: Oxford University Press, 1985.

Willis, Susan. "Wandering: Zora Neale Hurston's Search for Self and Method." In *Specifying: Black Women Writing the American Experience, 26–52.* Madison, Wis.: University of Wisconsin Press, 1987.

Wolfe, George C. *Spunk: Three Tales by Zora Neale Hurston.* New York: Theatre Communications Group, 1991.

Woll, Allen. *Black Musical Theatre: From Coontown to Dreamgirls.* Baton Rouge: Louisiana State University Press, 1989.

APPENDIX

Characteristics of Negro Expression

DRAMA

The Negro's universal mimicry is not so much a thing in itself as an evidence of something that permeates his entire self. And that thing is drama.

His very words are action words. His interpretation of the English language is in terms of pictures. One act described in terms of another. Hence the rich metaphor and simile.

The metaphor is of course very primitive. It is easier to illustrate than it is to explain because action came before speech. Let us make a parallel. Language is like money. In primitive communities actual goods, however bulky, are bartered for what one wants. This finally evolves into coin, the coin being not real wealth but a symbol of wealth. Still later, even coin is abandoned for legal tender, and still later cheques for certain usages.

Every phase of Negro life is highly dramatized. No matter how joyful or how sad the case there is sufficient poise for drama. Everything is acted out. Unconsciously for the most part of course. There is an impromptu ceremony always ready for every hour of life. No little moment passes unadorned.

Now the people with highly developed languages have words for detached ideas. That is legal tender. "That-which-we-squat-on" has become "chair." "Groan-causer" has evolved into "spear" and so on. Some individuals even conceive of the equivalent of cheque words, like "ideation" and "pleonastic." Perhaps we might say that *Paradise Lost* and *Sartor Resartus* are written in cheque words.

The primitive man exchanges descriptive words. His terms are all close fitting. Frequently the Negro, even with detached words in his vocabulary—not evolved in him but transplanted on his tongue by contact—must add action to it to make it do. So we have "chop-axe," "sitting-chair," "cook-pot" and the like because the speaker has in his mind the picture of the object in use. Action. Everything illustrated. So we can say the white man thinks in a written language and the Negro thinks in hieroglyphics.

A bit of Negro drama familiar to all is the frequent meeting of two opponents who threaten to do atrocious murder one upon the other.

Who has not observed a robust young Negro chap posing upon a street corner, possessed of nothing but his clothing, his strength, and his youth? Does he bear himself like a pauper? No, Louis XIV could be no more insolent in his assurance. His eyes say plainly "Female, halt!" His posture exults "Ah, female, I am the eternal male, the giver of life. Behold in my hot flesh all the delights of this world. Salute me, I am strength." All this with a languid posture, there is no mistaking his meaning.

A Negro girl strolls past the corner lounger. Her whole body panging* and posing. A slight shoulder movement that calls attention to her bust, that is all of a dare. A hippy undulation below the waist that is a sheaf of promises tied with conscious power. She is acting out "I'm a darned sweet woman and you know it."

These little plays by strolling players are acted out daily in a dozen streets in a thousand cities, and no one ever mistakes the meaning.

WILL TO ADORN

The will to adorn is the second most notable characteristic in Negro expression. Perhaps his ideas of ornament does not attempt to meet conventional standards, but it satisfies the soul of its creator.

In this respect the American Negro has done wonders to the English language. This is true, but it is equally true that he has made over a great part of the tongue to his liking and has his revision accepted by the ruling class. No one listening to a Southern white man talk could deny this. Not only has he softened and toned down strongly consonanted words like "aren't" to "ain't" and the like, he has made new force words out of old feeble elements. Examples of this are "ham-shanked," "battle-hammed," "double-teen," "bodaciously," "muffle-jawed."

*From "pang."

Appendix

But the Negro's greatest contribution to the language is: (1) the use of metaphor and simile; (2) the use of the double descriptive; (3) the use of verbal nouns.

1. Metaphor and Simile

One at a time, like lawyers going
to heaven.
You sho is propaganda.
Sobbing hearted.
I'll beat you till: (a) rope like okra,
(b) slack like lime, (c) smell like
onions.
Fatal for naked.
Kyting along.
That's a rope.
Cloakers—deceivers.
Regular as pig-tracks.
Mule blood—black molasses.
Syndicating—gossiping.
Flambeaux—cheap cafe (lighted by flambeaux).
To put yo'self on de ladder.

2. The Double Descriptive

High-tall.
Little-tee-ninchy (tiny).
Low-down.
Top-superior.
Sham-polish.
Lady-people.
Kill-dead.
Hot-boiling.
Chop-axe.
Sitting-chairs.
De watch wall.
Speedy-hurry.
More great and more better.

3. Verbal Nouns

She features somebody I know.
Funeralize.
Sense me into it.
Puts the shamery on him.
'Taint everybody you kin confidence.
I wouldn't friend with her.
Jooking—playing piano or guitar as
it is done in Jook-houses (houses of ill-fame).
Uglying away.
I wouldn't scorn my name all up on you.
Bookooing (beaucoup) around—showing off.

Nouns from Verbs

Won't stand a broke.
She won't take a listen.
He won't stand straightening.
That is such a compliment.
That's a lynch.

The stark, trimmed phrases of the Occident seem too bare for the voluptuous child of the sun, hence the adornment. It arises out of the same impulse as the wearing of jewelry and the making of sculpture—the urge to adorn.

On the walls of the homes of the average Negro one always finds a glut of gaudy calendars, wall pockets and advertising lithographs. The sophisticated white man or Negro would tolerate none of these, even if they bore a likeness to the Mona Lisa. No commercial art for decoration. Neither the calendar nor the advertisement spoils the picture for this lowly man. He sees the beauty in spite of the declaration of the Portland Cement Works or the butcher's announcement. I saw in Mobile a room in which there was an over-stuffed mohair living-room suite, an imitation mahogany bed and chifferobe, a console victrola. The walls were gaily papered with Sunday supplements of the *Mobile Register*. There were seven calendars and three wall pockets. One of them was decorated with a lace doily. The mantel-shelf was covered with a scarf of deep home-made lace, looped up with a huge bow of pink crepe paper. Over the door was a huge lithograph showing the Treaty of Versailles being signed with a Waterman fountain pen.

It was grotesque, yes. But it indicated a desire for beauty. And decorating a decoration, as in the case of the doily on the gaudy wall pocket, did not seem out of place to the hostess. The feeling back of such an act is that there can never be enough of beauty, let alone too much. Perhaps she is right. We each have our standards of art, and thus we are all interested parties and so unfit to pass judgment upon the art concepts of others.

Whatever the Negro does of his own volition he embellishes. His religious service is for the greater part excellent prose poetry. Both prayers and sermons are tooled and polished until they are true works of art. The supplication is forgotten in the frenzy of creation. The prayer of the white man is considered humorous in its bleakness. The beauty of the Old Testament does not exceed that of a Negro prayer.

ANGULARITY

After adornment the next most striking manifestation of the Negro is Angularity. Everything that he touches becomes angular. In all African sculpture and doctrine of any sort we find the same thing.

Anyone watching Negro dancers will be struck by the same phenomenon. Every posture is another angle. Pleasing, yes. But an effect achieved by the very means which a European strives to avoid.

The pictures on the walls are hung at deep angles. Furniture is always set at an angle. I have instances of a piece of furniture in the *middle* of a wall being set with one end nearer the wall than the other to avoid the simple straight line.

ASYMMETRY

Asymmetry is a definite feature of Negro art. I have no samples of true Negro painting unless we count the African shields, but the sculpture and carvings are full of this beauty and lack of symmetry. It is present in the literature, both prose and verse. I offer an example of this quality in verse from Langston Hughes:

> I ain't gonna mistreat ma good gal any more,
> I'm just gonna kill her next time she makes me sore.
>
> I treats her kind but she don't do me right,
> She fights and quarrels most every night.

I can't have no woman's got such low-down ways
Cause de blue gum woman aint de style now'days.

I brought her from the South and she's goin on back,
Else I'll use her head for a carpet tack.

It is the lack of symmetry which makes Negro dancing so difficult for white dancers to learn. The abrupt and unexpected changes. The frequent change of key and time are evidences of this quality in music (Note the St. Louis Blues).

The dancing of the justly famous Bo-Jangles and Snake Hips are excellent examples.

The presence of rhythm and lack of symmetry are paradoxical, but there they are. Both are present to a marked degree. There is always rhythm, but it is the rhythm of segments. Each unit has a rhythm of its own, but when the whole is assembled it is lacking in symmetry. But easily workable to a Negro who is accustomed to the break in going from one part to another, so that he adjusts himself to the new tempo.

DANCING

Negro dancing is dynamic suggestion. No matter how violent it may appear to the beholder, every posture gives the impression that the dancer will do much more. For example, the performer flexes one knee sharply, assumes a ferocious face mask, thrusts the upper part of the body forward with clenched fists, elbows taut as in hard running or grasping a thrusting blade. That is all. But the spectator himself adds the picture of ferocious assault, hears the drums and finds himself keeping time with the music and tensing himself for the struggle. It is compelling insinuation. That is the very reason the spectator is held so rapt. He is participating in the performance himself—carrying out the suggestions of the performer.

The difference in the two arts is: the white dancer attempts to express fully; the Negro is restrained, but succeeds in gripping the beholder by forcing him to finish the action the performer suggests. Since no art can ever express all the variations conceivable, the Negro must be considered the greater artist, his dancing is realistic suggestion, and that is about all a great artist can do.

NEGRO FOLKLORE

Negro folklore is not a thing of the past. It is still in the making. Its great variety shows the adaptability of the black man: nothing is too old or too new, domestic or foreign, high or low, for his use. God and the Devil are paired, and are treated no more reverently than Rockefeller and Ford. Both of these men are prominent in folklore. Ford being particularly strong, and they talk and act like good-natured stevedores or mill-hands. Ole Massa is sometimes a smart man and often a fool. The automobile is ranged alongside of the oxcart. The angels and the apostles walk and talk like section hands. And through it all walks Jack, the greatest culture hero of the South; Jack beats them all—even the Devil, who is often smarter than God.

Culture Heroes

The Devil is next after Jack as a culture hero. He can outsmart everyone but Jack. God is absolutely no match for him. He is good-natured and full of humour. The sort of person one may count on to help out in any difficulty.

Peter the Apostle is third in importance. One need not look far for the explanation. The Negro is not a Christian really. The primitive gods are not deities of too subtle inner reflection; they are hard-working bodies who serve their devotees just as laboriously as the suppliant serves them. Gods of physical violence, stopping at nothing to serve their followers. Now of all the apostles, Peter is the most active. When the other ten fell back trembling in the garden, Peter wielded the blade on the posse. Peter first and foremost in all action. The gods of no peoples have been philosophic until the people themselves have approached that state.

The rabbit, the bear, the lion, the buzzard, the fox are culture heroes from the animal world. The rabbit is far in the lead of all the others and is blood brother to Jack. In short, the trickster-hero of West Africa has been transplanted to America.

John Henry is a culture hero in song, but no more so than Stacker Lee, Smokey Joe or Bad Lazarus. There are many, many Negroes who have never heard of any of the song heroes, but none who do not know John (Jack) and the rabbit.

Examples of Folklore and the Modern Culture Hero

Why de Porpoise's Tail is on Crosswise

Now, I want to tell you 'bout de porpoise. God had done made de world and everything. He set de moon and de stars in de sky. He got de fishes of de sea, and de fowls of de air completed. He made de sun and hung it up. Then He made a nice gold track for it to run on. Then He said, "Now, Sun, I got everything made but Time. That's up to you. I want you to start out and go round de world on dis track just as fast as you kin make it. And de time it takes you to go and come, I'm going to call day and night." De Sun went zoomin' on cross de elements. Now, de porpoise was hanging round there and heard God what he told de Sun, so he decided he'd take dat trip round de world hisself. He looked up and saw de Sun kytin' along, so he lit out too, him and dat Sun!

So de porpoise beat de Sun round de world by one hour and three minutes. So God said, "Aw naw, this aint gointer do! I didn't mean for nothin' to be faster than de Sun!" So God run dat porpoise for three days before he runs him down and caught him, and took his tail off and put it crossways to slow him up. Still he's de fastest thing in de water. And dat's why de porpoise got his tail on crossways.

Rockefeller and Ford

Once John D. Rockefeller and Henry Ford was woofing at each other. Rockefeller told Henry Ford he could build a solid gold road round the world. Henry Ford told him if he would he would look at it and see if he liked it, and if he did he would buy it and put one of his tin lizzies on it.

ORIGINALITY

It has been said so often that the Negro is lacking in originality that it has almost become a gospel. Outward signs seem to bear this out. But if one looks closely its falsity is immediately evident.

It is obvious that to get back to original sources is much too difficult for any group to claim very much as a certainty. What we really mean by originality is the modification of ideas. The most ardent admirer of the great Shakespeare cannot claim first source even for him. It is his treatment of the borrowed material.

So if we look at it squarely, the Negro is a very original being. While he lives and moves in the midst of a white civilization, everything that he touches is re-interpreted for his own use. He has modified the language, mode of food preparation, practice of medicine, and most certainly the religion of his new country, just as he adapted to suit himself the Sheik haircut made famous by Rudolph Valentino.

Everyone is familiar with the Negro's modification of the whites' musical instruments, so that his interpretation has been adopted by the white man himself and then re-interpreted. In so many words, Paul Whiteman is giving an imitation of a Negro orchestra making use of white-invented musical instruments in a Negro way. Thus has arisen a new art in the civilized world, and thus has our so-called civilization come. The exchange and re-exchange of ideas between groups.

IMITATION

The Negro, the world over, is famous as a mimic. But this in no way damages his standing as an original. Mimicry is an art in itself. If it is not, then all art must fall by the same blow that strikes it down. When sculpture, painting, dancing, literature neither reflect nor suggest anything in nature or human experience we turn away with a dull wonder in our hearts at why the thing was done. Moreover, the contention that the Negro imitates from a feeling of inferiority is incorrect. He mimics for the love of it. The group of Negroes who slavishly imitate is small. The average Negro glories in his ways. The highly educated Negro the same. The self-despisement lies in a middle class who scorns to do or be anything Negro. "That's just like a Nigger" is the most terrible rebuke one can lay upon this kind. He wears drab clothing, sits through a boresome church service, pretends to have no interest in the community, holds beauty contests, and otherwise apes all the mediocrities of the white brother. The truly cultured Negro scorns him, and the Negro "farthest down" is too busy "spreading his junk" in his own way to see or care. He likes his own things best. Even the group who are not Negroes but belong to the "sixth race," buy such records as "Shake dat thing" and "Tight lak dat." They really enjoy hearing a good bible-beater preach, but wild horses could drag no such admission from them. Their ready-made expression is: "We done got away from all that now." Some refuse to countenance Negro music on the grounds that it is niggerism, and for that reason should be done away with. Roland Hayes was thoroughly denounced for singing spirituals until he was accepted by white audiences. Langston Hughes is not considered a poet by this group because he writes of the man in the ditch, who is more numerous and real among us than any other.

But, this group aside, let us say that the art of mimicry is better developed in the Negro than in other racial groups. He does it as the mocking-bird does it, for the love of it, and not because he wishes to be like the one imitated. I saw a group of small Negro boys imitating a cat defecating and the subsequent toilet of the cat. It was very realistic, and they enjoyed it as much as if they had been imitating a coronation ceremony. The dances are full of imitations of various animals. The buzzard lope, walking the dog, the pig's hind legs, holding the mule, elephant squat, pigeon's wing, falling off the log, seabord (imitation of an engine starting), and the like.

ABSENCE OF THE CONCEPT OF PRIVACY

It is said that Negroes keep nothing secret, that they have no reserve. This ought not to seem strange when one considers that we are an outdoor people accustomed to communal life. Add this to all-permeating drama and you have the explanation.

There is no privacy in an African village. Loves, fights; possessions are, to misquote Woodrow Wilson, "Open disagreements openly arrived at." The community is given the benefit of a good fight as well as a good wedding. An audience is a necessary part of any drama. We merely go with nature rather than against it.

Discord is more natural than accord. If we accept the doctrine of the survival of the fittest there are more fighting honors than there are honors for other achievements. Humanity places premiums on all things necessary to its well-being, and a valiant and good fighter is valuable in any community. So why hide the light under a bushel? Moreover, intimidation is a recognized part of warfare the world over, and threats certainly must be listed under that head. So that a great threatener must certainly be considered an aid to the fighting machine. So then if a man or woman is a facile hurler of threats, why should he or she not show their wares to the community? Hence, the holding of all quarrels and fights in the open. One relieves one's pent-up anger and at the same time earns laurels in intimidation. Besides, one does the community a service. There is nothing so exhilarating as watching well-matched opponents go into action. The entire world likes action, for that matter. Hence prize-fighters become millionaires.

Likewise love-making is a biological necessity the world over and an art among Negroes. So that a man or woman who is proficient sees no reason why the fact should not be moot. He swaggers. She struts hippily about. Songs are built on the power to charm beneath the bed-clothes. Here again we have individuals striving to excel in what the community considers an art. Then if all of his world is seeking a great lover, why should he not speak right out loud?

It is all in a view-point. Love-making and fighting in all their branches are high arts, other things are arts among groups where they brag about their proficiency just as brazenly as we do about these things that others consider matters for conversation behind closed doors. At any rate, the white man is despised by Negroes as a very poor fighter individually, and a very poor lover. One Negro, speaking of white men, said, "White folks is alright when dey gits in de bank and on de law bench, but dey sho' kin lie about wimmen folks."

I pressed him to explain. "Well you see, white mens makes out they marries wimmen to look at they eyes, and they know they gits em for just what us gits em for. 'Nother thing, white mens say they goes clear round de world and wins all de wimmen folks way from they men folks. Dat's a lie too. They don't win nothin, they buys em. Now de way I figgers it, if a woman don't want me enough to be wid me, 'thout I got to pay her, she kin rock right on, but these here white men don't know what to do wid a woman when they gits her—dat's how come they gives they wimmen so much. They got to. Us wimmen works jus as hard as us does an come home an sleep wid us every night. They own wouldn't do it and its de mens fault. Dese white men done fooled theyself bout dese wimmen.

"Now me, I keeps me some wimmens all de time. Dat's whut dey wuz put here for—us mens to use. Dat's right now, Miss. Y'll wuz put here so us mens could have some pleasure. Course I don't run round like heap uh men folks. But if my ole lady go way from me and stay more'n two weeks, I got to git me somebody, ain't I?"

THE JOOK

Jook is the word for a Negro pleasure house. It may mean a bawdy house. It may mean the house set apart on public works where the men and women dance, drink and gamble. Often it is a combination of all these.

In past generations the music was furnished by "boxes," another word for guitars. One guitar was enough for a dance; to have two was considered excellent. Where two were playing one man played the lead and the other seconded him. The first player was "picking" and the second was "framming," that is, playing chords while the lead carried the melody by dexterous finger work. Sometimes a third player was added, and he played a tom-tom effect on the low strings. Believe it or not, this is excellent dance music.

Pianos soon came to take the place of the boxes, and now player-pianos and victrolas are in all of the Jooks.

Musically speaking, the Jook is the most important place in America. For in its smelly, shoddy confines has been born the secular music known as blues, and on blues has been founded jazz. The singing and playing in the true Negro style is called "jooking."

The songs grow by incremental repetition as they travel from mouth to mouth and from Jook to Jook for years before they reach outside ears. Hence the great variety of subject-matter in each song.

The Negro dances circulated over the world were also conceived inside the Jooks. They too make the round of Jooks and public works before going into the outside world.

In this respect it is interesting to mention the Black Bottom. I have read several false accounts of its origin and name. One writer claimed that it got its name from the black sticky mud on the bottom of the Mississippi River. Other equally absurd statements gummed the press. Now the dance really originated in the Jook section of Nashville, Tennessee, around Fourth Avenue. This is a tough neighborhood known as Black Bottom—hence the name.

The Charleston is perhaps forty years old and was danced up and down the Atlantic seaboard from North Carolina to Key West, Florida.

The Negro social dance is slow and sensuous. The idea in the Jook is to gain sensation, and not so much exercise. So that just enough foot movement is added to keep the dancers on the floor. A tremendous sex stimulation is gained from this. But who is trying to avoid it? The man, the woman, the time and place have met. Rather, little intimate names are indulged in to heap fire on fire.

These too have spread to all the world.

The Negro theatre, as built up by the Negro, is based on Jook situations, with women, gambling, fighting and drinking. Shows like "Dixie to Broadway" are only Negro in cast, and could just as well have come from pre-Soviet Russia.

Another interesting thing—Negro shows before being tampered with did not specialize in octoroon chorus girls. The girl who could hoist a Jook song from her belly and lam it against the front door of the theatre was the lead, even if she were as black as the hinges of hell.

The question was "Can she jook?" She must also have a good belly wobble, and her hips must, to quote a popular work song, "Shake like jelly all over and be so broad, Lawd, Lawd, and be so broad." So that the bleached chorus is the result of a white demand and not the Negro's.

The woman in the Jook may be nappy headed and black, but if she is a good lover she gets there just the same. A favorite Jook song of the past has this to say:

Singer: It aint good looks dat takes you through dis world.

Audience: What is it, good mama?

Singer: Elgin* movements in your hips. Twenty years guarantee. And it always brought down the house too.

> Oh de white gal rides in a Cadillac,
> De yaller girl rides de same,
> Black gal rides in a rusty Ford
> But she gits dere just de same.

The sort of woman her men idealize is the type put forth in the theatre. The art-creating Negro prefers a not too thin woman who can shake like jelly all over as she dances and sings, and that is the type he put forth on the stage. She has been banished by the white producer and the Negro who takes his cue from the white.

Of course a black woman is never the wife of the upper class Negro in the North. This state of affairs does not obtain in the South, however. I have noted numerous cases where the wife was considerably darker than the husband. People of some substance, too.

This scornful attitude towards black women receives mouth sanction by the mud-sills.

Even on the works and in the Jooks the black man sings disparagingly of black women. They say that she is evil. That she sleeps with her fists doubled up and ready for action. All over they are making a little drama of waking up a yaller** wife and a black one.

A man is lying beside his yaller wife and wakes her up. She says to him, "Darling, do you know what I was dreaming when you woke me up?" He says, "No honey, what was you dreaming?" She says, "I dreamt I had done cooked you a big fine dinner and we was setting down to eat

---

*Elegant (?). [from the Elgin Watch, Ed.]
**Yaller (yellow), light mulatto.

out de same plate and I was setting on yo' lap jus huggin you and kissin you and you was so sweet."

Wake up a black woman, and before you kin git any sense into her she be done up and lammed you over the head four or five times. When you git her quiet she'll say, "Nigger, know whut I was dreamin when you woke me up?"

You say, "No honey, what was you dreamin?" She says, "I dreamt you shook yo' rusty fist under my nose and I split yo' head open wid a axe."

But in spite of disparaging fictitious drama, in real life the black girl is drawing on his account at the commissary. Down in the Cypress Swamp as he swings his axe he chants:

> Dat ole black gal, she keeps on grumblin,
> New pair shoes, new pair shoes,
> I'm goint to buy her shoes and stockings
> Slippers too, slippers too.

Then adds aside: "Blacker de berry, sweeter de juice."

To be sure the black gal is still in power, men are still cutting and shooting their way to her pillow. To the queen of the Jook!

Speaking of the influence of the Jook, I noted that Mae West in "Sex" had much more flavor of the turpentine quarters than she did of the white bawd. I know that the piece she played on the piano is a very old Jook composition. "Honey let yo' drawers hang low" had been played and sung in every Jook in the South for at least thirty-five years. It has always puzzled me why she thought it likely to be played in a Canadian bawdy house.

Speaking of the use of Negro material by white performers, it is astonishing that so many are trying it, and I have never seen one yet entirely realistic. They often have all the elements of the song, dance, or expression, but they are misplaced or distorted by the accent falling on the wrong element. Everyone seems to think that the Negro is easily imitated when nothing is further from the truth. Without exception I wonder why the black-face comedians *are* black-face; it is a puzzle—good comedians, but darn poor niggers. Gershwin and the other "Negro" rhapsodists come under this same axe. Just about as Negro as caviar or Ann Pennington's athletic Black Bottom. When the Negroes who knew the Black Bottom in its cradle saw the Broadway version they asked each other, "Is you learnt dat *new* Black Bottom yet?" Proof that it was not *their* dance.

And God only knows what the world has suffered from the white damsels who try to sing Blues.

The Negroes themselves have sinned also in this respect. In spite of the goings up and down on the earth, from the original Fisk Jubilee Singers down to the present, there has been no genuine presentation of Negro songs to white audiences. The spirituals that have been sung around the world are Negroid to be sure, but so full of musicians' tricks that Negro congregations are highly entertained when they hear their old songs so changed. They never use the new style songs, and these are never heard unless perchance some daughter or son has been off to college and returns with one of the old songs with its face lifted, so to speak.

I am of the opinion that this trick style of delivery was originated by the Fisk Singers; Tuskegee and Hampton followed suit and have helped spread this misconception of Negro spirituals. This Glee Club style has gone on so long and become so fixed among concert singers that it is considered quite authentic. But I say again, that not one concert singer in the world is singing the songs as the Negro songmakers sing them.

If anyone wishes to prove the truth of this let him step into some unfashionable Negro church and hear for himself.

To those who want to institute the Negro theatre, let me say it is already established. It is lacking in wealth, so it is not seen in the high places. A creature with a white head and Negro feet struts the Metropolitan boards. The real Negro theatre is in the Jooks and the cabarets. Self-conscious individuals may turn away the eye and say, "Let us search elsewhere for our dramatic art." Let 'em search. They certainly won't find it. Butter Beans and Susie, Bo-Jangles and Snake Hips are the only performers of the real Negro school it has ever been my pleasure to behold in New York.

DIALECT

If we are to believe the majority of writers of Negro dialect and the burnt-cork artists, Negro speech is a weird thing, full of "ams" and "Ises." Fortunately, we don't have to believe them. We may go directly to the Negro and let him speak for himself.

I know that I run the risk of being damned as an infidel for declaring that nowhere can be found the Negro who asks "am it?" nor yet his brother who announces "Ise uh gwinter." He exists only for a certain type of writers and performers.

Very few Negroes, educated or not, use a clear clipped "I." It verges more or less upon "Ah." I think the lip form is responsible for this to a great extent. By experiment the reader will find that a sharp "i" is very much easier with a thin taut lip than with a full soft lip. Like tightening violin strings.

If one listens closely one will note too that a word is slurred in one position in the sentence but clearly pronounced in another. This is particularly true of the pronouns. A pronoun as a subject is likely to be clearly enunciated, but slurred as an object. For example: "You better not let me ketch yuh."

There is a tendency in some localities to add the "h" to "it" and pronounce it "hit." Probably a vestige of Old English. In some localities "if" is "ef."

In story telling "so" is universally the connective. It is used even as an introductory word, at the very beginning of a story. In religious expression "and" is used. The trend in stories is to state conclusions; in religion, to enumerate.

I am mentioning only the most general rules in dialect because there are so many quirks that belong only to certain localities that nothing less than a volume would be adequate.

13. *Hurston with flowers.*

INDEX

Index

Bennet, Gwendolyn, 122
Berliner Ensemble, 173
Bhaba, Homi, 46
Bickerstaff, Aunt Judy, 164, 165
Big Sweet (*Polk County*), 187, 188
Billie Holiday Theater, 190
Birth of a Nation (film), 4
"Black America" (Du Bois), 41
Black Arts Movement, 2, 119
"Black Death," 72, 141, 153, 197: significance of, 150; sympathetic magic in, 128–131, 134–135; variations of, 132
Blacks, middle class intellectual vs. "folk," 106–107
Blake, Eubie, 48, 104
Blue Sink Lake, 85, 129
Blues, xxix, 30, 34, 123, 125; and folklore development, 79, 80–81; in *Mule Bone*, 172, 179; paradoxical humor of, 105; in *Polk County*, 187–188; in *Spunk*, 194, 195
Blues, Ideology and Afro-American Literature: A Vernacular Theory (Baker), xxix
"The Blues I'm Playing" (Hughes), 71
Boas, Franz, xviii, xix, xxviii, xxx, 14, 15, 39, 50, 73, 80, 90, 95, 178, 190: African Institute proposal, 37–38, 39; interracial relations, views of, 111; and Kossula interviews, 62–63; race and culture research, 4–7, 38, 65, 160; superstition research, 139
"The Bone of Contention," xxv, 179–180
Botkin, Benjamin A., xxx
Brecht, Bertolt, 173, 197
Briggs, Charles, 177, 178, 186
Bronson, Judy, 85
Brown, Gabrielle, 59
Brown, Sterling, 3, 16
Brown, William Wells, 114
Browne, Theodore, 97
Bruce, Richard, 122
Bunche, Ralph, 90
Burroughs, Edgar Rice, 148
Buttitta, Anthony J., 13, 14, 16
Byrd, Jim, 88

Cakewalk, 109–110
Cane (Toomer), 116
Caribbean culture, 31, 50, 159, 160
Carnegie, Andrew, 37
Carolina Dramatic Association, 54
Carolina Playmakers, 54
Cattaneo, Anne, 179, 182
Censorship, 176
Cesaire, Aime, 36
"Characteristics of Negro Expression," ix, xxxi, 11, 14, 29, 39, 65, 78, 81, 87, 99:

drama in, 9; ethnological terms in, 36; historical impact of, 1; ideological basis of, 5; Locke and Boas, influence of, 7; meaning of, 3; metaphors in, 83; parody in, 45–46, 47; prose style in, 15; scientific writing and, 30; themes, serious vs. frivolous, 42
Charfin, Norman, 95
Chesnutt, Charles, xxix, 3, 105
"The Chick With One Hen," 181
Chip Woman's Fortune, The (Richardson), 113
Clarke, Joe, xvii, xx, 184, 196
Class, 120: middle, black, 115, 118, 121–122; differences, 119; and Florida Folklore Project research, 87; issues of, 108–113
Clifford, James, 36–37, 200
Clotilde (ship), 70
Codification, in drama, 202
Cole, Bob, 106
Color Struck, xviii, 118: class and race issues in, 108–113
Comedy: in black entertainment, 104–105; in *Mule Bone*, 172; in *Polk County*, 187. *See also* Humor
Committee for the Establishment of a Permanent Negro Repertory Theater, 10
Conjure stories, xxv, xxxii, 142: "Black Death," 128; "Uncle Monday," 84–85, 152, 157
Connelly, Mark, 31, 106
Conversion, 92–96
"The Court Room," xix
Covarrubias, Miguel, xix
Creation stories, 100
Crevecoeur, Michel-Guillame Saint–Jean de, 101–102, 103
Crisis Guild of Writers and Artists, 112
Crisis of the Negro Intellectual, The, 117
Crittenden, Ned (*Jonah's Gourd Vine*), 32
Cross Creek (Rawlings), 193
Crossroads Theater, 180
Cruse, Harold, 117, 118, 119
"Cudjo's Own Story of the Last African Slaver," 61, 62
Cugoano, Ottobah, 102
Cultural performance, xxii–xxiii
Culture: African origins of, 159; black, characteristics of, 65; essentialist theories and, 2, 11–12; in Florida, diversity of, 81; and "Folklore," ideas reflected in, 78; historical debates over meaning of, xxx–xxxi; and identity, 101; political forces affecting, 40–41; race relations

262

Index

Lonnie (*Polk County*), 187, 188
Lying session, 183, 184
Lynching, 1
Lyricism. *See* Music
Lysistrata, 97

Ma Rainey's Black Bottom (Wilson), 123
Madame Veronica, 94
Magic, xxxii: in "Black Death," 128–131, 134–135; cultural traditions and, xxiv–xxv; Hurston's personal use of, 145–146; language and, 145; as distinct from science, 83; sympathetic, 137, 139, 151, 164, 199; in "Uncle Monday" story, 84–85
Malinowski, Bronislaw, 149
"Mama Don't Want No Peas" (song), 34
Man of the Mountain, 99
Marrant, John, 102
Marriage: interracial, 111; in *Polk County*, 187
Masking, xxiii, 41, 51, 105: in *Spunk*, 194
Mason, Charlotte Osgood, xix, 11, 105, 106, 107, 112, 117, 198: Kossula project sponsorship, 70; and Hurston, relationship with, 71–72, 75, 107–108, 145–146, 151; and "primitive ideal," 65
Mason, Ruth, 144
Mauss, Marcel, 36
Mead, Margaret, xviii, 90, 93, 95, 139: focus on sexual behaviors, 149
Mechling, Jay, 41
Melting Pot, The (Zangwill), 103
Melting pot theory, 38, 101, 103
Metaphors: archetypal, 127; Coca Cola/the real thing, 116; and ritualistic language, 131; serving platter, 81, 82; use of, 44; visual, 192, 200
Metraux, Alfred, 36, 136, 141
Meyer, Annie Nathan, xviii
Middle Passage, 31, 33
Mimesis and Alterity: A Particular History of the Senses (Taussig), 42
Mimicry, xxxi, 3, 7, 44, 48, 119, 184, 198: as communication, 42; universal, 8–9, 15, 105
Minstrel tradition, xxi, xxiii, xxx, 104, 106, 182
Mirrors: magical and ritual uses of, 129, 130, 131, 137–138, 140; in Hoodoo, 141, 142
Mitchell, Loften, 113
Mitchell, W. T. J., 124, 200
Modernism and the Harlem Renaissance (Baker), 105
Moses, 99

Mosher, Gregory, 122, 171, 177, 179
Mule Bone, a Comedy of Negro Life, xii, xix, xxv, xxvii, xxxii, 122, 123, 171, 202: conflict in, 172; costume design, 169; humor in, 182–183; production of, 171, 175–186; property rights and, 171, 172, 173; scene from, 166–168
"Mule on the Mount" (song), 89
Mules and Men, xix, 14, 15, 30, 46, 65, 77, 80, 89, 96, 120, 121, 133, 152, 183, 192, 201: culture, views of, 78; gender roles in, 74; Hoodoo in, 141, 144; music in, 79, 86; Noah tales in, 99; race and communication in, 93; women, empowerment of, 164
Mulira, Jessie Gaston, 133, 135
Music, 201: in *All De Live Long Day*, 30–32; black, market for, 123; blues, xxix, 30; in *Color Struck*, 110; in folklore, 79–80, 81, 83, 86, 89; gospel, 96; in *Jonah's Gourd Vine*, 33; in *Polk County*, 187–188; primitive, xxviii; ragtime, xxx; in *Singing Steel*, 34; in *Spunk*, 194, 195; verbal arts derived from, 105; work songs, xxix, 30
Musical theater: black, 33, 104; imitation and, xxi; Johnson/Cole team, 106
My Honey (*Polk County*), 187
"My People, My People," 134
Myth, Literature and the African World (Soyinka), 157
Myth of the Negro Past, The (Herskovits), 159
Myths, 132, 138, 152, 153, 203: defined, 154; male dominance and, 164–165; Yoruba, 157

Narrative forms, 128: autobiographical, 70; as community property, 131–132; first–person voice, 35; in *Spunk*, 195; in "Sweat," 196–198; verbal, xxix, 14–15, 47, 156; written, 14
National Association for the Advancement of Colored People (NAACP), 41
National Folk Festival, 97
National Urban League, 7
Naturalism, 115–116
Neal, Larry, 73, 75, 77, 118: conception of African–American culture, 124
Negro (Cunard), xxxi, 1, 2, 14, 16, 29–30, 77: perspectives on black culture, 33, 41, 44
Negro: distinctive features of, 61; new, 116; use of term, 7–8, 49
"Negro Folklore in North Carolina" (Buttitta), 13

266